The
English
Vision

The English Vision

The Picturesque in Architecture, Landscape and Garden Design

David Watkin

Icon Editions

1817

Harper & Row, Publishers, New York

Cambridge, Philadelphia, San Francisco,
London, Mexico City, São Paulo, Sydney

Designed and produced by
Breslich & Foss, London

The English Vision. Copyright 1982 by David Watkin

For information address Harper & Row, Publishers,
Inc., 10 East 53rd Street, New York, New York, 10022.
Published simultaneously in Canada by Fitzhenry &
Whiteside Limited, Toronto.

FIRST U.S. EDITION

LIBRARY OF CONGRESS CATALOG
CARD NUMBER: 82–47548

ISBN 0-06-438875-1   82 83 84 85 86 10 9 8 7 6 5 4 3 2 1

Frontispiece: Scotney Castle, Kent,
looking down the landscaped quarry
from Salvin's new house of 1835–43 to
the improved ruins of the moated
fourteenth-century castle. Here Edward
Hussey and W. S. Gilpin put into
practice the picturesque principles of
Payne Knight who had written in *The
Landscape* (1794);

Bless'd too is he, who, 'midst his tufted
trees,
Some ruin'd castle's lofty towers sees;
Imbosm'd high upon the mountain's
brow,
Or nodding o'er the stream that glides
below.

Contents

To John and Valerie

Preface

The title of the present book derives from the assumption that the theory and practice of the Picturesque constitute the major English contribution to European aesthetics. Deeply rooted in the country house, the Picturesque became the leading building-type in post-Reformation England and has long been recognised as the nation's principal contribution to the arts. Between 1730 and 1830 English poets, painters, travellers, gardeners, architects, connoisseurs and dilettanti, were united in their emphasis on the primacy of pictorial values. The Picturesque became the universal mode of vision for the educated classes. Thus for Horace Walpole in 1770 landscape gardening meant that 'every journey is made through a succession of pictures'.[1] Likewise at the estate village of Old Warden in Bedfordshire in the early nineteenth century the inhabitants were induced to wear red cloaks and tall hats to harmonise with the red paintwork and quaint dormers of their cottages; and William Gilpin, high priest of the Picturesque, even advised the tourist that 'Cows are commonly the most picturesque in the months of April, and May, when the old hair is coming off'.[2] Gilpin's numerous topographical books were essentially a preparation for intelligent critical visiting, for the Picturesque presupposed a society which was interested in nature and in art and, above all, in travelling.

The eighteenth century was not only the age of the continental Grand Tour but also of touring in search of picturesque scenery in England, Scotland and Wales. Curiously, this appreciation of their native scenery only became possible for the English in the eighteenth century after they had become accustomed to the landscapes of seventeenth-century painters such as Claude, Salvator Rosa, Hobbema and Ruysdael. The country-house-building mania and the passion for visually informed touring made the eighteenth century the greatest age of country-house-visiting before the twentieth century. In 1774, for example, 2,324 members of the public visited Wilton, while at Hawkstone in Shropshire there were so many visitors to the dramatically landscaped park that in c.1790 an hotel was built to accommodate them. At Horace Walpole's Strawberry Hill and Thomas Hope's London house there were printed catalogues and even printed tickets of admission. In 1780 Mrs Montagu was issuing admission tickets for her splendid house in Portman Square designed by 'Athenian' Stuart, and when the Picturesque reached Paris at Ledoux's Hôtel de Thélusson and at the Parc Monceau, laid out by Carmontelle and altered by Thomas Blaikie, it was again found necessary to make arrangements for public viewing. John Harris[3] has catalogued as many as ninety guides to English country houses and collections published between 1740 and 1840, including no less than thirty-one editions of guides to a single house, Stowe. We can thus see how far the Picturesque had helped foster a literary and intellectual approach to the appreciation of architecture, gardening and scenery. The cult of illustrated topography reached a climax in the books produced by Rudolf Ackermann (1764–1834), master of the aquatint, and by John Britton (1771–1857), topographer and gothicist. The technique of aquatint, invented in France in the 1760s and brought to England in 1774 by the water-colourist Paul Sandby, was especially well suited to convey the soft shades of the moist English landscape.

One of the dominant themes of the Picturesque was clearly stated by Edmund Burke (1729–97) in his claim that 'No work of art can be great, but as it deceives'.[4] The Picturesque thus represents the triumph of illusion in which architecture resembles scenery, gardens resemble paintings, and the natural landscape is assessed and criticised, by William Gilpin for example, as though it had been devised by a painter.

Make-believe and surprise also played a vital part in the Picturesque. Thomas Blaikie, the Scottish gardener and botanist, recorded in his diary an amusing incident which occurred in the *jardin anglais* he had designed in 1778 for the comte d'Artois in the grounds of the Bagatelle:

the 20th May the count gave a great fete at Bagatelle to the King and Queen and the court which was at this time at La Meutte; here was the Superbe Band of Musick placed upon a scaffold on a thicket of trees which as the company walked round to see the Gardins played which with the echo of the trees made an enchanting affects, and in different parts of the wood was Booths made of the Branches of trees in which there was actors who acted different pieces agreeable to the scene; on the further side towards Longchamp there was erected a Pyramide by which was a Marble tomb; this part of the wood being neuly taken in to the grounds there remained the wall of the bois de Boulogne, and to rendre this scene More agreeable Mr Belanger had an invention which made a Singulare effect by undermining the wall on the outside and placing people with ropes to pull the wall down at a word; at this pyramide there was an acteur who acted the part of a Majician who asked there Majestys how they liked the Gardins and what a beautiful vue there was towards the plaine if that wall did not obstruct it, but that there Majestys need only give the word that he with his inchanting wand would make that wall dissapear; the queen not knowing told him with a Laugh 'Very well I should wish to see it dissapear' and in the instant the signal was given and above 200 yards oposite where the company stood, fell flat to the ground which surprised them all.[5]

The ingenious pictorial device of the disappearing wall which opens up a prospect from a garden to the plains beyond combines French artifice with the impact of the English Picturesque. Indeed it anticipates the celebrated flaps over the watercolours in Repton's Red Books which were contrived so as to show the same view before and after improvement by Repton.

Is it merely accidental that the phenomenon of the Picturesque should be English in origin, or does it perhaps correspond, as at least one leading critic would have us believe, to deeply embedded traits in the national character? However sceptical we may wish to be on this point, there is little doubt that a moist and temperate climate is favourable to a gardening style dependent on grass and trees; and that the gentle valleys of a small island have provided a friendly rather than daunting setting in which it has been appropriate to lay out gardens that look like landscapes, and landscapes that look like gardens. Architecture in such a background is rarely what it seems, with houses resembling garden ornaments, and garden ornaments resembling houses or temples. These beautiful myths have been fostered in a country which has specialised in preserving the picturesque façades of ancient institutions whilst making fundamental changes to the reality behind them; for example the Anglican Church, a Protestant body expecting to be taken for part of the Catholic church; and the monarch, still crowned with full mediaeval panoply as the Lord's anointed yet neither exercising power nor wishing to do so. The element of make-believe has often been central to English architecture, and nowhere more so than in the romantic chain of sham castles which stretch from Tattershal and Hurstmonceux in the fifteenth century, through Bolsover in the seventeenth to Castle Drogo in the twentieth century: in differing degrees these are pictorial rather than functional statements and are made possible by the relative internal security of the island nation.

This preoccupation with the past and with the *genius loci* finds its classic expression in the eighteenth century. As early as 1709 the architect John Vanbrugh had argued for the preservation of Woodstock Manor not only for its historical associations but because judicious planting could make it resemble 'One of the Most Agreable Objects that the best of Landskip Painters can invent'.[6] Here in a nutshell is the whole picturesque programme. In his revolutionary book of 1757, *A Philosophical Enquiry into the Origin of our Ideas of the Sublime and the Beautiful*, the young Edmund Burke related Terror, Obscurity and the Infinite to aesthetic emotion and created the category of the Sublime to contain them. His emphasis on passion and emotion rather than reason encouraged the theory of Association by which, for example, architectural forms were adopted not for their beauty or functional appropriateness, but for what ideas they suggested. In his numerous tours, beginning with *Observations on the River Wye and several Parts of South Wales, etc., relative chiefly to Picturesque Beauty* (1782), Gilpin defined a category of Picturesque Beauty which made the word 'Picturesque' a popular tool for analysing nature in terms of the effects aimed at by seventeenth-century landscape painters. In their theoretical writings of the 1770s and 80s respectively, Robert Adam and Sir Joshua Reynolds applied these painterly and landscape principles to architecture which they treated as though it were landscape, a process in which they drew inspiration from the buildings of Vanbrugh. Sir Uvedale Price, who codified the principles of the Picturesque at the end of the eighteenth century in his *Essay on the Picturesque* (1794, enlarged 1810), claimed that when Vanbrugh was approached for suggestions as to the layout at Blenheim he said, 'you must send for a landscape-painter'.[7]

Price recognised the difficulty of defining the Picturesque succinctly, as did Ruskin and Pevsner after him. As early as 1794 Price could write: 'There are few words whose meaning has been less accurately determined than that of the word picturesque. In general, I believe, it is applied to every object, and every kind of scenery, which has been, or might be represented with good effect in painting'. Price made it his aim to expose the inadequacy of this broad application of the term and to demonstrate 'that the picturesque has a character not less separate and distinct than either the sublime or the beautiful, nor less independent of the art of painting'.[8] Indeed for him the principal attributes of the Picturesque – roughness, sudden variation and irregularity – were precisely the opposite of those of Beauty. Writing in 1849, Ruskin felt that 'Probably no word in the language, (exclusive of theological expressions), has been the subject of so frequent or so prolonged dispute; yet none more vague in their acceptance'. Ruskin's somewhat unpleasing definition of the Picturesque was 'Parasitical Sublimity', by which he meant 'a sublimity dependent on the accidents, or on the least essential characters, of the objects to which it belongs'. He felt that 'whatever characters of line or shade or expression are productive of sublimity, will become productive of picturesqueness ... [e.g.] angular and broken lines, vigorous oppositions of light and shadow, and grave, deep, or boldly contrasted colour; and all these are in a still higher degree effective, when, by resemblance or association, they remind us of objects on which a true and essential sublimity exists, as of rocks or mountains, or stormy clouds or waves'.[9]

There is no doubt that Price's account of the attributes of the Picturesque continued to colour the outlook and vocabulary of critics throughout much of the nineteenth century, though the gross buildings depicted in C. J. Richardson's *Picturesque Designs in Architecture* (1870) are picturesque only in name. However, Carroll Meeks showed in 1957[10] how each of the five principal characteristics of the Picturesque – variety, movement, irregularity, intricacy and roughness – is respectively echoed in the characteristics of the Baroque as defined by Heinrich Wölfflin (1864–1945): painterly, recession, open, unity, and unclearness. In Wölfflin's *visual* system of analysis, which in itself could be seen as a legacy of the Picturesque, these baroque characteristics were identified as the opposite of those of Classic art: namely linear, plane, closed, multiplicity and clearness. This, again, is a parallel to Price's contrast between the Beautiful and the Picturesque. Pevsner, who had done so much to rediscover and popularise the writings of Price and Knight, gave a lecture at the Royal Institute of British Architects in 1947 on 'The Picturesque in Architecture' in which he included buildings of such widely varied date and character that John Summerson was forced to exclaim afterwards that 'what Dr. Pevsner this evening described as picturesque architecture is simply architecture'.[11]

One method of appreciating the impact of the new picturesque vision is to observe the changing representation of architecture, especially of country houses, in paintings and drawings during the course of the eighteenth century. J. M. W. Turner (1778–1851), who had been taught perspective by the architectural draughtsman Thomas Malton, was a pioneer in the new pictorial representation of architecture by means of fetching watercolours. This picturesque technique had been further stimulated by the desire of those exhibiting architectural projects at the Royal Academy to save the expense of models and show their buildings in their settings. The totally different tradition prevailing in France is demonstrated by the history of the celebrated architectural competitions for the Grand Prix awarded by the French Academy and later by the Ecole des Beaux-Arts: from the first competition held in 1702 up until 1962 no site was ever specified. In England, however, the simple outline elevation in the form of a diagram on an otherwise blank background gradually gave way to drawings which show the building in its setting and eventually, as in the work of Blore for example, to fully developed watercolours of landscapes in which the house appears as an incident. This dethroning of architecture is a constant feature of the Picturesque with its subordination of architectural to associational values. One example of this is the emphasis on the evocative powers of natural or even artificial ruins; another is the insistence on seeing architecture as a part of its environment. Sensitive appreciation of the fortuitous characterises two unusual late-eighteenth-century publications: in his illustrated book, *A New Method of Assisting the Invention in drawing Original Compositions of Landscape* (*c*.1785), Alexander Cozens developed ideas suggested by partially planned blots to establish an instant technique for the expression of ideal conceptions; in 1798 James Malton published a volume of aquatint designs for cottages under the tendentious title, *An Essay on British Cottage Architecture: being an Attempt to perpetuate on Principle, that peculiar mode of Building, which was originally the effect of Chance.* Turner, however, was opposed to the view that in art blotches of light, shade and colour are sufficient to stimulate the aesthetic imagination of the viewer. The power of association of ideas through truth to nature, through imagery and through sentiment was always central to his art: 'Painting, for Turner', as John Gage has put it, 'was essentially another word for language'.[12]

The impact of landscape paintings and watercolours on our approach to architecture is still felt every time a photographer composes his view by framing it with branches à la Claude. The history of amateur sketching in the nineteenth century in the manner of De Wint and Cox affords another example of the way in which a particular mode of vision became established as a thing so 'natural' that its artificiality and its debt to the theories of Sir Uvedale Price were generally forgotten. Christopher Hussey wrote in 1927 of the picturesque tradition in which he was brought up: 'I remember clearly the shock with which I suddenly became conscious that it was only one of many aspects of reality . . . It was humiliating, at the time, to find my aesthetic impulses no more than the product of heredity and environment'.[13] Today, over fifty years later, Hussey's *The Picturesque, Studies in a Point of View* (1927) is still the only book which investigates the Picturesque in all its manifestations, literary and visual. It is hoped that the present book, which has architecture as its centre point, will complement Hussey's beautiful and pioneering study.

TUSCUM.

Plan of Pliny's garden at Tuscum, from Robert Castell's *Villas of the Ancients Illustrated* (1728). In this imaginative reconstruction of one of the younger Pliny's gardens, based on Pliny's letters, Castell claims that Pliny had adopted a style in which 'under the Form of a beautiful Country, *Hills, Rocks, Cascades, Rivulets, Woods, Buildings*, &c. were possibly thrown into such an agreeable Disorder, as to have pleased the Eye from several views, like so many beautiful Landskips'.

Early Landscape Gardens

T HE growth of irregular land-
scape gardening in the early eighteenth century was prompted by a variety of
motives ranging from the poetic and aesthetic to the practical and political. In its
earliest years, it was sometimes justified, especially by poets, in political terms as
expressive of English 'liberty' in contrast to French 'tyranny' and formality. This
explanation has naturally been emphasised by determinist art historians of recent
years, but it may be more accurate to see the political interpretation as a rhetorical
justification *after* the event, rather than as a guiding inspiration from the start.
More important, perhaps, was the romantic desire to create an Elysium or heaven
on earth, a kind of pagan Garden of Eden, and this was encouraged by a reading of
classical literature. In Homer the Elysian fields were not part of the realms of the
dead but a happy land with neither snow, nor cold, nor rain, while to the Latin
poets they were part of the lower world, the dwelling place of mortals made
blessedly immortal by the favour of the Gods. This desire was fortified by an
ambition to recreate the antique garden from the evidence provided by the
younger Pliny's accounts of his gardens at Tuscum and Laurentinum. Thus,
classical allusions were gradually translated into a pictorial approach to landscape
which drew on the impact of antiquity and on the effect of the Italian landscape on
artists such as Claude and Poussin. Not surprisingly, this tended to encourage a new
appreciation of the qualities of the English landscape and the relation to it of
architecture.

The new gardening and landscape movement, with its emphasis on turf and
woodland, coincided with practical developments: firstly the urgent need for
afforestation after the Restoration of Charles II; secondly the process of enclosure
which altered the face of the country by creating compact farms in place of the old
widely distributed holdings in open fields; and thirdly the rise of fox-hunting with
its characteristic and even spread of small coverts. Enclosure had a visually
unifying effect akin to that of landscape gardening itself. Another advantage, of
course, was that turf and woodland were easier and cheaper to maintain than the
elaborate topiary work and parterres of the French and Dutch formal garden. The
commercial value of improved turf for grazing was one significant factor in the
role which agriculture, estate and woodland management, played in the growth of
the national economy during the eighteenth century. The English climate is also
especially favourable to the growth of the luscious turf which was exploited so
successfully in the new gardens. None of this is to suggest that developments in
agricultural economy generated the new movement, but rather that they helped
encourage its acceptance.

The circumstances of the adoption and growth of the picturesque garden in
France were entirely different. Conceived at a time of political and economic
decline after the glories of the Grand Siècle, the new gardens represented an

PRESTRES ou MOINES DE FO,
tirés de Nieuhof.

Mendicant priests, from J. Nieuhof, *An Embassy . . . to the Grand Tartar Cham Emperor of China* (1665), the earliest full and illustrated account of Chinese civilisation, scarcely superseded before the mid-nineteenth century. In the text which accompanies this plate of picturesquely attired priests, Nieuhof explains, '[one] has commonly a gown on of several Colours, and full of Patches. Upon his Head he has a Cap, which on both sides hath long Feathers to defend him against the Sun and Rain . . . there are some who Heads are very long, and brought into that shape on purpose when they are Infants . . . being, as it is believed, somewhat more holy'.

escape by the individual into nature and into a wholly idealised concept of rural life. The strikingly different mood prevailing in England can immediately be appreciated in the pages of Arthur Young (1741–1820), agriculturalist, author, enthusiast for enclosure and dynamic promoter of the maximum net produce of British agriculture. His *Six Months Tour through the North of England* (4 vols., 1770) is marked by a lively commitment to 'improvement' whether in picture collecting, agricultural science, architecture or landscape gardening. He announces on the title-page that his book is illustrated with 'copper plates of implements of husbandry and views of picturesque scenes', and inside produces lists of cabbages and Carlo Dolcis impartially.

The irregularity and asymmetry which we especially associate with the picturesque garden were held up for admiration in an essay 'Upon the Gardens of

Epicurus' written as early as 1685 by the essayist and statesman Sir William Temple (1628–99), though not published until 1692. By 1700 Temple had already added a little wilderness with wiggly paths in one corner of the otherwise formally laid-out gardens of his Surrey seat, Moor Park, near Farnham. In 'Upon the Gardens of Epicurus', Temple had claimed that:

Among us the beauty of Buildings and Planting is placed chiefly in some Proportions, Symmetries, or Uniformities; our walks and our trees rang'd so as they answer one another, and at exact Distances. The Chinese scorn this way of planting . . . their greatest reach of imagination is employed in contriving Figures where the Beauty shall be great, and strike the eye, without any order of Disposition of parts that shall be commonly or easily observed: And though We have hardly any notion of this sort of Beauty, yet they have a particular word to express it; and where they find it hit their eye at first sight, they say the *Sharawadgi* is fine or is admirable . . .[1]

Sharawadgi, or Sharawaggi in the form in which Horace Walpole was to use it in 'The History of the Modern Taste in Gardening', is an exotic word of uncertain origin, possibly derived from the Chinese syllables Sa-ro-kwai-chi which signify 'the quality of being impressive or surprising through careless or unorderly grace'. Accounts of Chinese gardens, with their grottoes, temples, cascades and wildernesses, had been brought back to Europe during the seventeenth century by a number of travellers, but especially by French Jesuit missionaries. One of the earliest publications was Father M. Ricci's *Histoire de l'Expedition Chrétienne au Royaume de la Chine* (Lyon, 1616), while J. Nieuhof's *An Embassy . . . to the Grand Tartar Cham Emperor of China* (Amsterdam, 1665) contained drawings of Chinese gardens and landscapes which were, incidentally, used by Fischer von Erlach in his celebrated and influential *Entwurff einer historischen Architectur* (Vienna, 1721) and in Athanasius Kircher's *China Monumentis qua sacris qua profanis illustrata* (Amsterdam, 1667, French translation 1670). Lord Burlington's circle in England became familiar with Chinese gardens through a set of thirty-six engravings by the Italian Jesuit Matteo Ripa of the Emperor K'ang Hsi's palace and gardens at Jehol. Burlington bought these engravings from Ripa in 1724. In 1743 J.-D. Attiret, French Jesuit and painter to Emperor Chien Hsi, wrote a letter to a friend in Paris describing in detail the newly completed pleasure gardens and buildings at the Emperor's summer palace outside Peking. This was published in the *Lettres édifiantes* (XXVII, 1749, pp. 7–43) and enjoyed wide popularity in England where it appeared in several translations in the 1750s and 60s.

One of the earliest examples of an imaginative recreation of a Chinese garden occurs in the stage directions for the last act of Henry Purcell's 'Fairy Queen', first produced in 1692. These envisaged 'a transparent prospect of a Chinese garden, the architecture, the trees, the plants, the fruit, the birds, the beasts quite different to what we have in this part of the world'. In the *Spectator* for 25 June 1712 Joseph Addison asked the portentous question, 'why may not a whole Estate be thrown into a kind of Garden by frequent Plantations'. He justified his question by reference to the Chinese who, instead of placing

Trees in equal Rows and uniform Figures . . . chuse rather to shew a Genius in Works of this Nature, and therefore always to conceal the Art by which they direct themselves . . . Our *British* Gardeners, on the contrary, instead of humouring Nature, love to deviate from it as much as possible. Our Trees rise in Cones, Globes, and Pyramids. We see the Marks of the Scissars upon every Plant and Bush.[2]

Pope's grotto at Twickenham. Perhaps the most celebrated and influential of eighteenth-century grottoes, it was formed by Pope in *c.* 1725 and extended by him in 1740. Pope enhanced his grotto with optical illusion, with mirrors and waterworks, with ores and minerals chosen for their beauty not their rarity, yet he still considered it natural in comparison with the formality and artificiality of mannerist and baroque grottoes.

Alexander Pope, writing in the *Guardian* in the following year, argued that the principles of irregular garden design had been followed by the ancients themselves, and concluded that 'There is certainly something in the amiable Simplicity of unadorned Nature, that spreads over the Mind a more noble sort of Tranquility, and a loftier Sensation of Pleasure, than can be raised from the nicer Scenes of Art'.[3] It is attractive to find Pope's admiration for nature anticipating Winckelmann's praise of the 'noble simplicity and calm grandeur' of Greek art.

In an important publication of 1728, *The Villas of the Ancients Illustrated*, dedicated to Lord Burlington, Robert Castell united the views of both Pope and Addison by recommending the Chinese as well as the ancients (exemplified in Pliny's villas) for their understanding of 'Irregularity' and 'artfull confusion'. It should not be supposed that all proposers of the new informal garden justified it in terms of Chinese precedent – about which very little was known – but simply that it provided a helpful vocabulary and range of expectations. Later in the century in the 1740s and 50s a number of rococo chinoiserie gardens were in fact created, but these will be described in their proper chronological place in the next chapter.

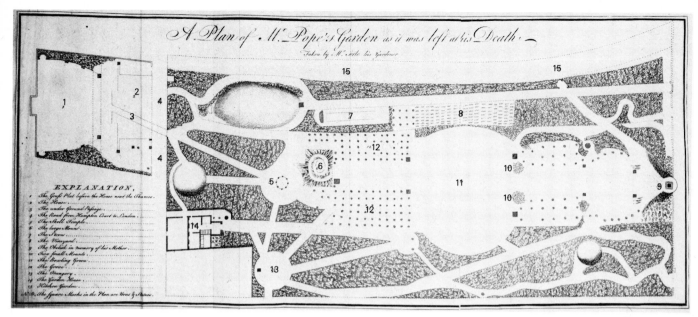

Pope's garden at Twickenham. Plan drawn by J. Serle, 1745. Mostly laid out in *c*. 1718-25, this vies with Chiswick as the first picturesque garden. Alexander Pope, whom Philip Southcote described as 'the first that practised painting in gardening', created a riverine paradise for the enjoyment of classical allusion, nostalgic reflection and the cultivation of friendship.

Key from the original plan: 1. The Grass Plot before the House next the Thames 2. The House 3. The underground passage 4. The road from Hampton Court to London 5. The Shell Temple 6. The large Mount 7. The Stoves [i.e. Hothouses] 8. The Vineyard 9. The Obelisk in memory of his Mother 10. Two small Mounts 11. The Bowling Green 12. The Grove 13. The Orangery 14. The Garden House 15. Kitchen Garden. N.B. The Square Marks in the Plan are Urns and Statues

One distinguished author who was not interested in any real or imaginary Chinese precedent was the 3rd Earl of Shaftesbury whose celebrated passage from *The Moralists, a Philosophical Rhapsody* of 1709 must here be quoted:

Your *Genius*, the *Genius* of the Place, and the GREAT GENIUS have at last prevail'd. I shall no longer resist the passion growing in me for Things of a *natural* kind; where neither *Art*, not the *Conceit* or *Caprice* of Man has spoil'd their *genuine Order*, by breaking in upon that *primitive State*. Even the rude *Rocks*, the mossy *Caverns*, the irregular unwrought *Grotto's*, and broken *Falls* of Waters, with all the horrid Graces of the *Wilderness* itself, as representing NATURE more, will be the more engaging, and appear with a Magnificence beyond the formal Mockery of princely Gardens.[4]

In his *Letter Concerning the Art or Science of Design* (1712) Shaftesbury called for the creation of a national style and a national taste based on the spirit of national freedom which he believed was enshrined in the Whig oligarchy. Burlington made it his aim to achieve this style, taking as his model the free commonwealth of republican Rome as well as the culture of China.

Addison, Pope and Burlington all essayed gardens in the new style. Addison's, at Bilton near Rugby, seems to have been a rather confused attempt at creating artificial wildness, but Pope's at Twickenham, where he had bought a house and five acres in 1719, rapidly acquired considerable fame. His garden was formed in the earliest 1720s on the other side of the road from the house itself, to which it was connected by a diagonal underground passage constructed in the form of a long grotto. This emerged into the garden by a circular shell temple near the edge of a tiny wilderness. Radial as well as serpentine paths conducted the visitor through carefully contrived vistas terminated with statues and urns, the whole intended to evoke a mood of quiet philosophical reflection. What Pope persisted in seeing as 'natural' seems to us as artificial as Rococo, although Walpole emphasised its pictorial qualities: 'The passing through the gloom from the grotto to the opening day, the retiring and again assembling shades, the dusky groves, the larger lawn and the solemnity of the termination at the cypresses that lead up to his mother's tomb [an obelisk inscribed Et in Arcadia Ego], are managed with exquisite judgement'.

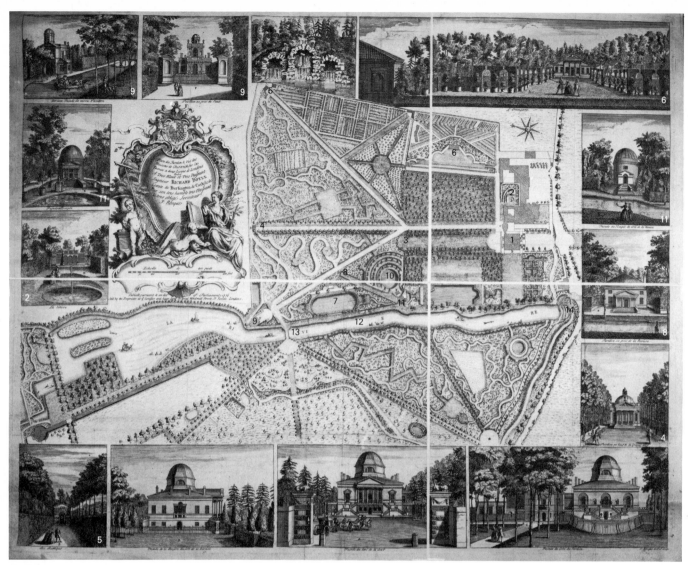

Chiswick House. Plan of the gardens engraved by J. Rocque, 1736. Lord Burlington had begun laying out a formal garden, probably with the help of Charles Bridgeman, in *c.* 1716 and extended it with William Kent's help in the early 1730s, adding the Italianate *exedra,* serpentining the river and opening up distant prospects. It thus became one of the earliest picturesque gardens, though with a strongly Italianate flavour recalling the arcadian gardens of classical antiquity and of the Renaissance.

Key: 1. House 2. Aviary 3. Exedra 4. Pavilion 5. Rustic Arch 6. Orangery 7. Oval pond 8. River Pavilion 9. Bagnio 10. Round Pond 11. Ionic Temple 12. Serpentine River 13. Stone Bridge 14. Cascade

Lord Burlington's garden at nearby Chiswick was of crucial importance in the development of picturesque garden design, though the history of its development is exceptionally complicated and still not entirely clear. On his return from his first Italian visit in 1716 he began laying out the gardens, perhaps with Bridgeman's help, dotting them with temples and garden buildings. This first phase, which was complete by 1724–5, was in a mixture of styles: sinuous rococo paths on the one hand, and on the other clipped hedges, trees in tubs and *pattes d'oie* (i.e. three straight avenues radiating from a single point). What was important for the future was that the vistas of the main *patte d'oie* terminated in an architectural feature. It has been suggested that this device owes something to stage and masque design, as for example in Scamozzi's celebrated scenery for Palladio's Teatro Olimpico at Vicenza which Burlington had recently seen. In *c.*1723–9 Burlington built from his own designs his elegant domed villa at Chiswick, closely modelled on Palladio and Scamozzi, as an art gallery and pleasure pavilion. He could now turn his attention to the gardens once more and in the early 1730s called on the services of his talented protégé and friend, William Kent (*c.*1685–1748). Kent, who had been trained as a painter in Italy, proceeded

to loosen the rather dense planting of the gardens in accordance with the free pictorial manner which he was beginning to make his own. Under Kent's hand the river assumed a serpentine form, distant prospects were opened up, a cascade (now demolished) was constructed in the form of a rocky tripartite grotto, and an *exedra*, which largely survives today, was laid out. Properly a hall with seats, the *exedra* at Chiswick consisted of a semi-circular hedge cut with niches for urns and for three statues supposedly taken from Hadrian's Villa at Tivoli. Features like the grotto and the *exedra* are based on seventeenth-century Italian gardens which Kent and Lord Burlington would have known at first hand, though they were also well illustrated in publications on gardens such as those by G. J. Rossi and G. B. Falda. Thus there are analogies to the *exedra* at the Villa Mattei in Rome, and to the cascade grottoes at the Villa Barberigo at Valzansibio and at the Belvedere Gardens at Frascati.

There are several complex layers of association in Burlington's approach which it is important to try to disentangle. There is, firstly, an intellectual, emotional and political attachment to Whiggish ideals of simplicity and freedom. Secondly, there is a belief that only by imitating the ancients can one hope to achieve 'natural' and objective ideals of beauty. Thirdly, there exists a deliberate reversion, in the absence of accurate archaeological evidence about the practice of

Chiswick House. The *exedra* laid out by William Kent for Lord Burlington in *c.* 1730. An Italian theme for which Burlington could claim antique precedent in Castell's *Villas of the Ancients Illustrated* and Renaissance precedent at the Villa Mattei. It shelters statues of Caesar, Pompey and Cicero supposedly brought from Hadrian's villa at Tivoli. Kent's Temple of British Worthies at Stowe is a more elaborate version of the same theme.

The Temple, Castle Howard, North Yorkshire. Vanbrugh's Temple, designed in 1724, 'really was a place to spend the afternoon with a good book, a bottle and Ciceronian thoughts', according to a recent biographer of Vanbrugh, Kerry Downes. Inspired by the younger Pliny and by Palladio it commands beautiful views in four directions and is approached by a grassed terrace walk, serpentine and statue-flanked, which until *c.* 1730 was the old village street of Henderskelfe.

the ancients, to the rules and practice of the sixteenth-century Italian masters of architecture and garden design. None of these is a specially romantic or picturesque ideal. Together they constitute a sober, classical programme of a markedly doctrinaire character. This, at any rate, is the interpretation proposed by Rudolf Wittkower in an important essay on 'English Neo-Palladianism, the Landscape Garden, China and the Enlightenment'.[5] But Wittkower perhaps under-estimates both the purely visual or pictorial appeal of Kent's contribution, as well as the romance of recreating under an English sky the sensations produced by an Italian garden warmed by an Italian sun.

As early as 1718 the gardener, nurseryman and author Stephen Switzer (1682–1745) published in three volumes his *Ichnographia Rustica*, in which he contrasted 'the regular designer' with the 'natural gardener'[6] who makes 'his Design submit to Nature, and not Nature to his Design'.[7] According to Switzer, the gardener 'ought to pursue Nature . . . and by as many Twinings and Windings as his *Villa* will allow',[8] make his design 'more rural, natural, more easy and less expensive'.[9] Switzer's first independent garden was probably his remodelling of Grimsthorpe, Lincolnshire, for the Marquess of Lindsey in 1711. He transformed a square wood near the house into a roughly hexagonal shape with an open circular centre from which new walks radiated outwards. With its low breast wall and its *fossé* or ditch, the terrace walk round the edge of the wood became a kind of mock fortification opening out at intervals into diamond-shaped bastions from which extensive views of the surrounding countryside could be enjoyed. This device is in effect a kind of ha-ha. Derived from the bastions of French fortifications, the ha-ha began to appear in a limited form in French gardens during the seventeenth century. But what in France had been associated with regularly placed openings or gateways in the fixed boundary of the garden, as at Grimsthorpe, was soon to be transformed in England into a continuous, invisible and frequently serpentine line. Vanbrugh may have become familiar with the form during his stay in France and began to exploit it in co-operation with Bridgeman by *c.*1709 at Blenheim and by *c.*1718 at Eastbury and Stowe. To Walpole, writing in 1770, the ha-ha was the fundamental corner-stone of the new gardening:

But the capital stroke, the leading step to all that has followed, was (I believe the first thought was Bridgeman's) the destruction of walls for boundaries, and the invention of

A View from Grimes walk in Grimsthorp gardens. 27 jul.1736.

Grimsthorpe Castle, Lincolnshire. View by William Stukeley in 1736 of the fortified wood laid out from 1711 by Stephen Switzer for the Marquess of Lindsey. Switzer surrounded a wood with a raised terrace walk punctuated by a series of bastions contrived so as to command views towards open parkland and the surrounding countryside. Here are the seeds of ideas developed later by Capability Brown.

fossés – an attempt then deemed so astonishing, that the common people called them Ha! Ha's! to express their surprize at finding a sudden and unperceived check to their walk.

Walpole spells out his precise reasons for attaching such significance to the ha-ha:

I call a sunk fence the leading step for these reasons. No sooner was this simple enchantment made, than levelling, mowing, rolling, followed. The contiguous ground of the park without the sunk fence was to be harmonized with the lawn within; and the garden in its turn was to be set free from its prim regularity, that it might assort with the wilder country without.

He is also clear about the specifically picturesque function of the ha-ha: 'How rich, how gay, how picturesque the face of the country! The demolition of walls laying open each improvement, every journey is made through a succession of pictures'.[10]

Stephen Switzer may have worked at the very start of his career with George London for Vanbrugh at Castle Howard from 1699, and in his *Ichnographia Rustica* he praises Castle Howard as the perfect example of 'Natural and Polite Gardening'. Vanbrugh's large pictorial and imaginative genius as displayed at Castle Howard, at Blenheim (with Wise, Switzer and Bridgeman) and at Stowe (with Bridgeman), deployed the elements of continental baroque garden design in impressive schemes which concentrated attention in an unaccustomed way on views of the existing landscape. At Castle Howard he was responsible for demolishing Henderskelfe church, castle and village so as to open up panoramic views of the countryside. In Wray Wood straight and irregular walks linked circular open spaces containing garden ornaments in a manner possibly influenced by the younger Pliny. Thanks to Vanbrugh's planning, the house itself is approached, by a dramatic coup, from the side and not frontally. Especially memorable at Castle Howard are Vanbrugh's Obelisk (1714) and Temple (1724–8), and Hawksmoor's Pyramid (1728) and Mausoleum (1729–36). Vanbrugh's Temple or Belvedere, inspired by Palladio's Villa Rotonda, is approached by a winding grassy path flanked by statues which followed the line of the former village street. Vanbrugh's biographer, Kerry Downes, has beautifully observed that the effect of these buildings in the landscape is to 'extend the aesthetic environment of the house far into the practical one, and . . . at one moment seen and at the next hidden by another hill, give the traveller that feeling of being silently observed which is stronger and deeper than the conventional sense of the *genius loci* of many an eighteenth-century garden peopled with classical statues and summer houses'.[11]

The relation of the Temple and Mausoleum at Castle Howard may have inspired the beautiful turfed ride or terrace at Duncombe Park, also in North Yorkshire, which is punctuated at each end by a classical temple. The open Ionic rotunda at the northern end is so close to Vanbrugh's at Stowe that it may well be the work of Vanbrugh and is probably of the same date, *c.*1719–20. The Doric temple to the south is doubtless a little later since it echoes Hawksmoor's mausoleum at Castle Howard, the form of which was not finally settled until 1729. More remarkable than the temples is the broad and embanked grassy terrace itself, running for half a mile in a gentle concave arc and commanding attractive views down into the narrow Rye valley. Arthur Young explained in 1770 how 'This view is beheld with moving variation as you walk along the terrass to the *Tuscan* temple.'[12] Following the contours of the land, the terrace forms a natural ha-ha ending in the two circular bastions containing the temples. Indeed, in order to enclose the northern section of the terrace on the west side away from the escarpment, a low stone retaining wall was constructed in a series of curves on one of which stands the Ionic rotunda. Though this arrangement lacks the ditch of the fully developed ha-ha, it corresponds to the kind of ha-ha envisaged by Switzer. It is thus unfortunate that its date is not precisely known. The house at Duncombe was built in 1713–18 in a bold Vanbrughian style by the local architect William Wakefield, and work on the gardens presumably began soon after.

One of the most revolutionary and, by now, best known of Vanbrugh's contributions to landscape gardening was his Memorandum of June 1709 on the preservation of the ruins of Woodstock Manor in the park at Blenheim. In it he adumbrated a picturesque approach to nature, architecture and the past which anticipated much English theory and practice for the next century. He argued for the preservation of buildings of distant times because 'they move more lively and pleasing Reflections (than History without their Aid can do) on the Persons who have Inhabited them; On the Remarkable things which have been transacted in them, Or the extraordinary Occasions of Erecting them'. In the park at Blenheim he considered that:

Buildings, And Plantations . . . rightly dispos'd will indeed Supply all the wants of Nature in that Place. And the Most agreable Disposition is to Mix them: in which this Old Manour *gives so happy an Occasion for*; that were the inclosure filld with Trees . . . Promiscuously Set to grow up in a Wild Thicket, So that all the Building left . . . might Appear in Two Risings amongst 'em, it wou'd make One of the Most Agreable Objects that the best of Landskip Painters can invent.[13]

Walpole was antagonistic to Vanbrugh and under-emphasised his contribution to the development of landscape gardening. To Walpole the pioneer was Charles Bridgeman (*c.* 1680–1738), whose approach was characterised by an understanding of the *genius loci*, and by a predilection for largeness of scale and for garden buildings. His biographer, Peter Willis, has described him as a pragamatist, no two of whose schemes were exactly alike but combining formal, transitional and progressive elements.

At Claremont, Surrey, Bridgeman co-operated with Vanbrugh from *c.*1717 on the improvement of the gardens for the Duke of Newcastle. Vanbrugh designed the remarkable castellated Belvedere on a hilltop set off from the axis of the house. It is one of the earliest mediaevalising follies of its kind and was surrounded by woodland pierced with winding paths and vistas. As Colen Campbell explained, in the text accompanying his plan of Claremont in *Vitruvius Britannicus* (III, 1725), 'The Situation . . . [is] singularly romantick, and from the high Tower has a most prodigious fine Prospect of the *Thames* and the adjacent villas'. Below the Belvedere, Bridgeman laid out a round pond with an elaborate grass amphitheatre on one side, though in the 1730s William Kent softened Bridgeman's lines, as he was also to do at Rousham and Stowe. After years of neglect Claremont has recently been wonderfully restored to something like the state that Kent left it in the 1730s.

In 1728 Bridgeman was appointed Master Gardener to George II, the year after he succeeded to the throne, but most of Bridgeman's royal work was carried out for Queen Caroline, a passionate gardener. At Kensington Gardens, which he laid out for her in 1726–33, the basic elements of his plan survive. Near the palace is the Round Pond with three rides radiating out through the woodland. A contemporary plan shows the pond flanked by two symmetrically placed mounts capped by circular temples. Separating Kensington Gardens from Hyde Park is Bridgeman's familiar Serpentine, constructed in 1730–2 and the forerunner of the more undulating lakes that were to be created by Capability Brown and Humphry Repton.

Concurrently with his improvements at Kensington, Bridgeman was also working for Queen Caroline at Richmond Gardens, which lay between Richmond Green and Kew Palace. Richmond Lodge was a modest irregular building which

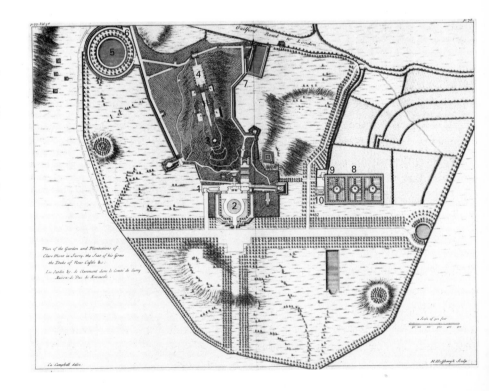

(*Above*) Claremont. Charles Bridgeman's amphitheatre as exposed in the
recent restoration of the garden. (*Right*)
Plan of the garden and plantations from
Vitruvius Britannicus III, (1725). This
shows the grounds as laid out by Bridgeman from 1716 for the 1st Duke of
Newcastle. There are formal avenues
and a parterre south of the house and a
round pool in the top left-hand corner of
the plan.

Key: 1. House 2. Parterre 3.
Belvedere 4. Bowling-green 5. Round
pond 6. Site of amphitheatre laid out by
1728 7. Terrace or ha-ha 8. Kitchen
garden 9. Gardener's cottage by Vanbrugh 10. Stables

she had occupied as Princess of Wales, and its gardens became her special delight. Bridgeman's unusual achievement here was to create a rural pastoral atmosphere where meadows were interspersed with undulating belts of trees and winding walks. Walpole wrote admiringly: 'As his [Bridgeman's] reformation gained footing, he ventured farther, and in the royal garden at Richmond dared to introduce cultivated fields, and even morsels of a forest appearance'.[14] In the early 1730s Bridgeman was joined by William Kent who added the picturesque hermitage and the even more bizarre Merlin's Cave.

The two finest surviving gardens where Bridgeman worked, Stowe and Rousham, are so overlaid by William Kent's additions of the 1730s that it is now virtually impossible to consider Bridgeman's contribution independently of Kent's. Kent was a successful architect of forty-six when he turned to garden design in *c.*1730. He had spent eight years in Rome from 1711 training to be a painter where he would, of course, have become familiar with the idealised landscapes of the Roman Campagna painted by artists like Claude and Gaspard Poussin. He would also have known the landscape park created at the Villa Borghese in the early seventeenth century, and he recorded in his diary his admiration for the Villa Pratolino near Florence with its groves, grottoes and views from the terrace over the adjacent countryside.

A letter of December 1734 from Sir Thomas Robinson to Lord Carlisle contains a fascinating contemporary reaction to the revolution which it was believed Kent had already effected in garden design:

There is a new taste in gardening just arisen, which has been practised with so great success at the Prince's garden in Town [i.e. at Carlton House, acquired by Frederick, Prince of Wales in 1733], that a general alteration of some of the most considerable gardens in the Kingdom is begun, after Mr Kent's notion of gardening, viz., to lay them out, and work without either level or line. By this means I really think the 12 acres the Prince's garden consists of, is more diversified and of greater variety than anything of that compass I ever saw; and this method of gardening is the more agreeable, as, when finished, it has the appearance of beautiful nature, and without being told, one would imagine art had no part in the finishing, and is, according to what one hears of the Chinese, entirely after their models for works of this nature, where they never plant straight lines or make regular designs. The celebrated gardens of Claremount, Chiswick, and Stowe are now full of labourers, to modernise the extensive works finished in them, even since every one's memory.[15]

Walpole hailed Kent as 'the father of modern gardening' and inventor of 'an art that realizes painting and improves nature'. For Walpole he was

painter enough to taste the charms of landscape, bold and opinionative to dare and to dictate, and born with a genius to strike out a great system from the twilight of imperfect essays. He leaped the fence, and saw that all nature was a garden. He felt the delicious contrast of hill and valley changing imperceptibly into each other, tasted the beauty of the gentle swell, or concave scoop, and remarked how loose groves crowned an easy eminence with happy ornament . . . By selecting favourite objects, and veiling deformities by screens of plantation; sometimes allowing the rudest waste to add its foil to the richest theatre, he realised the compositions of the great masters in painting.[16]

Though the profoundly picturesque character of Pope's garden at Twickenham has now been established by Morris Brownell in his *Alexander Pope and the Arts of Georgian England* (Oxford, 1978), neither Pope nor Addison mentioned Claude or indeed specified any painters in their writing on gardening. An important part of Kent's pictorial approach, which owed so much to Pope, was that he owned landscape paintings and drawings by Gaspard Poussin, Claude and Salvator Rosa, and it is impossible not to see traces of their influence in his work. However, Walpole was writing after the event and may have exaggerated the painterly basis of his design. Modern scholars, inspired by the Warburgian tradition of iconographical analysis, have tended to concentrate more on the symbolical and political allusions which, as we shall see, can be found in gardens such as Stowe and Stourhead.

The essence of Kent's contribution can be immediately grasped by comparing plans of Claremont, Stowe and Rousham before and after his arrival. He dissolved the massive almost architectural ordonnance of Bridgeman's gardens, in which temples and statues were anchored to a framework provided by terraces, hedges, and rides through woods pivoting on *rond-points*. He substituted an essentially painterly sequence of shifting perspectives which must have been envisaged from the start in a three-dimensional way, for, as Christopher Hussey was the first to point out, we do not know of any *plan* for a garden in Kent's hand. Since Stowe is the most extensive and spectacular picturesque garden in Europe we should discuss its development, which was carried out in five phases, in some detail.

The garden at Stowe was begun by the Whig Sir Richard Temple, 4th Baronet, soon after his dismissal by Queen Anne's Tories in 1713 from his army command in Flanders. With the arrival of the House of Hanover in the following year he was at once reinstated and created Baron Cobham. In 1714, aged forty, he married

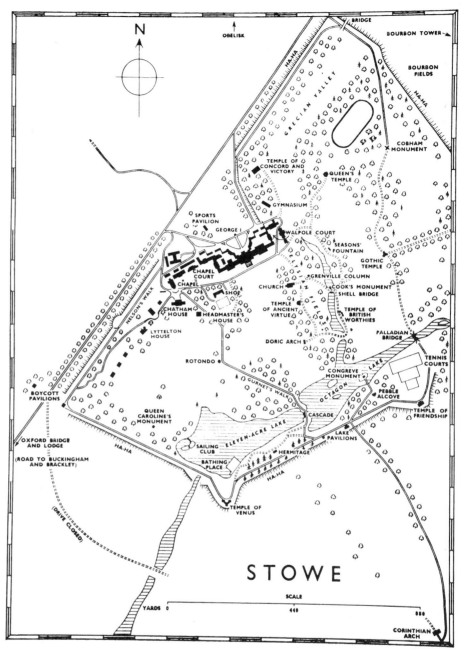

STOWE

SCALE

YARDS 0   440   880

Anne Halsey, heiress of a wealthy brewer, and three years later was advanced to the dignity of Viscount Cobham. Bridgeman was at work on the gardens west of the house in 1714, and two years later Vanbrugh, dismissed from Blenheim, was called in to remodel the late-seventeenth-century house itself. By 1719 Vanbrugh had also added the Temple of Venus and Nelson's Seat, while Bridgeman had placed statues, urns and a garden pavilion near the house, had laid out the Elm Walk leading to Nelson's Seat, and had raised two mounts at the north and south ends of an axis running through the centre of the house.

The second phase of the development of Stowe lasted from 1721–30 and was a continuation of what Vanbrugh and Bridgeman had achieved in the first phase. Fortunately, a detailed bird's-eye view of c.1720, attributed to Bridgeman, survives in the Bodleian Library. The gardens were greatly extended by an

Stowe, Buckinghamshire. Plan of the gardens. Between 1714 and 1779 Viscount Cobham and his nephew Earl Temple employed an impressive array of English and continental architects and garden designers, including Bridgeman, Vanbrugh, Kent, Gibbs, Capability Brown, Blondel, Valdrè, Borra and T. Pitt, to provide elaborate garden buildings and remodel the grounds into one of the wonders of eighteenth-century Europe.

15

Stowe. The Rotunda, *c.* 1719, by Sir John Vanbrugh, was placed at a focal point in the then still largely geometrical layout of the original gardens with a canal and avenues radiating out from it. However, towards the west it commanded views of open parkland across a bastion-like ha-ha. The present dome is by Giambattista Borra of 1752 and has a shallower profile than Vanbrugh's. This change was made to blend the building more smoothly into the surrounding landscape which had become more fluid than in 1719.

avenue leading south to a large octagonal lake flanked by two pavilions designed by Vanbrugh. From this lake another avenue led north-westwards to a prominently placed rotunda designed by Vanbrugh and commanding extensive views in different directions. This was an open Ionic temple similar to that which survives at Duncombe Park, North Yorkshire. A canal or rectangular basin ran eastwards from the temple towards the avenue on the main north–south axis. A contemporary visitor, Lord Perceval, has left an instructive account of his visit in 1724:

what adds to the bewty of this garden is, that it is not bounded by walls, but by a ha-Hah, which leaves you the sight of the bewtiful wooded country, and makes you ignorant how far the high planted walks extend. [There are] a great number of walks, terminated by summer houses & heathen temples of different structure, and adorned with statues cast from the Anticks . . . You think twenty times you have no more to see, & of a sudden you find your self in some new garden or walk, as finish'd & adorn'd as that you left. Nothing is more irregylar in the whole, nothing more regular in the parts, which totally differ one from the other.[17]

On Vanbrugh's death in 1726 he was swiftly replaced by James Gibbs (1682–1754), the distinguished baroque architect. Gibbs's contributions to Stowe began with the two Boycott Pavilions of *c.*1726 which were placed at the start of the new western approach road. This road, completed in 1731, was planned so as to approach the north entrance-front of the house obliquely – from the wings, as it were – a dramatic gesture inspired by Vanbrugh's plans for Castle Howard and Blenheim. The road also made redundant the old approach, known as the Hey Way, which led from Buckingham up to the south front of the house. Once this was closed, Cobham could begin to develop the eastern area of the estate as a garden. The work carried out here from 1731–40 constitutes the third and probably best-known phase in the design of the gardens at Stowe.

According to Philip Southcote (1699–1788) of Woburn Farm, 'Lord Cobham began in the Bridgeman taste: 'tis the Elysian Fields that is the painting part of his gardens'.[18] The Elysian Fields with their celebrated garden buildings by William Kent were laid out east of the main north–south axis of Stowe in *c.*1733–8. We cannot be sure how much of the design to attribute to Bridgeman, how much to Lord Cobham and how much to Kent. What is probably due to Bridgeman is the straight avenue connecting the southern end of the Elysian Fields with the Octagon Pond, and also the serpentine river running up the edge of the Elysian Fields. In attributing this river – which really consists of two narrow lakes forming the Alder River and the Styx – to Bridgeman, one should remember that he had recently laid out the rather similar Serpentine in Hyde Park. This little 'river' in the Elysian Fields was so shaped that Kent's two buildings on either side, the Temple of British Worthies and the Temple of Ancient Virtue, could each be seen from the other, perfectly mirrored in the water. This pictorial device is more characteristic of Kent the painter than of Bridgeman. However, the way in which the Temple of Ancient Virtue fulfils three visual purposes may be due to Bridgeman as much as to Kent. These roles of the Temple of Ancient Virtue are as a terminus to the great Cross Walk, as an answer to the Temple of British Worthies on the other side of the water, and as a pivot for the whole composition of the Elysian Fields. It is worth noting that Bridgeman had a hand with Vanbrugh in the similar siting of the Rotunda.

Now this scene may seem to be composed like a painting by Claude and may even be thought to point forward to the work of Capability Brown. However, we should remember that not only have the trees grown up but that originally there were many more little buildings dotted about; above the shell bridge (a disguised dam which still survives), there were formerly a grotto, two little domed temples with curly pillars, and a Chinese House. In other words, the effect was a great deal more rococo and, in fact, probably rather like the garden paintings of the topographical artist Thomas Robins.

To turn from the visual to the symbolical aspect of the Elysian Fields is to be reminded that the iconographical arrangement seems to have been directly inspired by a remarkable essay in the *Spectator* by Addison in 1709–10. This was an allegorical vision in which Addison described how in a dream he had found himself walking through a wood behind a group of people carrying the standard of Ambition. As George Clarke has recently pointed out,[19] the essential features of the Elysian Fields are all in Addison's Essay: a long straight path (i.e. the Great Cross Walk), is terminated by a Temple of Virtue (Ancient Virtue at Stowe), beyond which over the Styx lies a Temple of Honour (British Worthies at Stowe); nearby is a ruinous Temple of Vanity (Modern Virtue at Stowe, built deliberately and ironically as a ruin). The types of people mentioned in Addison's vision and also the effigies, correspond to the statues actually set up in the gardens at Stowe. Thus it seems clear that the layout of the Elysian Fields was not inspired by a wish to imitate the landscape paintings of Claude or Poussin, but by a fanciful literary or philosophical programme. If this is so, then it tends to diminish the contribution of Bridgeman and Kent, for such an iconographical impetus is more likely to have come from the literary members of Lord Cobham's circle: his nephew and heir Richard Grenville, who had just completed the Grand Tour and was an early member of the Society of Dilettanti, from his other poet nephews, Gilbert West and George Lyttelton, from William Pitt, and, indeed, from Alexander Pope himself who was a frequent visitor to Stowe. As a picturesque retreat dedicated to philosophic reflection, Pope's own garden at Twickenham may well have inspired the Elysian Fields at Stowe.

Kent's training in Rome had provided a first-hand knowledge of Italian Renaissance gardens which had often contained secluded and rather wild sections set apart from the maunderings of poets and philosophers. The creators of these gardens had been aware that groves, grottoes and nymphaea had been the delight of scholars and statesmen in classical antiquity. A wilder type of landscape garden had also appealed to the ancients as an appropriate setting for sacred architecture. Indeed, one such Roman sacred landscape survived, the so-called Temple of the Sybil set above the gorge at Tivoli. This romantically placed temple, frequently drawn and painted, had itself already become a garden ornament in classical antiquity when Hadrian created his own landscape garden around it in the extensive grounds of his villa. It is, of course, this temple which inspired Kent's Temple of Ancient Virtue at Stowe, which is adorned inside with statues of four heroes: Homer, Socrates, Epaminondas and Lycurgus.

The Temple of British Worthies on the other side of the river to the Temple of Ancient Virtue is directly inspired by buildings in sixteenth- and seventeenth-century Italian gardens. The theme had already been essayed by Kent in an unexecuted project for an *exedra* at Chiswick which seems to have been based on

the now destroyed circus in the grounds of the Villa Mattei in Rome. Two surviving sixteenth-century parallels in the Veneto, a part of Italy which Kent visited in 1714, are the groups of Roman emperors in niches in the gardens of the Villa Brenzone near Verona, attributed to Sanmicheli, and the nymphaeum by Palladio at the Villa Barbaro at Maser. In an oval niche at the top of the central pyramid at the Temple of British Worthies was the head of Mercury, the messenger of the gods who led the souls of the just across the Styx to the Elysian Fields.

Stowe. The Temple of British Worthies, 1733, by William Kent, looking across the Elysian Fields to Kent's Temple of Ancient Virtue. The bust, probably by Scheemakers, is of Sir John Barnard, M.P., an opponent of Sir Robert Walpole. The Temple of Ancient Virtue is inspired by Hawksmoor's mausoleum at Castle Howard, which itself owes something to the Temple of the Sybil (or Vesta) at Tivoli as restored by Palladio in his *I Quattro Libri* (1570).

We have seen four layers of association in the Elysian Fields: antique, Renaissance, visual or painterly, and allegorical. The fifth, which is an extension of the allegorical, relates to the vicissitudes of Cobham's political position. The days of his triumphant Whig apotheosis in which he had undertaken the gardens at Stowe ended painfully in 1733 while the buildings in the Elysian Fields were rising. In that year he fell foul of Walpole over the Excise Bill and was also dismissed from his regiment again. He now joined other prominent Whig peers in forming an opposition to the whiggery of Walpole. They called themselves the Patriots and claimed that they were defending British Liberty and the Constitution from the complacency and massive corruption which they attributed to Walpole and his followers. Stowe became an active centre of the new Whig opposition and the iconography of the gardens took on the additional character of a political manifesto in which traditional ideals of government were contrasted with the decadence of Walpole's administration. Thus the headless statue in the deliberately decayed Temple of Modern Virtue represented Sir Robert Walpole as Cobham wished to see him. In the Temple of Ancient Virtue the statues of the Greek heroes were given unequivocal inscriptions, such as that beneath Lycurgus which emphasised that he had 'planned a system of laws firmly secured against all corruption; and established in the state for many ages perfect liberty and inviolate purity of manners'.

The same theme was developed even more strikingly in the Temple of British Worthies with its busts by Rysbrack and Scheemakers of those on whom Cobham and his friends were prepared, for a variety of complex reasons, to smile. In the left arm were eight men of contemplation, and in the right eight men of action, including Edward, Prince of Wales, the Black Prince, who seems to have been intended as a counterpart to the contemporary Prince of Wales, Frederick, son of George II. It was around Prince Frederick that Cobham and the dissident Whigs gathered, Frederick having himself quarrelled with his father.

In 1737 Frederick, Prince of Wales, paid an ostentatious visit to Stowe as Cobham's guest at about the time that this extraordinary political garden was reaching completion. The visit seems to have stimulated Cobham to lay out further buildings in a valley immediately east of the Elysian Fields. At the southern foot of the valley, in fact in the south-east bastion of Bridgeman's ha-ha, Gibbs built in 1739 the Temple of Friendship (later remodelled by Blondel and Valdrè) to contain busts of the Whig Patriots, including the Prince of Wales, Lord Chatham and Lord Cobham himself. At the top or north end of the valley Gibbs built in *c.*1744 the Ladies' (or Queen's) Temple, where Lady Cobham and her friends could sit and sew while her husband talked Whig politics with his friends in the temple below. The most important architectural addition to this part of Stowe is the Gothic Temple designed by James Gibbs in 1741. This is important stylistically as one of the earliest garden buildings in the Gothic Revival style anywhere, but it is also significant in that the style was here overlaid with iconographical or political implications. The building was originally known not as the Gothic Temple but as the Temple of Liberty and was specifically dedicated to the Liberty of our Ancestors. These were supposed to be the Goths associated with the Germanic tribes who invaded Rome. Eighteenth-century antiquaries argued that when Hengist landed in Thanet he brought with him the democratic procedures described by Tacitus as typical of German assemblies. Thus

Stowe. Gothic Temple, 1741, by James
Gibbs. A startling pile of red ironstone
with a triangular Elizabethan-inspired
plan and elaborate Early English detail.
It is unique in Gibbs's executed *œuvre*
and a pioneering work in the history of
the Gothic Revival.

England's government was sometimes described in the eighteenth century as 'our
old Gothick constitution'. These northern Goths had also produced the
Reformation as a second attack on Rome. Thus Gothic could be seen in a number
of fanciful ways as conterminous with Liberty, Constitution and Enlightenment.
On the ceiling of the temple were painted the arms of Lord Cobham's Saxon
forbears; round it were placed the seven Saxon deities by Rysbrack, which had
been brought from the earlier western parts of the gardens; nearby paths were
named Thanet Walk and Gothic Walk, and, perhaps most significantly, Cobham
had placed over the door a quotation from *Horace* by Corneille: '*Je rends Grace au
Dieux de nestre pas Romain Pour concerver encore quelque chose d'humain*'.

The principal development of the landscape, aside from political connotations,
of this part of Stowe begins with the remodelling of the great valley in the 1740s.
This valley, with the Temple of Friendship at the foot, the Ladies' Temple at the
top and the Gothic Temple half way up the east or right-hand side, was reshaped
as part of the fourth phase of development which lasted from 1741–53. At the
hands of Kent, or possibly of Capability Brown who became head of the kitchen
gardens in 1740, the valley became a long funnel-shaped space eight-hundred
yards long from north to south. Known today as the Queen's Valley it probably
shows Kent's ideal of landscape gardening at this late stage in his career. In place
of rococo wiggles we have a bald area leading up very obviously to a centrally
placed object – Gibbs's Ladies' Temple – with clumps of trees down the edges

Stowe. View of the Grecian Valley looking towards the Temple of Concord, designed in 1748 probably by Richard Grenville and completed in 1762 by Borra. Like Gibbs's Gothic Temple this is one of the earliest examples of full-scale revivalism in the eighteenth century. Inspired by a peripteral Roman temple it contains a series of plaster reliefs based on medals, designed by James 'Athenian' Stuart, struck to commemorate the victories of the Seven Years War which gave England mastery over the New World.

rather like the wings on a stage. Like a stage set the whole thing is meant to be viewed from one or two points only. Underlining this theatrical character is the beautiful Palladian Bridge which closed the Queen's Valley where the river left it on the eastern side. This was built, possibly from designs by Gibbs, some time between 1737 and 1742 and is inspired by the one built at Wilton in 1737 by Lord Pembroke and Roger Morris. It is theatrical because originally its whole eastern wall was solid so that there was a colonnade on only one side. It may have been constructed in this form to help hide the cottages in the nearby village of Lamport. In 1762, when trees had grown up, this solid wall was replaced with an answering colonnade. The bridge is functional for wheeled traffic and was intended for visitors making the circuit of the gardens in carriages. The blank rear wall was adorned with a great sculptural relief by Scheemakers showing the four quarters of the world bringing produce to Britannia, while there were two paintings by Francesco Sleter in the side compartments showing Raleigh and Penn as examples of the imperial ideals of the Whig circle. These paintings have disappeared but the sculptured relief survives in the pediment of the Temple of Concord to which we should now turn our attention.

The Temple of Concord, sadly shorn of its peristyle in 1927, stands in the angle of a large right-angled valley laid out in the 1740s as the Grecian Valley. After Walpole's fall from power, the relationship of Cobham and his circle of Whig

Patriots became rather strained since their common enemy had now been removed. This new part of the gardens therefore lacks any political iconography. It is, nonetheless, an important part of the development of Neo-classicism and the Picturesque. The Grecian Valley used to be attributed to William Kent, but there is no documentary evidence that he was at work at Stowe in the 1740s and it is now thought more likely that it is due to Cobham and his nephew Richard Grenville, with assistance from their friends and from the young Capability Brown (1716–83). The intention was to create a Grecian vale of Tempe dominated by a large temple at one end, a triumphal arch at the other, and between there was to be lake with wavy lines of trees along the edge. Accounts show that in 1746–7 huge quantities of earth were excavated to shape the valley, and trees were brought to it from elsewhere in the gardens. The idea of the water and the triumphal arch was abandoned. In terms of so-called 'natural' landscape, this dog-legged or right-angled valley represents a decisive advance on the slightly earlier Queen's Valley, and perhaps contains the seeds of Capability Brown's mature style. Its charming undulations, with their subtle cross-vistas, blend into distant views screened and curved to suggest infinity, while its varied planting incorporates cedars, larch and Scotch firs as well as the beech, sycamore and yew that Bridgeman relied on.

By a stroke of imagination the great Grecian Temple was placed at the hinge of the two parts of the Grecian Valley and was aligned at a slight angle to the main part of the valley running eastwards. The temple seems to have been designed in 1748 by Richard Grenville, later Lord Temple, though it was not completed till 1762 by Giambattista Borra. It probably ranks as the first neo-classical building in Europe, modelled as it is on the Maison Carrée at Nîmes. With its Roman source it was thus Grecian only in name, like the *goût grec* in contemporary France. Indeed in 1763, after Pitt had brought the Seven Years War to a victorious conclusion, the temple's dedication was changed to that of Concord and Victory. Scheemaker's relief of Britannia on the Palladian Bridge was now installed in the pediment so that, even in the Grecian Valley, contemporary politics were eventually allowed to have their say.

Lord Cobham died childless in 1749 at about the time of the beginning of work on the Grecian Temple, and his nephew Richard Grenville, Lord Temple, inherited Stowe in 1752. The fifth and final phase of work on the gardens of Stowe now began, only to be terminated by Temple's death in a carriage accident in the park in 1779. He spent a fortune in modernising what survived of Bridgeman's and Vanbrugh's gardens and garden buildings, in princely hospitality, and in enlarging the house from designs by Borra, Adam, and his cousin Thomas Pitt. The 1760s were the decade in which Lord Temple finally eliminated Bridgeman's network of connected vistas, formal ponds with terraces and clipped hedges. The Octagon Lake became irregular in shape and was extended to the east; the eleven-acre lake, adjacent on the west, became similarly irregular; and, perhaps most striking, the whole area between the south front of the house and the Octagon Lake was gradually broadened and widened. It became a vast unbroken expanse of turf with all trees and walks eliminated, one of the most impressive open spaces in Europe, and in powerful contrast to the intimate shaded Elysian Fields to the east. So vast a vista required an impressive terminal point, so in 1765 Thomas Pitt designed the great Corinthian Arch on the skyline to the south, a trial run for the Arc de Triomphe.

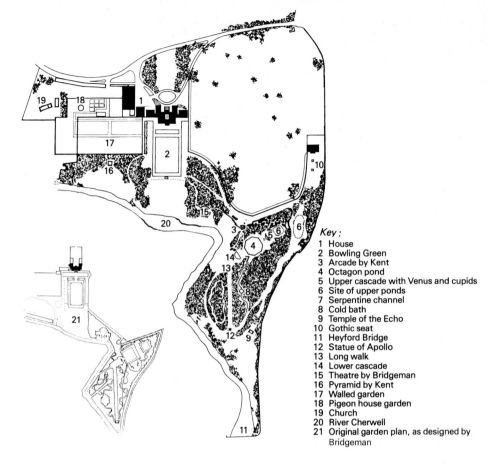

Rousham, Oxfordshire. (*Right*) Plan of the grounds laid out by Charles Bridgeman in *c*. 1720 and by William Kent in 1737-41. One of the most important features of Kent's garden was his incorporation of views of the open country and farmland which lie on the other side of the river Cherwell. Note also the simple paddocks which adjoin the house on the right.

(*Below*) Rousham. Drawing by William Kent for Venus's Vale, *c*. 1740. This part of the garden was laid out in exactly the form depicted and survives largely unaltered today. The upper cascade is presided over by a lead statue of Venus with swans and cherubs.

Key:
1 House
2 Bowling Green
3 Arcade by Kent
4 Octagon pond
5 Upper cascade with Venus and cupids
6 Site of upper ponds
7 Serpentine channel
8 Cold bath
9 Temple of the Echo
10 Gothic seat
11 Heyford Bridge
12 Statue of Apollo
13 Long walk
14 Lower cascade
15 Theatre by Bridgeman
16 Pyramid by Kent
17 Walled garden
18 Pigeon house garden
19 Church
20 River Cherwell
21 Original garden plan, as designed by Bridgeman

Rousham. The stone channel designed by William Kent, *c.* 1740. A rare survival of the highly artificial naturalness which characterised the earliest and still half-rococo phase of the landscape garden.

If Stowe is the grandest, perhaps Rousham, not far away in Oxfordshire, is the most charming of English landscaped gardens. Like Stowe it is an amalgam of work begun by Bridgeman in the 1720s and overlaid by Kent in the following decade. The appeal of Rousham is that it is that and nothing else, whereas at Stowe it is that and a dozen other and later things. Pope was a frequent visitor to Rousham and it is clear that the garden was inspired by his own at Twickenham. In September 1728 he wrote to Martha Blount: 'I lay one night at Rowsham which is the prettiest place for water-falls, jetts, ponds inclosed with beautiful scenes of green and hanging wood, that ever I saw'.[20] The small concave valley at Rousham sloping down to the river Cherwell was laid out by Bridgeman for Colonel Robert Dormer in *c.*1721 as a wilderness with tortuous paths and rectangular ponds. Dormer died in 1737 when the estate passed to his brother, Sir James Dormer, one of Marlborough's generals, a member of the Whig Kit-Kat club and a friend of Pope, Swift and Gay. He now called in William Kent to remodel the Jacobean house at Rousham in the new Gothick or castellated style, and also to soften or blur the lines of Bridgeman's garden. Kent opened up Bridgeman's wilderness to form the enchanting Venus's Vale, whose 'opening and retiring shades' reminded Walpole of Pope's garden at Twickenham. Kent transformed Bridgeman's principal pond from a square to an octagon, which reminds us how far even he was from the undulating lines that would be admired by Capability Brown. He also flanked the pond with an Upper and Lower Cascade, resembling Lord Burlington's at Chiswick and derived from Italian cascades such as that at the Villa Aldobrandini, Frascati, and the *fontana rustica* at the Villa Barbarigo. From the pond there leads one of those wiggly paths typical of the rococo reaction against formal symmetry. Curiously, it follows the line of a serpentine channel of water, a long masonry drain, which recalls the stone channels at the Villa d'Este, Tivoli, and the Torrent at the Villa Lante. If we follow this watery rill we come to a clearing dominated by the Temple of Echo built in 1738 and containing a Roman tombstone. This little temple is generally known as Townesend's Building after its builder, William Townesend, who adapted it from a more elaborate design by Kent with three porticos. It stands out against a background of yew, cedar and larch. The planting of conifers for ornament seems to have been an innovation of Kent's. They appear in all his drawings for garden buildings and were presumably intended to recall the cypresses and ilexes of classical landscape. Equally important were the views from the Temple of Echo. From the front one looks north along the river to the late-thirteenth-century Heyford Bridge carrying the Bicester to Enstone road over the Cherwell. The incorporation of romantic and historical buildings as terminal points in garden schemes is characteristic of this time. On the grandest scale we can see mediaeval abbeys being turned into garden ornaments: Fountains Abbey at Studley Royal, and Rievaulx Abbey at Duncombe Park. Kent evidently felt that mediaeval though Heyford Bridge was, it was insufficiently spectacular as a termination to his landscape. He therefore invented an amusingly foolish piece of Gothic icing sugar just beyond the bridge with the ironical name of the Temple of the Mill. As if this were not enough, he adorned the hill above with a sham ruin known as the Eye Catcher. Amongst the earliest sham ruins in any English landscape park, these two buildings have miraculously survived.

Also anticipatory of the future are Kent's remarkable designs of the 1730s for the park at Euston in Suffolk. Here, his reliance on isolated 'clumps' in rather bare undulating parkland which reaches right up to the windows of the house, foreshadowed Capability Brown's standard repertoire.

In the meantime, private owners or amateurs were discovering that they could play the game as well as the professionals. In *c*.1735 Philip Southcote began transforming his small estate at Woburn Farm near Weybridge in Surrey into a picturesque garden which became known as a *ferme ornée*. Visitors were confronted with cattle, sheep and poultry to emphasise the modest pastoral charms of rural life. From *c*.1743 the poet William Shenstone followed Southcote's example at The Leasowes near Hagley in Worcestershire. Such gardens lacked the grand classical allusions and symbolism of Stowe and were welcomed by contemporaries as examples of a new move to simplicity. Later, they especially appealed in France to a generation inspired by the sentiments of Rousseau. Southcote and Shenstone contrived pictorial circuits within a natural wooded arena with winding paths leading to carefully composed vistas and

(*Right*) Rousham. Temple of the Mill. An old mill cottage dressed up by William Kent in *c.* 1740 to serve as a Gothick eye-catcher beyond the northern extremity of the garden.

(*Below*) Euston Hall, Suffolk. Design for new house and park by William Kent for the 2nd Duke of Grafton. Dating from the 1730s, this scheme is important for showing *parkland* with clumps of trees, a rather different effect from that produced by the crowded *gardens* at Chiswick, Claremont and Rousham.

buildings. Shenstone, who seems to have invented the term 'landskip, or picturesque-gardening' in his 'Unconnected Thoughts on Gardening' (*Works*, II, 1764), argued that when the visitor had seen an object from the intended position he should never approach it by the same route but be conducted to it deviously or unexpectedly.

Stourhead, Wiltshire. The banker Henry Hoare (1705-85) and his grandson Sir Richard Colt Hoare, Bt. (1758-1838) developed Stourhead from the mid-1740s into what Hazlitt described as 'a sort of rural Herculaneum, a subterranean retreat'. Henry Flitcroft's Pantheon of c.1754, shown here, acts as a vital pivot on which most views of the lake and landscape turn. The Pantheon is also an early example of a sculpture museum, containing an antique *Livia Augusta as Ceres,* four modern casts and copies from the antique, and figures of Hercules and Flora by Rysbrack.

The finest example of the 'pictorial circuit' garden is Stourhead. From 1743 Henry Hoare created an exquisite series of shifting pictures from one building to another round the edge of a large artificial lake. The Temple of Ceres (now Flora) built in 1744 by Henry Flitcroft (1697–1769), was provided with an inscription over the door from the Sixth book of the Aeneid, thus establishing the lakeside Virgilian overtones at the outset. In 1748 Hoare was building an elaborate tripartite grotto on the other side of the lake. A rough irregular passage leads down into an impressive domed chamber encrusted with lava-like rock and spars. This is dramatically lit from above and from an extraordinary hole in the side which also gives a beautiful view across the lake. At the back is an alcove containing a white lead figure of the Nymph of the Grot lying across the source of the river Stour, carved from the antique by John Cheere. A suitable quotation from Pope, whose grotto at Twickenham this closely resembles, is carved below the marble bath at her feet. Looking along the grotto, our attention is captured by another statue by Cheere, brilliantly lit from above, of the River God with his flowing urn. In a letter of 1765[21] Hoare quoted Virgil's words '*facilis descensus Averno*' ('easy is the descent to Avernus') in connection with the steps leading down to the grotto, thus implying that the whole path round the lake can be interpreted as an allegory of Aeneas' journey in the underworld in the Sixth Aeneid.

Continuing our tour of the shores of Lake Avernus, as recreated at Stourhead, we arrive at the most important building in the whole landscape, the Pantheon (or Temple of Hercules) of c.1754 by Flitcroft. This building seems to have been inspired by the Pantheon temple in Claude's *View of Delphi with a Procession,* of which Hoare owned a version by Locatelli. Even closer to Stourhead is Claude's *Coast View of Delos with Aeneas* (now in the National Gallery), which was one of six paintings illustrating the story of Aeneas. Claude shows a Doric portico (corresponding to the Temple of Ceres at Stourhead), a Pantheon and a bridge which are close not only in form but in their relation to each other, to the corresponding buildings at Stourhead. On a higher level on the south side of the lake is Flitcroft's Temple of Apollo of c.1765, based on the late Roman Round Temple of Venus at Baalbek. This had been illustrated by Robert Wood in his

Coast View of Delos with Aeneas, 1672, by Claude Lorrain. The first of the set of paintings of the story of Aeneas which Claude painted in the last decade of his life as part of his personal artistic discovery of Virgil. This kind of haunting scene may have inspired Hoare's creation of Stourhead.

The Ruins of Balbec, published in 1757, and we know that Henry Hoare had purchased a copy of the book in 1757. As Christopher Hussey has pointed out, Flitcroft's temple is placed on an elevation from which one could gain, 'before the side-screening trees encroached on it, the most extensive view of the elysium, and the most beautiful, when, from the spectator's left, evening light casts over it the appropriate Claudian glow'.[22]

Below the classical Temple of Apollo Hoare indulged a charming game of pastoral make-believe. Near the edge of the lake the mediaeval tower of Stourton parish church rises above cottage roofs and the village green with its cross. In fact the cross is not the village cross but an urban market cross of 1373 from Bristol High Street transplanted to Stourhead in 1768; nor is the grass round it the village green but simply an extremity of the park. Nonetheless, Hoare's incorporation into his Virgilian dream of a romanticised picture of the English village is a remarkable foretaste of what John Nash was to achieve much later at Blaise Hamlet. Even here Hoare's approach was coloured by Gaspard Poussin as we can see in a letter to his daughter of October 1762 in which he claimed that 'the view of the Bridge, Village and Church altogether will be a charming Gaspard picture at the end of that Water'.[23]

Shugborough, Staffordshire. View from the west by Nicholas Dall, 1768. This shows one of the most celebrated of all picturesque parks in the making. The uncompromising body of the house, built in 1693, was elegantly remodelled by Samuel Wyatt in the 1790s. In Dall's time it stood out uncomfortably against the informal setting which had been laid out from the late 1740s with a Chinese House and two sets of mock ruins facing each other across the serpentine water. Between the ruins we can see the free-standing greenhouse designed by Athenian Stuart in 1764 and containing a painting by Dall based on views in Stuart's *Antiquities of Athens*. The greenhouse, pagoda and Palladian bridge have disappeared but the park is still rich in buildings by Stuart.

1762 also saw the publication of the epoch-making first volume of James Stuart's and Nicholas Revett's *Antiquities of Athens*, although, subsidised by the Society of Dilettanti, they had prepared the first measured drawings as early as 1751–5. In 1764, James 'Athenian' Stuart (1713–88) embarked on the widescale transformation of its engravings into brick and plaster, scattering them across the park at Shugborough, Staffordshire. His patron was the Whig, Thomas Anson (1695–1773), traveller and founder member of the Society of Dilettanti. Stuart's Greek Doric Temple, Tower of the Winds, Arch of Hadrian and Choragic Monument of Lysicrates fitted elegantly if surprisingly into a park which Anson had long been adorning with picturesque garden buildings in a more whimsical rococo mood. This new phase of development in the 1760s was made possible by the large inheritance which Thomas Anson received in 1762 from his brother, the Admiral Anson who had helped re-establish British naval supremacy. One of the first of the new garden buildings, the Arch of Hadrian, was thus a triumphal arch explicitly commemorating the Admiral and his wife. Christopher Hussey has seen in these monuments at Shugborough something of the political symbolism of those at Stowe. Greek political philosophy with its ideal of liberty encouraged the Whig members of the Society of Dilettanti to view the monuments of Athens with especial favour. Near the house Stuart provided an impressive orangery with a south-facing colonnade and an apse at the west end with a coffered semi-dome. As well as plants and classical sculpture the building contained a backcloth of architecture selected by Stuart and painted by Dall. Miss Anna Seward, the Swan of Lichfield, wrote of this orangery:

> See where the stately colonnade extends
> Its pillar'd length to shade the sculptured forms
> Of Demigods or Heroes, and protect
> From the cold northern blast each tender plant . . .
> Here while we breathe perfume, the ravish'd eye
> Surveys the miracles of Grecian art.

As left by Anson and Stuart, the park at Shugborough appears as the last great classically inspired English landscape. In fact, as the brief description of its history in the next chapter shows, it was a product of the numerous and varied influence of the age. The eclectic, haphazard composition of buildings and landscape reveals an attitude that is quintessentially picturesque and certainly English.

The Rococo
and Chinoiserie Phase

_____

THE pattern we traced in the previous chapter from Vanbrugh and Bridgeman via Kent to Stourhead is largely based on surviving gardens and is also in broad agreement with the argument in Horace Walpole's *Essay on Modern Gardening* of 1770. There thus appears to be an inevitable development culminating in the apparently 'natural' landscaped parks of Capability Brown. However, this pattern may only be the product of hindsight. It is important to recognise that gardens in the 1740s and 50s could still be obviously artificial, and in an entertainingly whimsical way. This mood is one that we especially associate with the post-Baroque decorative style known as Rococo, which was invented in Paris in the 1690s and arrived in other European centres, including London, in *c*.1730. Its essentially asymmetrical use of ornament such as S-shaped curves, flowers and abstract decoration rather like splashes of water, gives it obvious affinities with both Chinoiserie and Gothick. The serpentine patterns of gardens like Rousham and Stourhead might be interpreted as reflections of rococo sensibility, but there were many lesser gardens which, with their flimsy and fanciful chinoiserie and Gothick ornaments tend to be forgotten, not only because they have almost entirely disappeared but because their appearance was scarcely ever recorded by contemporary artists. Enthusiasm for the depiction of gardens was at its height between *c*.1705, when Leonard Knyff's views were engraved by Johannes Kip for *Britannia Illustrata* (1707), and 1739 when Badeslade and Rocque's fourth volume of *Vitruvius Britannicus* appeared. Thereafter, with the important exception of Sir William Chambers's orientalising *Plans, Elevations, Sections and Perspective Views of the Gardens and Buildings at Kew in Surrey* (1763), there was virtually nothing until the illustrations in W. Watts's *Seats of the Nobility and Gentry* of 1779. In France G.-L. Le Rouge engraved hundred of views of *jardins anglo-chinois* for his series of books published between 1776 and 1788 of which the first was called *Détails des nouveaux jardins à la mode*. However, something of the service performed for French gardens by Le Rouge was echoed in England by the work of the provincial topographical painter Thomas Robins (1716–70).

The discovery by John Harris in 1972 of an album of 133 watercolours and drawings by Robins, mainly of gardens, and his subsequent publication of the most interesting of them, has reminded us that the rococo and chinoiserie phase of gardening was more important than has been realised. It is now clear that the interest in the irregularity of Chinese gardening expressed by Temple and confirmed by Burlington's purchase of Ripa's engravings in 1724, bore some remarkable fruit in the 1740s and 50s. At Grove House, Old Windsor, the Hon. Dickie Bateman (*c*.1705–73) had lived like a pseudo-Mandarin during the 1730s and by the end of the decade had laid out a whimsically designed irregular garden adorned with a chinoiserie bridge, a China House in a bizarre amalgam of Oriental

(*Above*) Davenport House, Shropshire. Painting by Thomas Robins of the Long Water in the garden created in 1753 by Sharington Davenport. On the left is a Gothick alcove seat at the end of an *alleé* and on the right is a half-timbered farm-house romanticised by the addition of a castellated tower. The bucolic atmosphere of a *ferme ornée* is further underlined by the grazing sheep and the cows being milked.

(*Right*) Davenport House painted by Robins as a chinoiserie *capriccio*. Though the Gothick seat has been retained, the rawness and stiffness of the actual garden as shown in in the previous plate have been dissolved into a misty fantasy.

and English styles, and a substantial 'abbatial barn' in the Gothick taste. In 1744–8 Benjamin Hyett created a sinuous Sharawaggi garden at Marybone House, Gloucester, dominated by a striking pagoda painted blue and red. In the grounds of his country house about six miles away at Painswick, he had built by 1748 an octagonal Gothic pavilion in the spiky post-Kentian Gothic style associated with Walpole's latest work at Strawberry Hill. At Davenport House, Shropshire, Sharington Davenport laid out the grounds in the new taste in 1753 and at the same time commissioned Robins to paint a series of views of them. He did not alter the house itself, a solid baroque building of 1726, but concentrated his attention on landscaping the serpentine valley beneath it and providing an extraordinary series of garden buildings including a circular castellated tower, an artificial ruin, a grotto and cascade, and an octagonal Gothic temple on a mount. Robins painted an entrancing chinoiserie *capriccio* in which the gardens at Davenport are transformed into a mountainous Chinese landscape enlivened by a frail bamboo bridge and, more unexpectedly, by the mediaeval market cross from Bristol High Street! One of the most attractive garden views ever painted in England, this must also be one of the most prophetic for, as we have seen, Henry Hoare was shortly to grace the gardens at Stourhead with this very cross.

At Woodside House, Berkshire, in 1752–5 Hugh Hamersley Gothicised the house and laid out a rococo wilderness with an elegant Chinese kiosk which seems to have been inspired by the House of Confucius at Kew, designed by Chambers and decorated by the fan-painter Joseph Goupy. Numerous pattern books were produced at this time for the benefit of the amateur gardener with picturesque leanings: William Halfpenny's *New Designs for Chinese Temples &c.* (1750) and *Chinese and Gothic Architecture properly ornamented* (1752), Thomas Wright's *Six Original Designs of Arbours* (1755) and *Six Original Designs of Grottos* (1758), and Thomas Collins Overton's *Original Designs of Temples and other Ornamental Buildings for Parks and Gardens, in the Greek, Roman and Gothic Taste* (1766).

The last in the group of gardens known from the paintings of Thomas Robins is at the late-seventeenth-century Honington Hall, Warwickshire, where the grounds were modernised for Joseph Townsend from 1755 by Sanderson Miller. The park was enlivened with water formed by the river Stour as newly laid out by Miller to create a varied and irregular scene which well matched the intricate rococo plasterwork installed in the house by Townsend in the 1740s. As John Harris aptly observes, Robins 'captured a moment of perfection in rococo art with all the right architectural and decorative paraphernalia, Chinoiserie pavilions, classical temples, frothing cascades, Halfpenny wooden bridges, rock works and grottoes, encapsulating a world of happiness and beauty'.[1] It is eminently characteristic of the Picturesque that Robins's patrons should have wanted to see their gardens from the start through the eyes of a painter. In commissioning his views whilst they were in the process of laying out their gardens, they remind us that the Picturesque dissolves abstract formal design in both architecture and gardens and sees everything subjectively through the shifting viewpoint of the landscape painter.

The landscaped park created in the 1740s and 50s at Hagley, West Midlands, for Lord Lyttelton and his illegitimate half-brother Admiral Thomas Smith, became one of the most visited and most written about picturesque gardens in the country. George, 1st Lord Lyttelton (1709–73), was for many years secretary to

Frederick, Prince of Wales, and briefly Chancellor of the Exchequer. A friend of Pope, Thomson, Shenstone, Fielding and James Gibbs, he was also influenced by the extraordinary achievement at Stowe of his uncle, the 1st Viscount Cobham. As early as the summer of 1739 in a letter to Ralph Allen, Pope was claiming to have designed three buildings at Hagley. The park also contained urns dedicated to him and to Shenstone, while other seats were called after Milton and Thomson. Here Thomson finished revising his epic poem, the *Seasons*, and included 'Prospect from Hagley Park' as part of the long passage on 'Spring'. Though the Palladian bridge, hermitage, statue of Apollo, and grotto with its statue of the Medici Venus have disappeared, the Ionic rotunda, the lakes and cascade, the wiggly paths and spinneys still survive as an appropriately intricate setting for the contemporary rococo plasterwork in the house itself.

Sanderson Miller's Ruined Castle was an important addition of 1747–8 which we shall discuss more fully in the next chapter. No less significant was the Doric temple built only ten years later in 1758 by James 'Athenian' Stuart (1713–88), the earliest monument of the Greek Revival anywhere in the world. Built of red sandstone originally covered with stucco, Stuart's temple is not an exact copy of any Greek building, but is a Doric hexastyle temple with a column at each side of the cella entrance behind the front colonnade, probably inspired by the Theseum in Athens. The essentially picturesque way in which Greek architecture was approached at this moment is made clear in the letter Lord Lyttelton wrote to Elizabeth Montagu in October 1758: '[Stuart] is going to embellish one of the Hills with a true Attick building, a Portico of six pillars, which will make a fine effect to my new house, and command a most beautiful view of the country'.[2] Thus in true picturesque fashion the actual quality of the architecture is somehow subordinate to its relationship to a landscape which has already been created. It must, however, be admitted that even the keenest twentieth-century enthusiast for neo-classical architecture is likely to turn his back on Stuart's Greek Doric temple the minute he has ascended the steep slope on which its stands, in order to admire the breathtaking view which it commands of the Malvern Hills.

Another notable rococo landscape where, as we have already seen, Stuart was also to work, was Shugborough in Staffordshire, not far from Hagley. Here in 1747 Thomas Anson erected the charming Chinese House on an island to commemorate his brother's circumnavigation of the world which had included a visit to Canton. Its design was based on drawings made in China by Sir Percy Brett, one of Admiral Anson's officers in the *Centurion*. The interior was decorated in a fanciful rococo chinoiserie style. A pagoda of 1752, anticipating that at Kew, as well as a cascade and a Palladian bridge had all disappeared by 1800. In the house itself Anson had adorned the drawing- (now dining-) room by 1748 with a set of wall decorations consisting of ruin pieces painted on canvas in Bologna by the mysterious but talented Scandinavian artist, Nicholas Thomas Dall.

For the creation of three-dimensional – one can hardly say 'genuine' – ruins in the park Anson seems to have relied on the help of Thomas Wright (1711–86), the eccentric and attractive architect, mathematician and astronomer who has recently been rescued from oblivion by the careful researches of Eileen Harris. In 1750 Wright plotted the path of the Milky Way and designed a Chinese Pleasure Barge probably for Frederick, Prince of Wales. By 1750 he had also replaced

Shugborough, Staffordshire. The dining-room was the result of a collaboration in *c.* 1748 between the patron Thomas Anson, the Italian plasterworker Vassalli, the Scandinavian painter Nicholas Dall, and almost certainly, the landscape designer and mathematician Thomas Wright. Beneath Vassalli's magnificent rococo ceiling the walls are fitted with eight Italianate ruin-paintings painted in Bologna by Dall in the style of Panini and the Bibiena.

Badminton, Avon. Hermit's Cell or Root House, *c.* 1750, by Thomas Wright for the 4th Duke of Beaufort. One of the most elaborate of eighteenth century hermitages, of which Kent's at Richmond Gardens (1730) was perhaps the first, it incorporates thatch, knotted tree trunks and moss to suggest a building which is part of its natural environment.

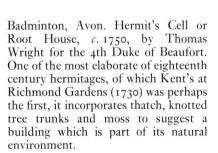

William Kent as garden designer at Badminton, Avon, where he provided garden buildings in a variety of styles, including Egyptian, Chinese, Greek Doric, Roman and Gothick, for the 4th Duke of Beaufort from 1748–56. Amongst his surviving buildings at Badminton are an elaborate Hermit's Cell or Root House, a castellated barn, thatched cottages with Gothic ornaments, and the Ragged Castle, a substantial stone folly with castellations and a circular turret in the style of Sanderson Miller's work at Edgehill. Wright also worked in the grounds of

Beckett Park, Culford, Oatlands, Stoke Gifford, Wallington and Shugborough, as well as publishing *Six Original Designs of Arbours* (1755) and *Six Original Designs of Grottos* (1758) as part of a projected *Universal Architecture*. His charming engravings are unusual for this date in showing the buildings in natural settings. Just to the west of the house at Shugborough there arose in 1747–9, on the banks of the river Sowe, a curious assembly of buildings known as the 'Ruins', supposedly incorporating fragments from the former palace of the Bishops of Lichfield. Wright seems to have provided the serpentine canal, Chinese bridge, green-house and a now demolished Gothic tower serving as a pigeon-house. Nearby on the opposite bank of the river stood a fragmentary Doric colonnade.

One of the most romantically evocative garden ornaments anywhere in England is the Shepherd's Monument at Shugborough, based on a plate in Wright's *Designs of Arbours* and in existence by 1758. Two primitivist Doric columns with a triglyph frieze, probably added later by James Stuart, shelter a rocky arch that might have strayed from some Mannerist grotto. This in turn frames a fine relief by Peter Scheemakers after Poussin's haunting painting, *Et in Arcadia Ego*. This is based not on the painting which was at Chatsworth by 1761 but on the rather different version with the same name in the French royal collection at the Louvre. The elegiac allegory of a group of shepherds deciphering an inscription on a tomb, thus discovering sorrow in the midst of beauty and happiness, was a favourite one at this time: George Keate, for example, published a poem in 1775 entitled 'The Monument in Arcadia'. A final touch of mysterious poetry is the inscription D O.U.O.S.V.A.V.V. M carved on a panel beneath Scheemakers's relief for which no explanation has yet been found, though the letters DM for '*Dis manibus*' seem to suggest the commemoration of some secret grief of Anson's.

It seems likely that in 1749 the young architect William Chambers (1723–96) met the Prince and Princess of Wales, Frederick and Augusta, and designed for them the octagonal Chinese pavilion at Kew Gardens known as the House of Confucius. Six years after Frederick's death in 1751 his widow continued his exotic tastes by commissioning Chambers to lay out Kew Gardens and by appointing him as architectural tutor to her son George, Prince of Wales, the future King George III. 1757 also saw the publication, probably with the Dowager Princess Augusta's support, of Chambers's handsome folio of *Designs of Chinese Buildings, Furniture, Dresses, Machines, and Utensiles . . . to which is annexed, a Description of their Temples, Houses, Gardens &c*, dedicated to George, Prince of Wales. Chambers did not claim in this book that Chinese architecture was equal to the antique, but picturesquely suggested that 'Variety is always delightful; and novelty, attended with nothing inconsistent or disagreeable, sometimes takes place of beauty'.[3] Nonetheless, he tends to classicise the form of the Chinese buildings he depicts, and it has been argued that had his book appeared a decade or so earlier it might have exercised a sobering and beneficial influence on the rococo fashion for buildings in the Chinese taste which was at its height in the 1740s and 50s: for example, the Chinese pavilions at Stowe, Shugborough, Wroxton, Virginia Water, Kew, Ranelagh and Vauxhall.

Chambers accompanied his designs with an account of Chinese gardening as well as with a statement of his own views on landscape gardening in general. He knew scarcely more about Chinese gardening than Sir William Temple at the end of the seventeenth century, and his knowledge of China was confined to the environs of Canton which he had visited in the 1740s whilst in the service of the Swedish East India Company. However, with the help of the descriptions of Attiret and of his own picturesque expectations of what Chinese gardens *ought* to be like, he was able to claim them as the ideal fulfilment of recent English practice. Chinese gardens are thus supposed to be painterly in conception, ingenious and artificial in execution, full of contrasts of forms, colours and shades, and provocative of sensations of terror, surprise and delight. The kind of intricate semi-rococo garden admired by Chambers, however, was shortly to be rendered old-fashioned by the blander 'naturalness' of Capability Brown. Chambers's answer was a thinly disguised attack on Brown published in 1772 as a *Dissertation on Oriental Gardening*, a book which did Chambers's reputation no good in England though it was widely admired on the Continent.

In 1750 when the fretwork House of Confucius was being erected, probably from Chambers's designs, at the command of the exotically-minded Frederick, Prince of Wales, an elaborate neo-Moorish pavilion known as the Alhambra was also being added to the gardens at Kew. The Alhambra has recently been attributed to the Swiss artist Johann Heinrich Müntz (1727–98), who was employed by Horace Walpole in the 1750s. From 1757–63 Chambers transformed the layout of the gardens into a kind of Kentian *ferme ornée* adorned with over twenty strikingly exotic garden buildings in classical, Chinese, Moorish and Gothic styles. Müntz designed the Gothic Cathedral, an impressive twin-towered façade fifty feet broad, while Chambers provided a second Alhambra as well as the circular Ionic Temple of Victory, the Ruined Arch, the fanciful Mosque, and the 160-foot high Pagoda, the most celebrated chinoiserie building in Europe. This provocative combination of historical styles seemed to realise the plates in Fischer von Erlach's remarkable *Entwurff einer Historischen Architectur* (Vienna, 1721), the first comparative history of world architecture. Chambers was proud enough of his eclectic extravaganza to announce it to the world in the form of a book entitled *Plans, Elevations, Sections and Perspective Views of the Gardens and Buildings at Kew in Surrey* (1763). Dedicated to Augusta, Dowager Princess of Wales, this seductive folio was paid for by her son, King George III.

The rococo chinoiserie enthusiasms of the short-lived Frederick, Prince of Wales, were inherited by his brother, the Duke of Cumberland, vile butcher of the Jacobites. Appointed Ranger of Windsor Great Park in 1746 he transformed the southern or Surrey parts of it along picturesque lines in 1748–57. With the help of the Deputy Ranger, Thomas Sandby (1721–98), he created in *c*.1750 the irregular artificial lake known as Virginia Water, partly to provide employment for the soldiers who had served under him. This was enlarged later in the century to its present size of about 120 acres. Sandby, who had been a member of the Duke's staff since 1743, was never a prolific architect but was nonetheless appointed Architect of the King's Works in 1777. The landscape gardening which he carried out at Virginia Water with his more celebrated brother Paul, may have been inspired by the lake landscape at Stourhead. Henry Flitcroft, who was working at Stourhead between 1744 and 1765, designed a wooden bridge at Virginia Water in *c*.1750 and also the triangular Belvedere Tower, the nucleus of Fort Belvedere which was enlarged by Wyatville in the 1820s to form a

Kew, Surrey. 'View of the Wilderness' from Sir William Chambers's *Plans . . . of the Gardens and Buildings at Kew in Surrey* (1763). Chambers laid out the grounds in 1757-63 for Augusta, Dowager Princess of Wales, the most celebrated area being the Wilderness approached through a Ruined Arch which still survives. The exotic buildings in this engraving (of which only the pagoda survives) are, from left to right, the Moorish Alhambra, the Chinese pagoda and the Turkish mosque. Despite Chambers's claims, these are rococo confections lacking in historical accuracy.

picturesquely irregular castellated house. Sandby adorned the edges of the lake with grottoes and artificial ruins which have now disappeared, though his cascade survives near the Wheatsheaf Hotel. He also had a project for re-erecting the Tudor 'Holbein' Gate from Whitehall which had been taken down in 1759, forty years after Vanbrugh's attempts to save it from demolition.

The chinoiserie elements of the picturesque landscape at Virginia Water have unfortunately totally disappeared. By a spectacular stroke of imagination they included an amazing chinoiserie yacht, *The Mandarine*, remotely inspired by a Chinese junk, which is known to us from drawings by Thomas Sandby and an engraving of 1753 by J. Haynes. This improbable vessel sailed on Virginia Water where an elegant chinoiserie pavilion was erected on an island in 1759. Mrs Lybbe Powys wrote in 1766:

we went to the Chinese Island, on which is a small house quite in the taste of that nation, the outside of which is white tiles set in red lead, decorated with bells and Chinese ornaments. You approach the building by a Chinese bridge, and in a very hot day, as that was, the whole look'd cool and pleasing, The inside consists of two state rooms, a drawing room and bed-chamber, in miniature each, but corresponds with the outside appearance.[4]

Two charming chinoiserie garden pavilions from the same period as the work at Virginia Water have survived at Harristown House, Co. Kildare (originally built in *c.*1750 in the grounds of Wotton House, Buckinghamshire, and transferred to Ireland in 1957), and at Arlesford House, Essex, where the little fishing-house of the late 1760s was painted by Constable in 1816. It is especially characteristic of the gay sparkle of chinoiserie buildings that they were frequently placed in conjunction with water, and none is more enchanting than Henry Holland's Chinese Dairy of *c.*1790 overlooking a pool in the grounds of Woburn Abbey, Bedfordshire. The dairy is decorated with fretted balustrades, an octagonal lantern, a verandah, and other ornamental details both inside and out which are based on plates in Chambers's *Designs of Chinese Buildings, Furniture, Dresses, &c.* (1757). What is not taken from Chambers is the attractive way in which the building is linked pictorially to its lakeside setting, and functionally to a range of buildings containing game larders, by a long curved colonnade or covered way

which echoes the design of the verandah. This picturesquely curved arm was a device later used for the design of elaborate conservatories at Dodington Park, Avon, by James Wyatt in the 1790s and by S. P. Cockerell at Sezincote, in Gloucestershire, in c.1805.

To mention Sezincote is to mention one of the most inspired creations of the taste for picturesque exoticism. Though its details are Moghul rather than Chinese, its air of festive fantasy more than justifies its inclusion in the present chapter. It was built for the retired nabob Charles Cockerell who had made a great fortune in the East India Company and was made a baronet in 1809. He conceived the picturesque idea of creating an English house that would yet remind him of his Indian past, designed by his architect brother with the help of Thomas and William Daniell's drawings of Indian buildings and with further landscaping advice from Humphry Repton. The main entrance front with its pronounced and convincingly Indian *chujja* or cornice is of a golden local stone, supposedly stained artificially to a correct Indian hue, and is crowned by the 'stately pleasure dome' of Xanadu, an amazing onion dome of turquoise copper. Elsewhere picturesque asymmetry reigns supreme as the long curved conservatory sweeps round to meet an octagonal pavilion. Thomas Daniell seems to have designed the Indian Bridge, with its octagonal columns copied from the Elephanta Caves, which

Woburn Abbey, Bedfordshire. Chinese Dairy, *c.* 1790, by Henry Holland for the 5th Duke of Bedford. With its quadrant timber loggia by the side of a pool this vernacular but sophisticated composition has something in common with the Hameau laid out from 1783 at the Petit Trianon by Richard Mique and Antoine Richard for Marie-Antoinette.

39

Sezincote, Gloucestershire, *c.* 1805, by S. P. Cockerell for his brother Sir Charles Cockerell, Bt. A similar composition to the dairy at Woburn in a parallel oriental style. A high point of the Picturesque where, in order to translate his pictorial and evocative fantasy into reality, the architect required the assistance of a landscape designer, Humphry Repton, and a topographical artist, Thomas Daniell.

carries the main drive over an exotic water garden in a steep wooded dell. Standing on the bridge, its balustrade crowned with cast-iron Brahmin bulls, one looks up the Temple Pool at the head of the little valley where, surrounded by rock-work caves, an Indian shrine contains a Coade-stone statue of Souriya. Like many owners of picturesque houses Cockerell could not fully appreciate his achievement until it had been translated back by a painter into pictorial form. Thus in 1810 he commissioned the visionary artist John Martin (1789–1854) to make a series of aquatints of the house and gardens. Especially characteristic of picturesque make-believe is the aquatint of the front door where the landscaped park, to which the painter has his back, is fully but ambiguously reflected in the glazed doors.

The Prince Regent who visited Sezincote, probably in 1807, was captivated by its charms and could not wait to transform the Brighton Pavilion along similar lines. Born in 1762, he had been brought up in the shadow of Chambers's pagoda at Kew, a building for which his father had an affection so intense as to become positively embarrassing during his periods of mental derangement. The prince had already created a Chinese drawing-room at Carlton House by 1790 and a gift of Chinese wallpapers in 1801 is supposed to have encouraged him to add the Chinese Gallery at Brighton Pavilion in 1802–3 for their display. Henry Holland, who had designed the pavilion for him in 1787 in a simple neo-classical style, now

Sezincote. View by John Martin of the entrance door in the east front. The last refinement of the picturesque process: the creator of a building and landscape garden, which were already dependent for their design on the art of the watercolourist, (i.e. Thomas Daniell), wishes finally to enjoy them through the medium of aquatint.

Brighton Pavilion, East Sussex, 1815-21, by John Nash for the Prince Regent. Interior of the Music Room, one of the two domed rooms which Nash added in 1816-17 at either end of Henry Holland's east front. All is illusion: the oriental detail is historically inaccurate, and the arches and dome non-structural.

prepared alternative designs for remodelling it as a chinoiserie palace and as a *cottage orné*. In 1803 Holland's pupil William Porden presented another chinoiserie design and three years later Humphry Repton, fresh from his experience at Sezincote, presented an elaborately fanciful Hindu design which, it seems, the prince fully intended to carry into execution. Indeed an impressive domed riding-school ornamented in the Saracenic taste arose in the grounds of the pavilion in 1804-8 from designs by Porden, but it was not until 1815 that attention was given to remodelling the pavilion itself, by which time John Nash (1752-1835) had become the prince's architect.

In 1815-21 the theatrical hand of Nash transformed Holland's chaste pavilion into a Hindu dream by clapping on to it an assortment of minarets, bulbous domes

Dropmore, Buckinghamshire. Aviary and pergolas, perhaps *c.* 1850. The long, low white house with its elegant bows is largely by Samuel Wyatt of 1792-4 for Lord Grenville, George III's prime minister. C. H. Tatham extended it and added garden buildings in 1806-9. Later it was continued in the form of the pergolas, trellised Doric pavilions and domed chinoiserie aviary seen here.

and traceried loggias. The interior, by contrast, resembled more the chinoiserie taste ornamented in hotly exotic colours by the decorator Frederick Crace (1779–1859) and his assistants. As the brilliant realisation of fantasy there can be little in Europe to touch these interiors, except perhaps for the dream palaces of Ludwig II of Bavaria. They did not, however, set a fashion and it is probably right to see them as late examples of an especially royal taste associated in the mid-eighteenth century with the Prince Regent's great uncles, the Duke of Cumberland and Frederick, Prince of Wales, and with the latter's widow Augusta. The Prince Regent developed his chinoiserie enthusiasms at St James's Park and at Virginia Water. It seems to have been on his suggestion that in order to commemorate the Peace of 1814 Nash spanned the canal in St James's Park with a Chinese bridge surmounted by a tall pagoda. At the opening ceremony on the night of 1 August this was rashly illuminated with myriads of small oil lamps and became the centrepiece of an unusually abandoned firework display. The inevitable happened, and shortly after midnight the upper storeys fell sizzling into the water, never to be replaced. At Virginia Water an extensive Chinese Fishing Pavilion was built in 1826 for George IV with three octagonal cupolas inspired by the House of Confucius at Kew. Wyatville was the nominal architect but the designs of this elaborately painted structure were supplied by Frederick Crace. It was carefully repaired in 1860 by the Victorian rogue architect Samuel Sanders Teulon, but was demolished before the end of the century and replaced by a Swiss cottage.

The enchanting Dropmore, Buckinghamshire, contains a Chinese aviary and garden of uncertain and probably different dates in the first half of the nineteenth century. The aviary of red-painted iron lattice-work ornamented with green glazed Chinese tiles is connected to long wooden trellis pergolas with conservatories and verandahs. In the Chinese garden are stone cairns, Oriental flowering plants and glazed Chinese pottery stools.

One of the last and in some ways most elaborate chinoiserie garden was created at Alton Towers, Staffordshire, in 1814–27 for the romantically-minded and Roman Catholic 15th Earl of Shrewsbury, shy, musical and married to an Irish wife. A steep-sided and densely-planted rocky valley north of the house was

adorned with an astonishing variety of garden buildings placed in unusually close proximity to each other. Surviving buildings include a seven-arched bridge designed by John Buonarotti Papworth (1775–1847), a miniature Stonehenge, a replica of the Choragic Monument of Lysicrates and a *cottage orné* designed by Thomas Fradgley of Uttoxeter; this last was provided for the specially imported blind harpist whose music was supposed to induce in visitors to the neo-Gothic Alton Towers an appropriately feudal and nostalgic mood. There are also a number of buildings by the architect Robert Abraham (1774–1850) namely the enchantingly romantic conservatory with its seven glass domes, the Gothick Prospect Tower with its three storeys of diminishing size and, most fantastic of all, the Pagoda in the lake, with its three latticed storeys hung with bells. This was built in *c.*1824–7 in imitation of Chambers's illustrations of the To-ho pagoda in Canton. By a pleasing conceit it acts as a fountain spurting a fine jet of water from its top, though originally it was to have been twice as high and ornamented with forty Chinese lanterns lit from a gasometer discreetly hidden from view inside the building.

One of the most important Early Victorian gardens is that at Biddulph Grange, Staffordshire, laid out from 1842 by John Bateman (1811–97) on a rocky site above the Trent valley. Though carrying something of the mood of the *jardin anglo-chinois* into the nineteenth century, it can also be interpreted as a parallel to the increasing stylistic eclecticism of Victorian architecture. It is, in effect, a museum of styles in the manner adumbrated by Repton, and later by Loudon. It

Biddulph Grange, Staffordshire. Pavilion and bridge (since simplified in design) in the Chinese Garden laid out from 1842 for J. Bateman. Newly imported plants and trees from North America and the Himalayas, orchids, camellias, rhododendrons and conifers were combined with Chinese and Egyptian features in a circuit garden containing a series of incidents and surprises which owed much to eighteenth-century picturesque technique.

includes a Chinese rock garden approached by a mysterious grotto passage and containing a pool, joss house, pagoda pavilion and willow-pattern bridge; a pinetum; a Cheshire cottage; a cedar avenue; and a bizarre Egyptian court with a massive entrance of clipped yew.

Yet Biddulph, for all its elegant fantasy, is not truly picturesque. Bateman created an inward-looking garden centred entirely on its own monuments and exotic trees, flowers and shrubs, the whole forming simply a succession of surprising but self-contained incidents. For the Picturesque implies something more than wilful eclecticism. One of its distinguishing characteristics is that sensitivity to the *genius loci* which ensures that alien features never invade a particular spot, but harmonise with and indeed enhance their surroundings.

3

The Cult
of the Ruin

THE foundation of the Society of Antiquaries in 1717 appears as the climax of a process of historical contemplation which had increasingly preoccupied many squires, clergy and professional men during the preceding century. A new appreciation of the mediaeval past and the losses of the Reformation lay behind works like Sir William Dugdale's *Monasticon Anglicanum* (1655–73), Anthony Wood's *Antiquities of Oxford* (1674), and also behind eighteenth-century antiquaries in Horace Walpole's circle such as George Vertue, William Cole and James Essex. William Stukeley (1687–1765), first secretary of the Society of Antiquaries, was the author of *Itinerarium Curiosum . . . an Account of the Antiquities and Remarkable Curiosities in Nature or Art observed in Travels through Great Britain* (1724) which contained plans of mediaeval buildings. In his garden at Stamford he built a Gothic Temple of Flora in 1738 ornamented with mediaeval stained glass windows.

This heightened historical consciousness coincided with the rise of the picturesque gardening movement described in the opening chapter. One of the first fruits of this conjunction is the romantic mediaevalising structure at Cirencester Park, Gloucestershire, known as Alfred's Hall which was begun in 1721 for the 1st Earl Bathurst (1684–1775). Bathurst was a cheerful man, a Tory with Jacobite leanings and a good friend of Alexander Pope with whom he shared a passion for landscape design and silviculture. From 1715 onwards he laid out his extensive property at Cirencester, consisting of the Home Park and Oakley Park, in a handsome if rather old-fashioned way as a forest cut through with great rides and glades like those at Fontainebleau or Compiègne. Thus, by bypassing altogether the formalities of Le Nôtre he almost anticipated in some ways the picturesque parkscapes of the future. Garden buildings were an essential part of Bathurst's vision and on 24 July 1732 he wrote to Pope: 'I have now almost finished my hermitage in the wood, and it is better than you can imagine . . . I will venture to assert that all Europe cannot show such a pretty little plain work in the Brobdingnag style as what I have executed here'.[1] This hermitage or Wood House, which must be the first of all castellated ruined follies, came to be known as Alfred's Hall. King Alfred was supposed to have shown tolerance to the Danes at Cirencester after his victory over them at Edington in Wiltshire, and contemporary political satirists contrasted him favourably with George II as a dutiful constitutional monarch. In its present form Alfred's Hall dates from a remodelling of 1732 carried out with advice from Alexander Pope. Its round tower and adjacent hall incorporate Tudor windows and stonework from Sapperton Manor which Bathurst had just demolished. In October 1733 Mrs Pendarves (later Delany) explained in a letter to Swift that 'My Lord Bathurst has greatly improved the wood-house, which you may remember but a cottage, not a bit better than an *Irish cabbin*. It is now a venerable castle and has been taken by an

Cirencester Park, Gloucestershire. Alfred's Hall, 1721-32, by Lord Bathurst and Alexander Pope. Perhaps the earliest mock ruin in an English park, the building grew over a number of years in a characteristically picturesque way. Originally its setting was more formal or theatrical since it terminated the central topiary allée in a three-pronged *patte d'oie* similar to Burlington's at Chiswick.

antiquarian for one of King *Arthur's*, "with thicket overgrown, grotesque and wild"'.[2] Not surprisingly, such a building attracted the attention of the topographical artist Thomas Robins. The drawing he made of it in 1763 was published as an engraving by Thomas Major with the presumably ironical caption: 'This appears to have been a very Antient Building, and by an Inscription thereon is said to have been repaired in the Year 1085'.

Pope and Bathurst thus anticipated the more celebrated ruin designer Sanderson Miller, to whom we shall turn shortly. But first we should move from an invented ruin at Cirencester Park to a real ruin, Fountains Abbey, at Studley Royal in North Yorkshire. The noble water gardens at Studley Royal were laid out in a mile-long valley with steep wooded sides from *c.*1716–40 for John Aislabie (1670–1742). Aislabie was Chancellor of the Exchequer in 1720 at the time of the collapse of the South Sea 'Bubble' scheme for liquidating the national debt, and must have been relieved to be able to retire to his Yorkshire Elysium. He had shown himself sympathetic to the preservation of historic buildings when Vanbrugh successfully enlisted his support in 1719 to spare the Tudor 'Holbein' Gate in Whitehall from demolition. At Studley Royal, Aislabie was anxious to add the historic Fountains Abbey to his estate, and though this was not actually achieved until 1768 by his son William, the presence of the superb ruins acted as a constant stimulus to him in laying out and adorning the adjacent property. According to Christopher Hussey, John Aislabie himself had probably planned the formal way in which the ruins would be approached from the south end of the Studley water gardens. The canalised river runs in its straight wooded valley, of which the sides have perhaps been artificially straightened, and directs the eye irresistibly to the closing vista formed by the east end of the abbey church, symmetrical and magnificently preserved. The incorporation into a planned Augustan landscape of a great slice of mediaeval monastic England creates an atmosphere charged with poignant beauty.

It was doubtless the landscape garden at Studley Royal converging on Fountains Abbey that, in the 1750s, prompted Thomas Duncombe to incorporate views of the ruined Rievaulx Abbey into his own landscaped grounds at

Rievaulx Abbey, North Yorkshire. The view down on to the ruins of the Cistercian abbey which inspired Thomas Duncombe in c. 1758 to construct the second turfed ride or terrace at Duncombe Park in imitation of the one which his grandfather had created over thirty years earlier.

Duncombe, also in North Yorkshire. Rievaulx Abbey lies three miles west of Duncombe Park and it seems that his original scheme may have been to connect the two with a scenic drive crossing the Rye valley with a viaduct. Instead of carrying out this grandiose project Duncombe duplicated on the slopes above the abbey the same kind of sinuous grass terrace serving as a viewing platform which, as we saw in the last chapter, already existed at Duncombe Park itself. The new undulating terrace walk, half a mile long, is punctuated at each end with Doric and Ionic temples just as at Duncombe itself. Groups of trees recede and advance creating a pleasing variety of vistas so that, in Arthur Young's beautiful description written in 1770 twelve years after its completion:

You look through a waving break in the shrubby wood, which grows upon the edge of a precipice, down immediately upon a large ruined abbey, in the midst, to appearance, of a small but beautiful valley; scattered trees appearing among the ruins in a stile too elegantly picturesque to admit description. It is a bird's-eye landscape; a casual glance at a little paradise, which seems as it were in another region.[3]

Similar work was carried out by Capability Brown at Sandbeck Park in South Yorkshire where the 4th Earl of Scarbrough invited him in 1766 to landscape the grounds so as to incorporate the ruins of Roche Abbey. In his contract, not drawn up till 1774, Brown undertook 'to finish all the Valley of Roach Abbey in all its parts, according to the Ideas fixed on with Lord Scarbrough (With Poet's feeling and with Painter's Eye)'.[4] The phrase in brackets, incidentally, is a direct echo of a line in William Mason's poem *The English Garden*, of which the first three volumes had been published in 1772. Brown grassed over the bases of the piers and other foundations so that the tall arches could rise majestically from a green sward. He also altered the course of the stream which ran nearby and dammed it to form shallow cascades. His bold scenic treatment of both ruins and nature as occasions for picturesque improvement is a parallel to the idealised approach to landscape of William Gilpin in his celebrated tours. However, on his visit to Roche in 1776 Gilpin complained that:

This is the first subject of the kind he has attempted . . . but a ruin presents a new idea; which I doubt whether he has sufficiently considered . . . [His lake] is too magnificent, and too artificial an appendage, to be in unison with the ruins of an abbey. An abbey, it is true, may stand by the side of a lake; and it is possible that *this* lake may, in some future time, become its situation; when the marks of the spade and the pick-ax are removed, – when its osiers flourish; and its naked banks become fringed and covered with wood . . . the ruin stands now on a neat bowling-green like a house just built, and without any kind of *connection* with the ground it stands on.[5]

In the grounds of his celebrated *ferme ornée*, The Leasowes, Worcestershire, William Shenstone had contrived by *c*.1750 a ruined priory incorporating fragments from the mediaeval Halesowen Priory nearby. This has now almost entirely crumbled away though its original appearance is recorded in an engraving by D. Jenkins of *c*.1770. In the 1750s Horace Walpole's friend Dicky Bateman destroyed the Norman church of Shobdon in Herefordshire and replaced it with a rococo Gothick fantasy. However, he re-erected the richly carved chancel arch and two doorways on a neighbouring hill to serve as an eye-catcher in the form of a screen from his house, Shobdon Court. Similarly at Cranbury Park, Hampshire, in *c*.1760 Thomas Dummer re-erected portions of the north transept of Netley Abbey on Southampton Water, the ruins of which he had recently purchased. A handsome arch forms a picturesque group in the landscape with an adjacent cottage added by Dummer in the form of a Gothic tower. In 1770 Dummer managed to acquire the delightful, mediaeval Butter Cross in Winchester High Street from the citizens of that city with a view to re-erecting it in the park at Cranbury in emulation of Henry Hoare's success with the Bristol Cross at Stourhead. Fortunately, the inhabitants of Winchester prevented him from dismantling it. Many years later, when the fourteenth-century chapel on the bridge at Wakefield, Yorkshire, was completely renewed by Sir Gilbert Scott, the ruins of the original façade were bought in 1847 by the Hon. George Chapple Norton who took them away to the shores of his serpentine lake at Kettlethorpe Hall to serve as the most improbable boat-house in the country.

Sanderson Miller (1716–80), country gentleman and amateur architect, was a key figure in the 1740s in promoting an historical if sentimental awareness of the mediaeval past and in translating that awareness into buildings set in landscapes. The son of a prosperous Banbury wool merchant, he inherited at the age of twenty

(*Above*) Cranbury Park, Hampshire, *c.* 1780, by George Dance for Thomas Dummer. In the foreground are mediaeval remains from Netley Abbey re-erected in *c.* 1760 by Dummer. This Gothic scenery in the park is echoed in the house by the neo-antique drama of Dance's picturesque groin-vaulted ballroom.

(*Left*) Kettlethorpe Hall, West Yorkshire. The boat house erected in 1847 for the Hon. G. C. Norton, incorporating the fourteenth-century chantry chapel from the bridge at Wakefield. A Victorian survival of an eighteenth-century picturesque practice.

Edgehill, Warwickshire. Sham castle, c. 1746-7, by Sanderson Miller. Country gentleman and amateur architect, Miller was a pioneer in the use of architecture to promote nostalgic, though historically imprecise, reflection.

an estate on Edgehill, Warwickshire, with a modest Elizabethan house, Radway Grange, which his father had bought in 1712. Miller had become interested in antiquarian matters whilst an undergraduate at St. Mary Hall, Oxford, where, falling under the influence of the distinguished Principal of the college, the Jacobite William King (1685–1763), he acquired a romantic attitude to the English mediaeval and seventeenth-century past. Royalist troops had passed through the grounds of Radway Grange in December 1642 on their way to the disastrous and bloody battle of Edgehill which was fought near the neighbouring village of Kineton. Before he was twenty-two, Sanderson Miller had constructed on the hill above the house cascades and a viewing platform from which the battlefield could be seen. The improvements which he subsequently carried out in the house and neighbourhood were intended to accentuate and heighten the existing historical associations. Thus in 1743–7 he enlarged and gothicised Radway Grange in a style derived from Batty Langley, and, at Edgehill, built a thatched and asymmetrical Gothic cottage and a castellated tower with a turreted gateway, the first of his sham ruins. The cottage is remarkable for its rocky ruinated stonework front and its two round bastions at the back. The octagonal tower, which is visible from the grounds of Radway Grange, is built on the spot where King Charles I is supposed to have raised his standard on the morning of the battle. Based on the design of Guy's Tower at Warwick Castle, its principal upper room was provided with Gothic niches, painted glass and a vaulted ceiling (since replaced) decorated with the royal arms and those of the kingdoms of the Saxon heptarchy. Virtually the only precedent for this building is Vanbrugh's impressive curtain wall with towers and bastions at Castle Howard of c.1723–4.

Wimpole, Cambridgeshire. Drawing by Sanderson Miller for the Ruined Castle. Designed 1749 and built by Capability Brown in 1768, this is considerably larger than its model, also by Miller, at Hagley. Two ruined walls project at right angles from a round tower behind which trees conceal the absence of real architectural substance.

Vanbrugh's construction, however, was not ruined and was a mediaevalising reminiscence of the city walls of Chester.

Sanderson Miller's little building at Edgehill must surely be seen as the parent of Payne Knight's Downton Castle of 1772–8 and thus of the romantic asymmetrical castles of John Nash. Its immediate progeny were Miller's own sham castles at Hagley, Wimpole and Ingestre. His Ruined Castle of 1747–8 at Hagley Hall, West Midlands, for the 1st Lord Lyttelton was one of the first and most important buildings to adorn that celebrated park. As early as January 1749 Lord Dacre remarked to Miller, 'You have got everlasting fame by this castle at Hagley, so that I hear talk of nothing else'.[6] In the previous June the poet William Shenstone had written of it that 'It consists of one entire Tow'r and three stumps of Tow'rs with a ruined wall betwixt them. There is no great art of variety in ye Ruin, but the situation gives it a charming effect'.[7] Mediaeval windows from the ruins of the nearby Halesowen Abbey were installed in the curtain wall, while Henry Keene was employed to make Gothic furniture from Miller's designs. In his *Letters on the Beauties of Hagley, Envil, and the Leasowes* (1777), Joseph Heely was confident that visitors would wonder 'what sieges it had sustained, – what blood had been spilt upon its walls: – and would lament that hostile discord, or the iron hand of all-mouldering time, should so rapaciously destroy it'.[8] Such an approach would not have surprised Vanbrugh who had envisaged the genuinely mediaeval Woodstock Manor as provocative of just such a train of thought. The most celebrated reaction was Horace Walpole's: 'There is a ruined castle, built by Miller, that that would get him his freedom even of Strawberry: it has the true rust of the Barons' wars . . . I wore out my eyes with gazing, my feet with climbing and my tongue and my vocabulary with commending!'.[9]

Lyttelton's friend, Lord Chancellor Hardwicke, was anxious to have a ruined castle of his own at Wimpole, Cambridgeshire, and in June 1749 Lyttelton approached Sanderson Miller on his behalf. 'He wants no house or even room in it', Lyttelton explained, 'but mearly the walls and semblance of an old castle to make an object from his house. At most he only desires to have a staircase carried up one of the towers, and a leaded gallery half round it to stand on and view the prospect. It will have a fine wood of firrs for a backing behind it and will stand on an eminence at a proper distance from his house'.[10] Four drawings for the castle, presumably by Miller, survive at Wimpole of which one is a fine perspective sketch showing the ruins intermingled with conifers in the manner recommended exactly forty years before by Vanbrugh. In fact the castle was not erected in the 1st Earl of Harwicke's lifetime but was built for his son by Capability Brown from Miller's suggestions when he was landscaping the park from 1769–72. Unlike its parent at Hagley, the castle can be seen clearly from the house. Somewhat surprisingly, it is placed in line with the central axis of the house at the southern end of the great Bridgeman avenue of the 1720s. This obviously artificial position tends to prevent the visitor from taking it for a genuine mediaeval ruin. However, the original intention was to call it Chicheley Castle in an historical allusion to the family who had acquired the manor of Wimpole in the mid fifteenth century. Humphry Repton, more practical in his approach than Sanderson Miller, suggested in his Red Book for Wimpole of 1801 that the building could be 'made more useful, by adding floors in the Tower . . . to form a Keeper's lodge'.[11] This advice was evidently taken, for the ruin was still occupied by the head gamekeeper in the early years of this century in conditions of bizarre if picturesque discomfort.

In his important book of 1770, *Observations on Modern Gardening*, Thomas Whately had included a separate section on the value of ruins in a landscape in which he emphasised their associational value as a stimulus to sentimental reflection. Though content to see the erection of artificial ruins where genuine ones did not exist, Tintern Abbey was for him the ideal. One of the most enthusiastic creators of artificial ruins was Henry Fox, 1st Lord Holland, who between 1762 and 1774 covered the cliffs at Kingsgate, Kent, with a remarkable array of flint ruins and follies, including an extensive castle and a cloistered convent. Their exposed position made them subject to continuous and at times alarming storm damage. They also attracted the hostility of William Gilpin in his *Observations on the Coasts of Hampshire, Sussex, and Kent, relative chiefly to Picturesque Beauty: made in the Summer of the year 1774* (1804):

It consists of a complete set of ruins, which compose the house and offices. The brew-house is a fort – the stable, a monastery – the pigeon house a watch tower, – and the porter's lodge a castle. Another strange building appears which you know not what to make of; but as you approach it you find it to be an inn. Even buildings, which all wish to conceal, are here ostentatious objects, in the form of ruins. Among all the crude conceptions of depraved taste, we scarce ever met with anything more completely absurd than this collection of heterogeneous ruins. Nothing can equal the caprice of bringing such a motley confusion of abbies, forts, and castles together, except the paltry style in which they are executed.[12]

Our attention so far has principally been engaged by the rise of interest in ruins and garden buildings as part of the growth of antiquarianism, the Gothic Revival and landscape gardening. This expressed itself in a mania for follies and garden buildings frequently contrived in the form of shams or ruins. There is almost a temptation to think that the English went completely insane in the course of the eighteenth century as one turns the pages of Barbara Jones's *Follies and Grottoes* (1953; rev.ed. 1974). This book records over 830 buildings designed with scenic rather than functional ends in mind, ranging from inhabited hermitages and Druidic altars to sham church towers. However, in the mid-eighteenth century an artistic movement centred largely on Rome was encouraging a picturesque interest in ruins from a rather different angle.

The neo-classical attempt to revive the antique tradition by a return to the original sources was profoundly coloured by the growing romantic sensibility of the eighteenth century. This responded strongly and imaginatively to the evocative appeal of the ruinous and half-buried state of those antique sources. It might be argued that love of the past is instinctive in man. Certainly every generation finds something to be dissatisfied with in the present, which is surprising since it can have no direct knowledge of any other period. The Christian doctrine of the Fall supports the view that in our endless quest for perfection in material as in spiritual matters, we are somehow trying to recapture a perfection which has already existed in the past and of which some obscure knowledge is implanted within us. Fired by the visions of artists like Panini, Piranesi and Hubert Robert, as well as by the rapid development of archaeology, the eighteenth century became intoxicated with the romance of the past. The painter Giovanni Paolo Panini (*c*.1692–1765/8) played a leading role in inventing a pictorial language expressive of the obsession with a half-real, half-imaginary world of vanished Roman grandeur. He acquired a range of imaginative scenographic skills in the circle of the Galli Bibiena family and from his work on stage designs for Juvarra in the 1720s. He was already applying these skills by the 1720s to the production of picturesque ruin scenes inspired by the *vedute ideate* of Giovanni Ghisolfi (1623–83). Panini's seemingly endless flow of immensely popular paintings incorporating genuine or invented Roman ruins relied on an increasingly familiar repertoire of stage effects such as obelisks, arches, urns and pyramids based on the Monument of Caius Cestius in Rome.

Panini was a potent influence on Piranesi and on the young Frenchmen who came to study architecture at the French Academy in Rome. Patronised by the French Cardinal Polignac and married to a French wife, Panini became professor of perspective at the French Academy where designers such as Le Lorrain, Challe, Jardin, Dumont and Petitot helped create the style of international classicism during the 1740s. They looked for inspiration not only to Panini but to the young architect Giovanni Battista Piranesi (1720–78) who arrived in Rome from Venice in 1740 and set up a print shop four years later in the Corso opposite the French Academy. In 1743 he produced the *Prima Parte di Architetture e Prospettive*, the first of his many books of etchings which took Europe by storm. The book contains imaginative ruin scenes inspired by Giuseppe Bibiena and the Venetian Marco Ricci (1676–1730) whose *capricci* fused the tradition of the topographical view with that of baroque stage design. One of the most powerful plates in the book depicts a slightly ruinous Ancient Mausoleum, blending elements from the imperial mausolea, Borromini's S. Ivo and Fischer von Erlach into an overwhelmingly evocative funerary vision. Even more sensational is 'Part of a Great Harbour' from *Opere Varie di Architettura, Prospettiva, Groteschi, Antichità* (*c*.1750). This is the kind of plate Horace Walpole must have had in mind in 1771 when he hoped that:

our artists would study the sublime dreams of Piranesi, who seems to have conceived visions of Rome beyond what it boasted even in the meridian of its splendour. Savage as Salvator Rosa, fierce as Michelangelo, and exuberant as Rubens, he has imagined scenes that would startle geometry, and exhaust the Indies to realize. He piles palaces on bridges,

(*Above*) 'Part of a Great Harbour' by G. B. Piranesi from his *Opere Varie di Architettura, prospettiva, groteschi, Antichità* (*c.* 1750). Piranesi's creative attitude to the antique, which was inspired by Marco Ricci, Bibiena, Panini and Fischer von Erlach, is explained in his dedication to his *Prima Parte di Architetture, e Prospettive* (1743): 'These speaking ruins have filled my spirit with images that accurate drawings such as those of the immortal Palladio, could never have succeeded in conveying'.

(*Left*) *Iphigenia in Aulis*, 1716–18, by G. P. Panini. A characteristic *capriccio* by one of the most architecturally influential of all eighteenth-century artists, including buildings inspired by the Arch of Constantine, the pyramid of Caius Cestius, Trajan's Column and, more remotely, by the Mausoleum of Hadrian.

and temples on palaces, and scales heaven with mountains of edifices. Yet what taste in his boldness! What grandeur in his wildness! What labour and thought both in his rashness and details![13]

In June 1749 there arrived at the French Academy in Rome the young Charles-Louis Clérisseau (1721–1820) who, though relatively undistinguished as an artist,

Ruins of the Great Gallery of the Louvre, 1796, by Hubert Robert. Robert was so obsessed by the romance of ruins that he recorded not only antique ruins but more recent buildings damaged in his lifetime by fire or vandalism. Here, uniquely, he envisages the future decay of an intact building: a *frisson* which Soane also enjoyed.

was to become influential throughout Europe as a ruin painter. While the great *veduta* and *capriccio* canvases of Panini and the etched plates of Piranesi inspired architects and visionaries with their compelling evocations of the Roman world in ruins, Clérisseau in the meantime reduced this to manageable form in over 1700 watercolours in a technique which architects and artists could and did imitate. Perhaps the principal ruin artist was Hubert Robert (1733–1808) who arrived in Rome from Paris in 1754 to live at the French Academy. He quickly began painting architectural scenes and ruins in the style of Panini and Piranesi, and probably accompanied the latter on a visit to Cora. In 1760 he travelled to Naples, Herculaneum and Pompeii with the Abbé de St. Non making drawings for the latter's *Voyage pittoresque dans . . . Naples et Sicile.* Returning to Paris in 1765 he painted decorations for several houses and public buildings, was appointed Designer of the King's Gardens in 1778 in which capacity he designed the celebrated rockwork grotto at the Petit Trianon, and became the first keeper of the museum which was established in the Louvre in 1784. One of his most remarkable works was his visionary painting of 1796 depicting the Grande Galerie of the Louvre in ruins.

In 1750, the year after Clérisseau's arrival in Rome, William Chambers (1723–96) began his own five-year stay in the city. He had spent a year from the autumn of 1749 studying architecture at J.-F. Blondel's celebrated Ecole des Arts in Paris which produced such distinguished neo-classical architects as Peyre, Ledoux, Gondoin and De Wailly. In January 1755 the sculptor Joseph Wilton told Robert Adam, who was in Italy between 1754 and 1758 on his Grand Tour, that Chambers 'owes all his hints and notions' to Clérisseau, 'to whom he behaved ungratefully'.[14] Even allowing for some professional jealousy on Wilton's part, it seems likely that Chambers's first architectural project – a mausoleum for Frederick, Prince of Wales – owes something in both conception and technique to Clérisseau. The prince died in March 1751 and between that date and the

February 1752 Section of The Mausoleum for the P of Wales

Mausoleum for the Prince of Wales,
1751-2, by Sir William Chambers. The
short-lived elder son of King George II,
Prince Frederick was keenly interested
in the exotic and the Rococo, and his
mausoleum is shown, significantly, in
romantic decay in this drawing. It was
doubtless intended for Kew where
Chambers worked extensively for the
prince's widow.

following February Chambers produced eight designs for a grandiose mausoleum
in the Franco–Italian neo-classical style recently developed by the French
pensionnaires. He also drew on Renaissance as well as on antique sources such as
the circular tomb of Cecilia Metella illustrated and restored by Piranesi in his
Antichità Romane of 1748. Chambers's mausoleum thus has some claim to be
regarded as the first neo-classical design in English architecture. However, its
special significance for our present purpose is that one of the designs seems to be
the first instance of an architect presenting a highly finished elevation *in a
landscape setting.* The origin of this treatment probably lies in the sketches of
William Kent, whose ubiquitous conifers Chambers also borrows. In an even
more remarkable drawing, dated February 1752, Chambers actually shows his
building as a ruin – and again it seems that no one before had presented a design of
his own as it would appear when time and decay had reduced it to a ruinous state.
The mausoleum is thus quintessentially picturesque because Chambers
presented it as part of both a natural and an historical environment: historical in
that the building is shown as part of the process of history and as indicative of the
vanity of human wishes, and natural in that it is an incident in a landscaped
setting. The architect who presents a project for a building as a ruin thereby
dethrones architecture, which becomes a thing narrative, reflective, and evocative
of a mood.

On his return to England Chambers was unable to persuade potential clients to
abandon the well-trodden path of Palladianism in favour of adventures in the
international neo-classical style. Instead, as we have already seen, he turned
perhaps surprisingly to chinoiserie exoticism at Kew. Of his six surviving garden
buildings there the most interesting, apart from the Pagoda, is the Ruined

56

Robert Adam. Proposed ruin at Kedleston, Derbyshire, *c*. 1759–61 for Sir Nathaniel Curzon, Bt. Inspired by antique buildings such as the Serapaeum of Hadrian's Villa at Tivoli and the Temple of Minerva Medica at Rome, as well as by the illustrative techniques of Piranesi and Clérisseau, this must be one of the most imposing mock ruins ever proposed.

Triumphal Arch of 1759. Designed, according to Chambers, 'to imitate a Roman Antiquity, built of brick, with an incrustation of stone', it also served as a picturesque bridge to bring sheep and cattle from the Kew Road into the meadows inside the ha-ha. Owing something to Clérisseau, it is important as an early and prominently situated example of a built ruin, 'confined between rocks, overgrown with briars and other wild plants, and topped with thickets amongst which are seen several columns, and other fragments of buildings'.[15]

Chambers followed his ruined arch at Kew with plans of *c*.1762, probably not executed, for an even more picturesquely decayed bridge to be erected in the grounds of The Hoo, Hertfordshire. Designs for ruins of this kind had been published as early as 1728 by the prolific architectural author Batty Langley (1696–1751) in his *New Principles of Gardening: or, the Laying out and Planting Parterres, Groves, Wildernesses, Labyrinths, Avenues, Parks, &c. after a more Grand and Rural Manner than has been done before.* Langley took up Switzer's pleas for a kind of rococo variety and irregularity, but his proposals for ornamental ruins are remarkably early for this date. William Kent's Hermitage at Richmond Gardens, built for Queen Caroline in *c*.1735, was a small pedimented classical building with three round-arched entrances which, according to Rocque's engraving of 1736, appears to have been conceived from the start as a ruin.

Close to Chambers's designs for ruins are those of the 1760s by Robert Adam (1728–92) for ruined bridges at Bowood and Syon and for a ruined temple at Kedleston inspired by the apses of the so-called Temple of Minerva Medica in Rome. The Kedleston temple, known to us from a superb watercolour by Adam of 1761, was developed from two drawings made by Adam in the 1750s when a pupil of Clérisseau: they are inscribed '*Coté du Temple Ruiné et restoré avec les fragments antiques*' and '*Une Autre Temple Frequenté par un Hermi*[*t*] *et par Lui Changé en Chappelle*'. The whole conception of this building as well as the French inscriptions recall Adam's drawing master, Clérisseau. Robert Adam spent much of his Grand Tour studying Imperial Roman and Renaissance architecture and

Romantic Composition by Robert Adam.
One of the numerous *capricci* produced
by Adam in the 1780s when he let his
architectural imagination run free in a
wild landscape inspired by his native
Scotland. Picturesque architecture here
echoes the form of the rocks from which
it rises. The improbably close proximity
of the two castles was realised in the
1840s when Salvin built Peckforton
Castle on a neighbouring eminence to
that occupied by Beeston Castle.

decoration under Clérisseau from 1755–7, as his brother James was to in 1760–3.
Adam, who also spent much time in the company of Piranesi, an incomparably
greater artist than Clérisseau, wrote enthusiastically of a 'most valuable and
ingenious creature called Clérisseau who draws ruins in Architecture to
perfection',[16] and explained to his brother James in February 1755 that 'I found
out Clérisseau a Nathaniel in whom tho' there is no guile, Yet there is the utmost
knowledge of Architecture, of perspective, and of Designing and Colouring I ever
Saw, or had any Conception of; He rais'd my Ideas, He created emulation and fire
in my Breast. I wish'd above all things to learn his manner, to have him with me at
Rome, to Study close with him and to purchase of his works'.[17]

There can be no doubt that Clérisseau's essentially picturesque approach to the
antique helped determine the course of Adam's life and work. It was under the
influence of Clérisseau that Adam conceived the notion of his great book, *Ruins of
the Palace of the Emperor Diocletian at Spalatro, in Dalmatia*, begun in 1757 and
published seven years later. Another project, which was also to have been carried
out with Clérisseau's support, was a completely new version of Desgodetz's *Les
édifices antiques de Rome* (1682), though this was never realised. It was also at this
time that Adam began producing the watercolours and drawings of architectural
fantasies, generally depicting imaginary buildings in dramatic landscapes, of
which there are large collections in the print rooms of British, Continental and
American museums. These drawings, which Adam never exhibited, became more
striking as his career progressed and some of the most arrestingly picturesque of
them seem to date from the 1770s and 1780s. A recurrent theme was an elaborate
ruined castle with an irregular skyline echoing and blending into the forms of its
hilly or mountainous setting. By this time there were already sham castles in
several English landscapes which, as we have seen, were largely due to Sanderson
Miller's impetus. Indeed the feeling for mediaeval architecture was such that
when, in the 1760s and 1770s, large Palladian mansions were built at Tabley,

Cheshire, and Wardour, Wiltshire, by Carr of York and James Paine respectively, the mediaeval buildings they replaced were preserved and incorporated into views in the landscaped parks.

Although Adam never chose to exhibit any of his drawings of architectural and landscape fantasies, they may have served as the basis of the decorative panels and overdoors painted by his assistants in many of his interiors. In his engraving of the Long Gallery at Syon he depicts paintings of this kind over the bookcases. The tradition of decorative wall painting had been brilliantly developed in seventeenth-century Italy where Gaspard Poussin himself had painted whole landscape-rooms in the Palazzo Pamphili at Valmontone and in the Palazzo Doria-Pamphili in Rome, though it is doubtful whether these were known to his English admirers in the eighteenth century. Decorative artists came to be known as *quadraturisti* (architectural specialists) or *vedutisti* (painters of picturesque landscapes, topographical views or ruin pieces). Giovanni Antonio Pellegrini and Marco Ricci both worked in England for a number of years from 1708, while Panini himself arrived in the 1720s and achieved success as a scenographer at the Opera in the Haymarket, as well as working as a mural painter in other so far unidentified places. The impressive ruin *capricci* of *c.*1730 on the staircase at 20, Cavendish Square, London, are attributed to the Italian artist John Devoto who had settled in this country by 1708. The Irish playwright Owen MacSwinney moved to Venice in 1720 where he conceived the idea of commissioning leading Venetian and Bolognese artists to paint a series of twenty-four imaginary 'monuments' to distinguished Englishmen of Whig sympathies around the year 1700. These extraordinary picturesque *capricci* or tomb pictures with their crumbling ruins and spreading foliage, by painters like Sebastiano and Marco Ricci, Pittoni and Canaletto, form an exact parallel to the Whig garden monuments we have seen at Stowe. Canaletto paid three visits to England between 1746 and 1754 where he provided permanent wall decorations at Farnborough Hall, Warwickshire, in the form of Venetian views, and at Oockham Park, Surrey, in the form of landscape *capricci* containing Palladian villas, English steeples and Roman ruins.

In the meantime Robert Adam, seeing Clérisseau as a possible rival paid him a retainer for two or three years from 1757 to keep him out of England until the reputation for originality of the Adam firm had been established! However, the Clérisseau manner was brought to England by the Venetian artist Antonio Zucchi (1726–95) who became an indispensible part of the Adam design machine. Following his meeting with James Adam in Venice in 1761, Zucchi made a tour of Italy with James and Clérisseau. James tried unsuccessfully to persuade Zucchi to come to England in 1763 but three years later he accepted Robert's invitation to become his chief decorative painter. Characteristic Adam interiors enlivened with picturesque architectural *capricci* by Zucchi are the dining-room at Osterley, where the two large panels are dated 1767, and the music room at Harewood House, where the panel representing a view of Naples is dated 1771. Clérisseau himself eventually arrived in England in 1771 and stayed until 1775, maintaining his association with the Adam brothers and probably co-operating with Zucchi in interiors like the Harewood music room. In the 1760s Clérisseau had been concerned with two eminently picturesque projects in Italy. For the Abbé Farsetti at Sala near Venice he planned an astonishingly elaborate garden laid out

(*Above left*) *Monument to Sir Clowdisley Shovell* by Sebastiano and Marco Ricci. An imaginary monument to a Whig hero painted in the 1720s for Owen MacSwinney, from 1706-13 manager of the Haymarket Theatre, the London home of Italian opera. The figures are by Sebastiano Ricci, the talented Italian baroque painter; the architecture and landscape by his nephew Marco.

(*Above right*) Harewood House, West Yorkshire. Music Room, *c.* 1765–71, by Robert Adam for the 1st Earl of Harewood. The four inset panel paintings by Antonio Zucchi are of architectural fantasies with romantic figures and include picturesque views of Rome and Naples and 'the Ruins of Dalmatia'.

to resemble the ruins of a Roman Imperial residence such as Hadrian's Villa. This was not executed, but the Roman ruin room he painted for two friends of Winckelmann, the Abbé Le Sueur and Abbé Jacquier, still survives in the convent behind the church of S. Trinità dei Monti at the top of the Spanish Steps in Rome. This room was intended to recall the effect of the flux of centuries on the cella of a Roman temple crumbled into decay and occupied by hermits, exactly like Adam's contemporary ruin for Kedleston. Though small and not especially imposing in its present state, Clérisseau's interior so impressed Piranesi that he planned to make engravings of it. Piranesi also contributed to the painting of a similar Ruin Room, which has since disappeared, for the Maltese Ambassador in Rome.

The staircase hall and adjacent top-lit vestibule at Bretton Hall, South Yorkshire, are spectacularly decorated with ruin *capricci* which take us back to the world of Panini and Piranesi. Almost certainly the work of Agostino Aglio (1777–1857), they are the ideal complement to the imaginative neo-classical interiors designed by Jeffry Wyatville (1766–1840) in *c.*1815. Aglio had received an excellent training in Milan under the leading neo-classical painters, sculptors and architects, and met the architect William Wilkins (1778–1839) in Rome with whom he travelled to Sicily, Greece and Egypt in 1799. Wilkins subsequently used the drawings Aglio made on this tour to illustrate his own *Antiquities of Magna Graecia* (1807) and *Atheniensia, or Remarks on the Topography and Buildings of Athens* (1816). In 1804 Aglio came to England at Wilkins's invitation and remained here for the rest of his life.

(*Left*) Design for ruin room at the convent of S. Trinità dei Monti, Rome, *c.* 1765, by C.-L. Clérisseau. A contemporary wrote after visiting the room: 'one imagined that one was seeing the cella of a temple. . . that had survived the ravages of time . . . all the furniture was in keeping: the bed was a richly decorated basin . . . the desk a damaged antique sarcophagus . . . Even the dog was housed in the remains of a vase'.

(*Below*) Bretton Hall, South Yorkshire. Staircase hall, *c.* 1815, by Jeffry Wyatville for Col. T. R. Beaumont. Great arched panels of ruin paintings, attributed to Agostino Aglio, fill three of the walls of the square domed vestibule adjacent to the staircase.

Architectural Ruins – a Vision, c. 1832, by Joseph Gandy. A watercolour depicting Soane's Rotunda and, immediately north of it, the 4 and 5% (or Old Shutting) Office at the Bank of England in ruins. This hangs in the upper part of the Monk's Room at Sir John Soane's Museum. When exhibited at the Royal Academy in 1832 the catalogue entry quoted *The Tempest*:

The cloud-capt towers, and gorgeous palaces,
The solemn temples, the great globe itself,
Yea, all of which it inherits shall dissolve.

The late neo-classical architect Sir John Soane (1753–1837) was also deeply influenced by Piranesi's haunting vision of the ruined antique world. Soane's obsession with domed top-lit interiors even, as at Wimpole, in a private house, surely owes something to Piranesi's shadowy etchings of vaulted or domed Roman interiors partially buried below ground-level as a result of the lapse of centuries. More specifically Piranesian is Soane's commissioning of his talented draughtsman Joseph Gandy (1771–1843) to paint the Rotunda and Dividend Warrant Office at the Bank of England as they would appear when in ruins. In Gandy's arresting watercolour, exhibited at the Royal Academy in 1832, Soane's building resembles a crumbling Roman ruin as depicted by Piranesi or Panini. As an imaginative tour de force it is in the direct tradition of Chambers's section of his royal mausoleum in ruins and Hubert Robert's painting of the Grande Galerie of the Louvre in ruins. In *c.*1830 Gandy painted a cut-away aerial perspective of the whole Bank of England apparently intended as an imaginative way of showing its plan and construction but, in the process, making it look like an extensive Roman ruin. Gandy exhibited numerous architectural fantasies in a heady style developed from Piranesi at the Royal Academy from 1789–1838. His favourite subjects were not ruins but subterranean temples, shrines, mausolea and cloud-capped palaces. His preoccupation with the funereal, like that of his master Soane, is deeply rooted in the picturesque obsession with the buried past. At Pitzhanger Manor Soane designed a group of sham ruins as the top half of buildings supposedly buried underground. These crumbling arches and columns were intended to interest his teenage son John in classical architecture, but they failed in their purpose and have long since been demolished.

Perhaps the most surprising and extensive of all landscaped ruins in England, the Temple of Augustus at Virginia Water, is due to Sir Jeffry Wyatville. The Temple is concocted from fragments of the Late Roman city of Lepcis Magna in North Africa. Nearly forty granite and marble columns together with other architectural fragments had been presented to the Prince Regent in 1816 by the Bey of Tripoli at the suggestion of Colonel Hanmer Warrington, the English Consul General at Tripoli, and with the active support of Captain W. H. Smyth, later the Director of the Society of Antiquaries. The columns were conveyed to London in March 1818 where they reposed for eight years in the forecourt of the British Museum. It seems to have been at the suggestion of one of the Trustees of the Museum, Sir Charles Long, a keen amateur of the arts, that the columns were eventually transported to Virginia Water at the south-east corner of Windsor Great Park, already an eminently picturesque area thanks to the activities of the Duke of Cumberland and Thomas Sandby.

In 1826 to 1827, when George IV was inspecting the site with Wyatville, over £12,000 was spent on re-erecting the columns according to Wyatville's master plan. The full extent of the ruin is initially concealed from the visitor since it is divided into two parts by the road from Virginia Water to Ascot, which is carried on an arch at a high level so that the king could pass under it. In the southern

Columns from Lepcis Magna re-erected at Virginia Water for King George IV under the direction of Jeffry Wyatville in 1826-7. A rare instance of genuine antique remains imported from abroad to a more picturesque setting in England and arranged for pictorial effect without attempt at archaeological accuracy. Virginia Water, one of the largest artificial lakes in the country, was laid out from *c.* 1746 by Thomas Sandby.

section, in the grounds of Fort Belvedere, the columns are disposed in a semi-circular apse with a ruined wall following its line at a distance of about ten feet to suggest the remains of the supposed outer wall of the whole imaginary building. To the north, in Windsor Great Park, the columns form two parallel colonnades. Several columns, presumably more by now than Wyatville intended, are lying on the ground so that the combination of natural and induced decay is conducive to a variety of reflections. Wyatville had doubtless read *The Landscape, a Didactic Poem* (1794) where, emphasising the good fortune of those whose grounds contain a ruined abbey or an ivy-clad cottage, Payne Knight argues that:

> Still happier he (if conscious of his prize)
> Who sees some temple's broken columns rise,
> 'Midst sculptured fragments, shiver'd by their fall,
> And tottering remnants of its marble wall; –
> Where every beauty of correct design,
> And vary'd elegance of art, combine
> With nature's softest tints, matured by time,
> And the warm influence of a genial clime.
>   But let no servile copyist appear,
> To plant his paltry imitations here;
> To show poor Baalbec dwindled to the eye,
> And Paestum's fanes with columns six feet high![18]

It may, however, be thought surprising that in an age when classical archaeology was being taken seriously these historic fragments from a great Roman city should have been distributed at Virginia Water in a wholly fanciful way as though they were stage props. Wyatville's actions are certainly a powerful example of the strength of picturesque sentiment and remind us that when, in 1768, William Aislabie finally added Fountains Abbey to his Studley Royal estate he was not content to leave the magnificent ruins alone but turned them into a Gothick garden with a parterre and classical sculpture. However, in his *Observations . . . on . . . Cumberland, and Westmoreland* (1786) William Gilpin complained bitterly of Aislabie's treatment of Fountains that since 'his busy hands were let loose upon it . . . He has pared away all the bold roughness, and freedom of the scene, and given every part a trim polish'. He goes on to emphasise that 'A Ruin is a sacred thing. Rooted for ages in the soil; assimilated to it and become, as it were, a part of it; we consider it as a work of nature, rather than of art'.[19] A later picturesque tourist, Prince Pückler-Muskau, also disliked its trim condition, suggesting on his visit in 1827 that it needed 'a little more artificial wildness' in order to achieve the 'half decayed grandeur which has the greatest power over the imagination'.[20]

The great landscape gardener Humphry Repton (1752–1818) seems, on the other hand, to have been frankly embarrassed by the Norman priory church of St Germans at Port Eliot, Cornwall. Invited to make alterations to Port Eliot he ingenuously explained in his Red Book of 1792 that

The situation of Port Eliot is apparently oppressed by the neighbourhood of St. Germans and its stupendous Cathedral, whose magnitude makes it impossible to be removed, while its more lofty situation prevents its being made subordinate to the mansion. Rather (therefore) it will be advisable to attempt such a union as may extend the influence of this venerable pile to every part of the mansion and form of the two objects, now at variance with each other, one picturesque and magnificent whole.[21]

He planned to achieve this unity by linking the house to the church with a porte-cochère and attached cloister containing a billiard room on the first floor. This proposal was not carried out and it was left to Sir John Soane to remodel the house in 1804–6 in a modest castellated style. Repton's near panic when confronted with St. Germans priory reminds us that the Picturesque did not necessarily encourage an appreciation of mediaeval architecture but only of *ruined* mediaeval architecture. Unfortunately for Repton, St. Germans was in perfect working order!

Another more modest attempt to unite a modern building with a mediaeval one in an effort to heighten the charms of both was indulged at Benington Lordship, Hertfordshire, in 1832. With the help of a local landscape gardener, neo-Norman additions were made to the Georgian house in order to blend with the few surviving remains of Benington Castle which were themselves elaborated with neo-Norman details. A substantial neo-Norman gatehouse was also constructed as a link between house and keep. It is a surprise to find that Pugin lent himself to a similar process, if rather more happily conceived, at Peper Harow, Surrey, in 1841–8 for Lord Midleton. Pugin's mock ruins, inspired by the remains of Oxenford Priory, are dominated by a characteristically accurate traceried window in the Decorated style; nearby are farm buildings, also by Pugin, picturesquely sited by a pond. Pugin even made neo-Norman additions to the parish church at Peper Harow, departing from his usual hostility to that style in order to harmonise with a building which was partly Norman.

A late and supremely successful example of tinkering with an historic building to make it look more picturesque is Scotney Castle, Kent, in some ways the *ne plus ultra* of the whole Picturesque movement. Here from 1835, Edward Hussey dismantled a substantial seventeenth-century manor house attached to the small fourteenth-century moated castle at the foot of the valley, so as to make the whole group more picturesque when viewed from the new house which Salvin built for him at the top of the hill. Stone for the new house was quarried from the hillside, which became a suitably picturesque approach to the old castle once its newly abrupt slopes had been judiciously planted with trees and shrubs. Advice on this work was given by the landscape architect William Sawrey Gilpin, nephew of the Rev. William Gilpin who had published his important *Three Essays: on Picturesque Beauty . . .* in 1792. Edward Hussey also knew Payne Knight's *The Landscape* which contains enthusiastic descriptions of the picturesque charm of the combination of water, quarries and ruined castles:

> The quarry long neglected, and o'ergrown
> With thorns, that hang o'er mouldering beds of stone,
> May oft the place of natural rocks supply,
> And frame the verdant picture to the eye . . .
>   Bless'd too is he, who, 'midst his tufted trees,
> Some ruin'd castle's lofty towers sees;
> Imbosom'd high upon the mountain's brow,
> Or nodding o'er the stream that glides below.[22]

At Belsay Castle, Northumberland, Sir Charles Monck built a startlingly austere Greek Revival house from 1807–17, quarrying stone from a corner of the grounds which then became a picturesque feature. As at Scotney the quarry leads to a fourteenth-century castle with a Jacobean domestic wing attached, and

Scotney Castle, Kent. Created from 1835 by Edward Hussey and W. S. Gilpin, Scotney is a late and lovely example of a picturesque house and landscape. The seventeenth-century conical roof crowning the round tower of the fourteenth-century moated castle curiously resembles some of the farm buildings in Claude's paintings.

Christopher Hussey has suggested that since Salvin knew Belsay the idea of forming a romantic quarry at Scotney may be due to him. Scotney has a double significance for us, because it was here in the early 1920s that Christopher Hussey rediscovered the Picturesque. Sitting in the library with the writings of Uvedale Price and the other Picturesque theorists on its shelves, and looking at the composed view down to the old castle so carefully contrived by his grandfather nearly a century before, Hussey found the key which was to unlock many long-closed doors in the history of eighteenth- and nineteenth-century architecture and design.

4

Theory and Practice
in Garden Design:
Capability Brown to J. C. Loudon

OUR expectations of what the grounds of a great country house should look like have been formed more by Capability Brown (1716–83) than by anyone else, if only because during the course of his prodigiously successful career he landscaped the parks of a majority of the most important English seats. He ushered in a period of consolidation, not of innovation, by finding a popular formula in the 1740s which he repeated, without alteration, during the next thirty years for an audience of contented landowners who liked to know what they were paying for.

Born in a Northumberland village in 1716, in what were presumably modest circumstances, Brown rose to the position of head gardener to Lord Cobham at Stowe in 1741, where he remained until 1751. In this crucial decade at Stowe, those responsible for laying out the Queen's Valley, and especially the Grecian Valley, gradually abandoned the crowded rococo effect of Kent's Elysian Fields, which must originally have recalled a painting by Thomas Robins, in favour of the broader sweep we now associate with Brown. How far the change was due to Brown and how far to William Kent, Lord Cobham, Richard Grenville and their friends, is still not entirely clear. Certainly Brown's *architectural* style, particularly in his garden buildings, is heavily dependent on Kent, so it is likely that his *gardening* style is as well. What we have called Brown's formula was established by 1750 in an early commission for the grounds of Warwick Castle, and was repeated consistently until his last important park at Heveningham, Suffolk, of 1782, regardless of whether the house were mediaeval like Alnwick Castle, Tudor like Burghley, Baroque like Blenheim, or Palladian like Wardour. Brown was able to create an extraordinary sense of amplitude and of opulence, enshrining an ideal image of the rural scene from which he had eliminated ploughed fields, cowsheds, kitchen gardens and all the evidence of toil. His parks are not calculated to stimulate philosophical or historical reflections like early-eighteenth-century gardens, but to create a sense of almost physical well-being, a beneficent calm rooted in the pride of land-ownership. His great expanses of turf are ideally planned for their patrician owners who appreciated the landscape as the fitting background to the inspection of prize livestock or to exercise on the back of a horse. Thus the scene is not dominated by bizarre follies or grottoes, statues or inscriptions, and there are no abrupt contrasts or loose ends. He always conceals the ends of artificial water, for example, by trees or contours, rather than drawing attention to them with a grotto as Kent would have done. He summons up an ideal timeless state of nature by the selection of generalised representative forms, and by removing accidents, a process which has been seen as analagous to

Burke's views in *A Philosophical Inquiry into the Origin of our Ideas of the Sublime and the Beautiful* of 1757. Burke's aesthetic of sentiment had emphasised as the qualifying attributes of Beauty: 'Smallness, Smoothness, Gradual Variation and Delicacy of form'. Like Brown, he was influenced, at any rate in the second edition, by Hogarth's waving or serpentine 'Line of Beauty' in *The Analysis of Beauty* (1753). Burke described smoothness as 'A quality so essential to beauty, that I do not now recollect any thing beautiful that is not smooth. In trees and flowers, smooth leaves are beautiful; smooth slopes of earth in gardens; smooth streams in the landscape'. Indeed he came close to citing Brownian landscape as the natural type of beauty when he remarked that 'Most people must have observed the sort of sense they have had, on being swiftly drawn in an easy coach on a smooth turf, with gradual ascents and declivities. This will give a better idea of the beautiful, and point out its probable cause better than almost any thing else'.[1]

For unexpected confirmation of an interpretation of Brown's art in physical and materialist terms we can turn to the Edwardian novelist Robert Hugh Benson (1871–1914), who was a master at describing the disturbing impact of Roman Catholicism on members of the English landed classes. In his highly original novel, *The Conventionalists* (1908), Benson hit by coincidence on Burke's analogy between the sensations produced by a Brown landscape and by rapid but comfortable wheeled transport. As two Catholic priests are being driven through the grounds of an impressive Georgian country house in order to convey to its proprietor the unwelcome news that his eldest son is about to enter the Charterhouse as a contemplative monk, one of them reflects that:

a well-padded motor and an English park are perhaps, above all else, the two things most calculated to induce a materialistic frame of mind. They are so supremely comfortable, so adequate to lower needs, so entirely representative of imagination fettered to the requirements of the body . . . I saw woods and bracken slip noiselessly by, and I knew that every branch was, so to speak, named and numbered. I saw a few anxious rabbits see-sawing back to their holes in the autumn light and knew that these too were the private possession of the man we were coming to see – his little incarnate interests. And the errand on which we came was to the effect that his son proposed to relinquish all rights to these things and all that they stood for and to devote himself to praising God. It was grotesque.[2]

Contemporary documents confirm that Brown's easy smoothness was exactly what his clients found so satisfying. An interesting early patron was Thomas Lennard Barret (17th Lord Dacre from 1755), an antiquarian and a friend of Sanderson Miller whom he employed in 1745–7 to 'Gothicise' his Tudor house, Belhus, Essex. In 1752 Barret called in Capability Brown who carried out improvements in the park during the following decade. In a letter to Sanderson Miller of February 1761, Lennard explained: 'You will find the Place, if not much altered since you was there; yet a good deal improved, by the Turff being got older and consequently smoother and greener, and by the Shrubberys being now in good measure come to perfection . . . I know that that coarse meadow and moory sided canal might be converted into a very pleasing scene: And Brown is of the same opinion'.[3]

In the mid-1750s Brown was also working in the grounds of the great Elizabethan houses of Burghley, Northamptonshire, Sherborne Castle, Dorset, Burton Constable, Humberside, and Longleat, Wiltshire. At Burghley he also

Basildon Park, Berkshire. Parkland laid out by Capability Brown in 1778 for Sir F. Sykes, Bt., a standard example of his unvarying manner. However, there is drama on the other side of the Palladian mansion by Carr of York where the park falls to the Thames Valley.

Gothicised some interiors, built the Gothick Orangery and the neo-Jacobean Bath House – modelled surprisingly on the Banqueting House at Chipping Camden – and laid out the superb park with its characteristic belts, clumps and thirty-two acre lake. Even more spectacular was the creation of the park at Longleat from 1757, since this involved the destruction of the especially fine formal garden of the seventeenth century shown in Kip's engraving. The draining, levelling and sowing of meadows, the laying out of sunk fences, new roads, and the planting of clumps of trees, had proceeded so rapidly that when Mrs Delany visited the place in 1760 she wrote, evidently with no great enthusiasm, 'There is not much alteration in the house, *but the gardens are no more!* they are succeeded by a fine lawn, a serpentine river, wooded hills, gravel paths meandering round a shrubbery, *all modernised* by the ingenious and much sought after *Mr. Brown*.'4

At Corsham Court, Wiltshire, a gabled Elizabethan mansion, Brown extended the south front in a matching Elizabethan style in the early 1760s, though his new east front was classical. The lake he proposed in the park was not formed until the 1790s under the direction of Repton. More spectacular was his park at Bowood, Wiltshire, where his plan of 1763 refers to a rockwork cascade at the head of the new lake. This was elaborated about twenty years later from designs by the Hon. Charles Hamilton of Painshill, Surrey, who is supposed to have taken a painting by Poussin as his model. Prior Park, Bath, is another especially attractive and instructive example of Brown's art. The beautifully modulated funnel-shaped valley which descends from Ralph Allen's impressive porticoed villa so as to converge on the dreamy Palladian bridge, is often thought of as quintessentially Brownian. However, when Brown worked here in the mid-1760s, the bridge, built by Richard Jones in imitation of that at Wilton, had already been in existence for a decade as the conclusion of an elaborate system of cascades and shaped basins descending the hillside. Brown destroyed this rococo setting, which is recorded in a recently discovered painting by Thomas Robins, though he brilliantly incorporated its principal feature, the bridge, into his own softly undulating landscape.

In 1778 Brown received payments from Sir Francis Sykes for plans for the kitchen garden at Basildon Park, Berkshire, so it is likely that the planting in the especially lovely and hilly park was also carried out at his suggestion. His clumps of chestnuts, beeches and limes create diagonal vistas through the park which is encircled by equally characteristic belts. Below the east or garden front of the house, which was built from designs by John Carr of York in 1776–83, the park drops steeply down to merge with the vast sweep of the Thames Valley. The principal drawing-room is an octagon picturesquely devised by Carr with three bays projecting on the centre of the east front so as to form a great three-sided bay window which commands panoramic views of the valley and rising beechwoods.

Brown's tranquil landscapes are animated by constant but small-scale patterns of movement: the slow drift of sheep or cattle, and the passing clouds which cast their shifting shadows on sun-lit uplands or their reflections in the calm waters of the inevitable lake. The formation of a lake in the middle distance, fringed with trees which were themselves reflected in its waters, was invariably Brown's principal ambition. The passion for artificial water goes back to the start of the landscape movement and beyond, to Wise at Blenheim and Bridgeman at Chiswick.

There is scarcely any need here to describe in detail the seemingly effortless and repetitive flow of great but reassuringly familiar landscapes by Brown at Blenheim (where his spectacular aggrandisement of the river Glyme is supposed to have led him to explain, 'Thames, Thames, you will never forgive me!'), at Claremont (where he designed the neo-Palladian house for Clive of India), and at Croome, Petworth, Chatsworth, Audley End, Castle Ashby, Holkham, Melton Constable, Milton Abbey (where he planted out the village), Temple Newsam, Trentham, Chillington, Euston, Luton Hoo, Dodington, Prior Park, Broadlands, Wimpole, Compton Verney, Syon, Alnwick, Brocklesby, Grimsthorpe, Harewood, Clandon, Wardour, Wilton, Ickworth, Heveningham and Nuneham Courtenay, to name only those at the more prestigious seats.

A small indication of Brown's success is that he sent his son Lancelot to Eton in 1761 where the poor boy was dubbed 'Capey', after his father's nickname. Brown did not set his principles down on paper himself, but he did not lack literary supporters, even though his phenomenal success naturally aroused envious hostility as well as admiration. Those who supported him in writing included the author of an anonymous poem of 1767 on *The Rise and Progress of the Present Taste in Planting Parks, Pleasure Grounds, Gardens, &c*; Horace Walpole in his *The History of the Modern Taste in Gardening*, written in 1770 but not published till ten years later; Thomas Whately in his *Observations on Modern Gardening* (1770); and William Mason in his four-volumed poem, *The English Garden* (1772–9).

Thomas Whately, M.P., secretary to George Grenville and Shakespearean scholar, had written his lively and attractive book on gardening in 1765, though it

Prior Park, Bath, Avon, looking from the house down Capability Brown's parkland of 1764 to the Palladian Bridge built by Richard Jones for Ralph Allen in 1755-6. It is rare to be able to see a town from a Brown park, but this was a remodelling by Brown of an existing park which had been crowded with rococo incident. The curvaceous balustrade in the foreground is part of Goodridge's staircase of 1829-34.

was not published for five years. It had reached its fifth edition by 1793 and also proved popular in France, where a translation had appeared as early as 1771. Whately intended it to be a comprehensive treatise on the aims, methods and achievements of landscape gardening which would rival French treatises on painting produced at the end of the seventeenth century by Roger de Piles, for example. He begins by defining the five materials at the disposal of the landscape gardener: ground, wood, water, rocks and buildings, and passes on to a description of a perfect example of their use at Moor Park, Hertfordshire, by Capability Brown (whom he does not mention by name). Other Brown parks described are Claremont, Blenheim, and Wotton, Buckinghamshire. As might be expected from an admirer of Brown, Whately is insistent on the importance of water and on not providing too many garden buildings. Though he is opposed to the introduction of obvious allegory into garden design, he is especially sensitive to the moods and emotions which he believes that buildings and scenery can induce. His section on rocks distinguishes between those which are simply majestic, as at Matlock Bath, Derbyshire, and those which provoke sensations of terror, as at New Weir on the Wye, or of amazement, as at Dovedale. After accounts of the Leasowes, Woburn Farm, Painshill, Hagley and, especially, Stowe, Whately concludes his book with a highly original chapter on the 'Seasons', which is a sensitive account of the effect of changing light and changing seasons on landscape and buildings. One of the classic documents of picturesque sensibility, it ought to be better known. It builds up to a purple patch describing the effect of sunset on the Temple of Concord and Victory at the angle of Brown's dog-legged Grecian Valley at Stowe, a building which Whately had rightly singled out as of central importance in the history of landscape architecture:

The temple of concord and victory at Stowe has been mentioned as one of the most noble objects that ever adorned a garden; but there is a moment when it appears in singular beauty; the setting sun shines on the long colonade which faces the west; all the lower parts of the building are darkened by the neighbouring wood; the pillars rise at different heights out of the obscurity; some of them are nearly overspread with it; some are chequered with a variety of tints; and others are illuminated almost down to their bases. The light is gently softened off by the rotundity of the columns; but it spreads in broad gleams upon the wall within them . . . the rays of the sun linger on the sides of the temple long after the front is over-cast with the sober hue of evening; and they tip the upper branches of the trees, or glow in the openings between them while the shadows lengthen across the Grecian valley.[5]

William Mason (1724–97), parson, poet, painter and landscape-gardener, was slightly more ambiguous in his support of Brown in that he was opposed to all systematised landscape gardening. A friend of Gray, Hurd, Warton and Walpole, and an admirer of Rousseau, he was an advocate of flowers, sensibility and sentiment. He proposed replacing undue reliance on systems with, firstly, an empirical approach derived from Gilpin's principles for studying the characteristics of a region, and secondly a strongly horticultural bias involving a new emphasis on flower gardens. He put both of these into practice at Nuneham Courtenay, Oxfordshire, for the 2nd Earl of Harcourt, beginning in 1772 with a striking Reptonian-looking flower garden, and later in the decade breaking up an avenue so as to form a series of framed landscape views of the Thames, the Berkshire Downs and the distant towers and spires of Oxford. At the end of this avenue stood the domed and porticoed church of All Saints, designed in 1764 by

'Athenian' Stuart and Lord Harcourt's father, the 1st Earl Harcourt. Mason's pictorial treatment of the grounds transformed this Greek Revival building into a picturesque garden ornament, a process noted by Horace Walpole when he wrote to Mason in 1782 that 'This place is more Elysian than ever, the river full to the brim, and the church by one touch of Albano's pencil is become a temple, and a principal feature of one of the most beautiful landscapes in the world'.[6]

Opposition to Brown came initially from Sir William Chambers in *A Dissertation on Oriental Gardening* (1772). We have already noted the circumstances in which Chambers, as a protagonist of rococo Chinoiserie both at Kew and in his *Designs of Chinese Buildings . . .* (1757), seems to have felt threatened by the success of the blander style of 'Capability' Brown. His *Dissertation* was thus more of an attack on Brown, though he did not mention him by name, than it was a serious account of Chinese gardening. In fact Chambers painted a near fictional picture of the lively variety of Chinese gardens in order to condemn, by contrast, the insipid monotony of Brown's. He emphasised the limitations of Brown's art caused by the rejection of 'the assistance of almost every extraneous embellishment' in favour of 'an indiscriminate application of the same manner, upon all occasions, however opposite, or ill adapted'. He found Brown's uneventful vistas anodyne and mentally stultifying, arguing that 'the attention [of the spectator] is constantly to be kept up, his curiosity excited, and his mind agitated by a great variety of opposite passions'.[7] Bored by Brown's smooth turf stretching from the distant horizon to the drawing-room windows, he was anxious to experience the contrast between the wilder scenes of nature at a distance from the house, and the more formal, regular and symmetrical layout immediately adjacent to it. This is precisely one of the points taken up in the 1790s by Uvedale Price who launched a new assault on Brown. Chambers was not heeded when he made the same criticism twenty years earlier because he chose to present his arguments under cover of a defence of Chinese gardening, a cause which was then *vieux jeu* in England though gaining in popularity in France where Chambers's book was taken far more seriously. Nor did he help matters by implying that English gardeners should emulate those Chinese landscapes where, apparently:

Bats, owls, vultures and every kind of bird of prey flutters in the groves; wolves, tigers and jackalls howl in the forest; half-famished animals wander upon the plains; gibbets, crosses, wheels, and the whole apparatus of torture are seen from the roads; and in the most dismal recesses of the woods . . . are temples dedicated to the king of vengeance, deep caverns in the rocks, and descents to subterraneous habitations, overgrown with brushwood and brambles; near which are placed pillars of stone, with pathetic descriptions of tragical events.[8]

Chambers's categories of 'the pleasing, the terrible, and the surprizing' are, of course, derived from Burke's *Essay on the Sublime* to which we have already referred in discussing Brown. Burke's emphasis on Terror, Obscurity and the Infinite as related to aesthetic emotion, helped provide a range of expectations on which romantic artists and architects were increasingly to draw. One of the most dramatically sublime of all picturesque gardens was Hawkstone, Shropshire, created by successive generations of the Hill family until well into the nineteenth century. Before his death in 1783 Sir Rowland Hill, 1st Baronet, had been extending his park to include a great expanse of red sandstone cliffs, rocks and woodland scenery to the west of the house, a red-brick Georgian baroque edifice.

Hawkstone Park, Shropshire. Looking south from Grotto Hill along the Terrace. Grotto Hill is a precipitous rocky promontory at the northern end of the main Hawkstone ridge of which the Terrace constitutes the wooded western face. Hawk Lake is behind us and the mediaeval Red Castle is on our right. The chalet just observable in the middle distance was not built until the 1920s, though near this spot in the eighteenth century was a sign-post inscribed 'Au Pont Suisse'.

He added an immense labyrinthine grotto perched high above a formidable precipice so that even Dr Johnson was bowled over by the 'terror' of the scene on his visit in 1774. The first guidebook appeared as early as 1776, and in 1783 T. Rodenhurst had produced *A Description of Hawkstone* which reached its tenth edition in 1811 and was still being printed in the 1850s. More remarkably, a substantial hotel was built in *c.*1790 for the accommodation of the increasing numbers of tourists. Prince Pückler-Muskau, one of the most perceptive and experienced of all picturesque travellers, wrote in 1827 that he 'must in some respects give Hawkstone the preference over all I have seen', noting that it is 'a spot whose beauties are so appreciated even in the neighbourhood, that the brides and bridegrooms of Liverpool and Shrewsbury come here to pass their honeymoon'.[9]

Sir Richard Hill formed the extensive Hawk Lake in 1783–7 and gradually added a range of delights such as the painted windmill with its adjacent cottages, trees and water recalling a scene by Ruysdael; a 'Scene in Switzerland' with a rustic bridge spanning a rocky crevice; a 'Scene in Otaheite'; a Hermitage with a live hermit gazing at a skull; and a menagerie. The Hills were fortunate that their park already contained a genuine mediaeval castle – the ruined Red Castle – whose various towers were divided by a steep glen. Not content with this, a modern castle, known as the Citadel, was added in *c.*1785 and rebuilt in 1824 by the 3rd Baronet, Sir Rowland Hill, with the celebrated Thomas Harrison of Chester as architect. Harrison's triangular fort with round towers at the corners is perhaps derived from Adam who, as we shall see in Chapter 5, realised that triangular planning was productive of the qualities of 'movement' which he so much desired in architecture.

The Hawkstone gardens are now totally neglected and overgrown, which in some ways has only added to their sublimity. They surely must have appealed to Uvedale Price and Payne Knight who, united in their opposition to Brown, both drew on and went beyond the theories of Burke to attempt the most detailed explanation to date of the qualities of the Picturesque.

The Rev. William Gilpin (1724–1804), Vicar of Boldre in the New Forest, had pointed the way to the new term in his *An Essay upon Prints* (1768), in which he defined Picturesque as 'a term expressive of that peculiar kind of beauty, which is agreeable in a picture'.[10] Gilpin may be regarded as the link between the writings of Burke and those of Price and Knight, though of course he also exercised a very considerable influence of his own as can be seen, for example, in William Combe's parody of him in *The Tour of Dr Syntax in Search of the Picturesque, a Poem* (1812). Arguably the first conscious critic of landscape, Gilpin undertook his tours of England, Scotland and Wales in the 1760s and 1770s and published the results of them between 1782 and 1809, beginning with *Observations on the River Wye, and Several Parts of South Wales &c. relative chiefly to Picturesque Beauty.* Especially sensitive to the changing effects of light and shade in mountain scenery, he analysed landscape systematically in terms of the ideals of seventeenth-century landscape painters, illustrating his points with oval aquatints on a brownish-yellow tinted ground. These charming little views did not reproduce the actual landscapes described in the text but rather composed them into a generalised ideal from which all visually distracting details had been removed. Cottages he particularly disliked, as well as artificial ruins and representation of motion near the eye.

With his more conceptual approach, Sir Uvedale Price (1747–1829) found Gilpin's broad definitions of the Picturesque inadequate. In *An Essay on the Picturesque . . .* (1794) he used the term as a precise category to include those aesthetic qualities which he felt were not comprised in the current terms, Sublime and Beautiful. He must have been impressed by Sir Joshua Reynolds's 13th Discourse delivered to students at the Royal Academy in 1786 in which he recommended architects to take advantage of 'accidents' rather than to rely on regularity, and also to imitate the scenic skills of Sir John Vanbrugh, 'an architect who composed like a painter'. At the core of Reynolds's bold argument is the following claim:

It often happens that additions have been made to houses, at various times, for use or pleasure. As such buildings depart from regularity, they now and then acquire something of scenery by this accident, which I should think might not unsuccessfully be adopted by an Architect, in an original plan, if it does not too much interfere with convenience. Variety and intricacy is a beauty and excellence in every other of the Arts which address the imagination; and why not in Architecture?[11]

It can hardly be a coincidence that variety and intricacy are also central to Price's definition of the Picturesque. He writes:

Engraving by T. Hearn from Payne Knight's, *The Landscape* (1794) of a house and park in the manner of Capability Brown. Knight criticises this placid and unadventurous scene as essentially unnatural.

The second engraving shows the same house and park treated in what Knight regarded as a truly picturesque manner so as to emphasise in both nature and architecture qualities of roughness, variety and intricacy.

There are few words whose meaning has been less accurately determined than that of the word picturesque. In general, I believe, it is applied to every object, and every kind of scenery, which has been, or might be represented with good effect in painting . . . I hope to shew in the course of this work, that the picturesque has a character not less separate and distinct than either the sublime or the beautiful, nor less independent of the art of painting.

A few pages later he emphasises that 'the two opposite qualities of roughness, and of sudden variation, joined to that of irregularity, are the most efficient causes of the picturesque'.[12] It was, of course, the absence of just these qualities that Price found so regrettable in the work of Capability Brown. He complained that:

modern improvers . . . overlook two of the most fruitful sources of human pleasure; the first, that great and universal source of pleasure, variety, whose power is independent of beauty, but without which even beauty itself soon ceases to please; the other, intricacy, a quality which, though distinct from variety, is so connected and blended with it, that the one can hardly exist without the other. According to the idea I have formed of it, intricacy in landscape might be defined as that disposition of objects, which, by a partial and uncertain concealment, excites and nourishes curiosity . . . As intricacy in the disposition, and variety in the forms, the tints, and the lights and shadows of objects, are the great characteristics of picturesque scenery; so monotony and baldness are the greatest defects of improved places.[13]

It is a tribute to the enduring influence of Alexander Pope that Price's views should echo his advice to Lord Burlington:

> Let not each beauty ev'rywhere be spy'd
> When half the skill is decently to hide.
> He gains all points who pleasingly confounds
> Surprizes, varies and conceals the Bounds.[14]

Uvedale Price inherited a large fortune on the death of his father in 1761 and was able to put his theories into practice on his estate, Foxley, Herefordshire. His main contribution was the creation of a drive one and a half miles long through the woods, but surprisingly he did not 'improve' the immense red-brick mansion in the Georgian baroque style. Now demolished, this house must have been strikingly inappropriate in the subtle picturesque setting recorded for us in a charming drawing by Price's friend, Thomas Gainsborough, *Beach Trees in Wood at Foxley with Yazor Church in distance*. Price advised Sir George Beaumont on

Downton Castle, Herefordshire. The Gorge of the river Teme. Payne Knight's appreciation of the picturesque qualities of the site he selected for his new house at Downton is reflected in the numerous watercolours of the river Teme which Thomas Hearne painted for him in 1784–6 as one of the earliest and most important of such pictorial records. Knight, who especially admired the setting of his cousin's house at Hafod (p. 101) and also Hawkstone (p. 74) had to admit that the rocks at Downton were 'very inferior in Form, Colour and Intricacy' to those at Hawkstone, though he consoled himself with the thought that the clear running water at Downton was 'a Beauty for which nothing can compensate'.

the layout of the park at Coleorton, Leicestershire, and wrote to Lady Beaumont in 1804 in praise of beech trees that they were 'of great lightness and playfulness in their style of growing'.[15] Gainsborough's lively sketch of Foxley seems designed to illustrate Price's point. Another friend of Price's was Charles James Fox whom he had met at Eton and whom he accompanied on a Grand Tour in 1767–8. Price was a lifelong Whig as was his friend and fellow Herefordshire squire, Richard Payne Knight (1750–1824).

A few months before the publication of Price's *Essay on the Picturesque* in 1794, Knight produced a similar polemical study which was addressed to Price, *The Landscape, a Didactic Poem in Three Books* (1794). Whereas Price's intellectual interests were centred almost entirely on the Picturesque, Knight's were far wider. He never married, but published books on a wide variety of subjects ranging from sexual symbolism to Greek philology. With his original, not to say perverse, mind, preoccupied with the symbolical meaning of religious forms, he was one of the most significant figures in the history of eighteenth-century taste. Grandson of a wealthy Shropshire ironmaster, he came of age in 1771 and inherited a 10,000 acre estate in Herefordshire where he began to build Downton Castle in the following year. Downton is a remarkable essay in a Claudian picturesque style, its castellated asymmetrical form serving as a powerful influence on the architect John Nash. The immediate surroundings of Downton Castle, set on the steep bank of the river Teme, were so naturally and dramatically picturesque that it was scarcely necessary for Knight to 'improve' them. A rocky path flanked by whirlpools and wooden hills leads along the gorge in which a cave with rock-hewn windows and two bridges are due to Knight.

Knight's first Grand Tour, in which he travelled as far south as Naples, began in 1767 and lasted for about four years. Before work on Downton was quite finished he set off on a second tour in 1776 with the young landscape artist John

Robert Cozens, with whom he travelled extensively in Switzerland. By the following spring he was in Rome, which he left for a tour of Sicily in April accompanied by two friends of Goethe, the landowner and artist Charles Gore (1729–1807), and the Prussian artist J. P. Hackert. In his journal of this tour, which was partly published by Goethe,[16] Knight was already describing the Doric temples at Paestum as 'picturesque'. In 1781 Knight was elected to the Society of Dilettanti, described by Walpole as 'a club, for which the nominal qualification is having been in Italy, and the real one, being drunk'. Nonetheless, as we have seen, it subsidized the first accurate survey of Greek architecture, Stuart and Revett's *Antiquities of Athens* of which the first volume appeared in 1762. It also arranged for the publication and distribution (to members of the Society only) of Knight's first book, an idiosyncratic and daring study entitled *An Account of the Remains of the Worship of Priapus lately existing in Isernia, to which is added a Discourse on the Worship of Priapus, and its Connexion with the Mystic Theology of the Ancients* (1786). The release into Georgian society of an illustrated account of phallic worship was bound to cause controversy and the Society attempted to withdraw the book. However, Knight repeated much of its subject-matter in *The Symbolical Language of Ancient Art and Mythology* (1818), a book which also makes clear his pantheism and hostility to all organised religion.

More widely read was his *An Analytical Inquiry into the Principles of Taste* (1805) which was important for its long second section entitled 'Of the Association of Ideas'. This emphasis on associationism with its logically argued but essentially subjective approach to the causes of beauty, led him away from Price and towards some of the dominant romantic moods of the nineteenth century.

Although Knight's poem, *The Landscape*, is the real reason for his inclusion in the present chapter, we need not dwell too long on it since it seems to be heavily dependent on discussions with Price and contains little that we have not already seen in Price's *An Essay on the Picturesque*. However, in the Advertisement to the second edition of 1795, Knight made it clear that he did not agree with Price's easy distinctions between the Sublime, the Beautiful and the Picturesque. He accepted the existence of picturesque qualities but not the term Picturesque, partly because in aesthetics, as in religion, he disliked rigid rules and partly because of his increasingly subjective approach, based on Hume, to the origins of our sensations of beauty. Thus, for Knight, the Picturesque was a way of looking, not a quality inherent in particular objects.

Despite its jejune rhymes, *The Landscape* is an entertaining attack on Brown as well as a spirited defence of variety and intricacy. It derives much of its cogency from the pair of telling engravings by Thomas Hearn, whom Knight also employed to paint a series of watercolours of the gorge at Downton. One of the two engravings in *The Landscape* depicts a typical Palladian house and park as improved by Brown. This relates to passages by Knight such as:

> Oft when I've seen some lonely mansion stand,
> Fresh from th'improver's desolating hand,
> 'Midst shaven lawns, that far around it creep
> In one eternal undulating sweep . . .[17]

The other engraving shows a rough landscape littered with weeds and stones,

ferns and branches, and containing in the distance an Elizabethan mansion with a balustraded terrace and a many-gabled roof echoing the outline of a clump of trees. This reflects Knight's advice to the designer of the ideal picturesque estate, which was to proceed:

> Through the rough thicket or the flowery mead;
> Till bursting from some deep-imbowered shade,
> Some narrow valley, or some opening glade,
> Well mix'd and blended in the scene, you shew
> The stately mansion rising to the view.
> But mix'd and blended, ever let it be
> A mere component part of what you see.[18]

This blending of architecture with scenery lies, of course, at the heart of the whole picturesque movement.

Both Price and Knight included in their strictures not only Brown but their contemporary Humphry Repton (1752–1818). Having followed various professions with no great measure of success, Repton decided in the course of a sleepless night in 1788 to try landscape gardening, a subject which seems to have been a guiding influence in his life for some years. His aim must have been to fill the gap left on Brown's death five years before. One of his earliest commissions, at Sheffield Park, East Sussex, in 1789 was to develop a park begun by Brown thirteen years earlier. The work of the two men merges into a single lovely whole, linked by artificial lakes and enriched by nineteenth- and twentieth-century

Sheffield Park, East Sussex. The irregular Gothic house built by James Wyatt in the 1770s and 1780s for the 1st Earl of Sheffield merges into its landscaped setting by Capability Brown and Humphry Repton. Much of the planting with coniferous trees and shrubs is late nineteenth and early twentieth century.

additions. In general Repton was content to follow Brown's practice, though he preferred wooded hills to belts of trees, and he did not allow the parkland to come right up to the house but introduced a transitional area of terraces, gravel walks and even flower beds. He liked to create an atmosphere of mild but pleasing disarray and was anxious to draw out the inherent character of a place rather than to impose a standard pattern as Brown had often done.

Unlike Brown, Repton was a talented artist who put his gifts to brilliant use in the charming Red Books of which over seventy survive. In these he illustrated his proposals for improving country seats and parks in a series of eye-catching watercolours accompanied by an explanatory and often fulsome text. The watercolours were often fitted with a flap, or Slide as Repton called them, depicting the prospect as it existed at the time, which, when lifted, revealed it as it would be when improved by Repton. This delectable and eminently practical device, which could scarcely fail to appeal to Repton's patrons, is a classic instance of the pictorial or picturesque approach. At the same time, Repton was flexible, practical and eclectic. Indeed, his lack of dogmatism and readiness to compromise, upset a passionate amateur theorist like Uvedale Price. In fact Repton was in agreement with Price on most of the important issues, as can be appreciated in his *Sketches and Hints on Landscape Gardening* (1794), where he defined the 'sources of pleasure in landscape gardening' as: 'I Congruity – II Utility – III Order – IV Symmetry – V Picturesque Effect – VI Intricacy – VII Simplicity – VIII Variety – IX Novelty – X Contrast – XI Continuity – XII Association – XIII Grandeur – XIV Appropriation – XV Animation – XVI The Seasons'.

However, in the writings of Price and Knight, Repton saw a potential threat to his independent professional status as a landscape gardener. He was thus obliged to disagree with three central points in Price's argument: the importance of landscape painting as a model for the gardener; the value of decay and neglect in buildings; and the overriding importance of picturesque theory as a solution to all problems. Repton's exceptional visual sensitivity, his awareness of space, of optical illusion and of the shifting tonal values of the changing seasons and times of day, made him conscious that the framed landscape painting must ultimately be inadequate as a guide to anyone entrusted with the shaping of earth, air, water, trees and buildings. He also had to deal with clients, unlike Price and Knight who were simply wealthy amateurs. This made him particularly alive to the need for compromise, so that he was able to claim, in words that shocked Price, 'I have discovered that *utility* must often take the lead of beauty, and *convenience* be preferred to picturesque effect, in the neighbourhood of man's habitation'.[19] His friendly personal relations with Price and Knight were shattered by the latter's poem, *The Landscape*, which contained a long footnote ridiculing Repton's pretentious proposals for placing the owner's coat of arms on the milestones at Tatton Park, Cheshire. Repton referred to this dispute in his *Sketches and Hints* of 1794, while Knight returned to it in the second edition of *The Landscape* in the following year. The differences between Repton, Price and Knight seem to us today comparatively trifling, especially in comparison with the range of important matters on which they were in complete agreement. Nonetheless, the debate was eagerly followed by the educated public, with the literary journals of the day taking different sides. Repton returned to the defence in subsequent books based on his Red Books, *Observations on the Theory and Practice of Landscape Gardening* (1803) and *An Inquiry into the Changes of Taste in Landscape Gardening* (1806). He was also mentioned enthusiastically in Jane Austen's *Mansfield Park* (1814) and appears as 'Marmaduke Milestone' in Thomas Love Peacock's *Headlong Hall* (1815). It was in a celebrated passage in this novel that Peacock punctured the concept of surprise, so dear to practitioners of the Picturesque:

'Allow me,' said Mr. Gale (who, with Mr. Treacle, was a very profound critic from Edinburgh), 'I distinguish the picturesque and the beautiful and add to them, in the laying out of grounds, a third and distinct character, which I call *unexpectedness*.' 'Pray, sir,' said Mr. Milestone, 'by what name do you distinguish this character when a person walks round the grounds for a second time?'.

Between 1789 and *c.*1815 Repton worked on nearly two hundred commissions, many of them being adaptations of existing parks. Though fewer of his parks have survived than Brown's, fine examples of his work can still be seen at Antony, Cornwall, Luscombe and Endsleigh, Devon, Newton Park, Somerset, Corsham Court, Wiltshire, Gayhurst and Tyringham, Buckinghamshire, Panshanger and Ashridge, Hertfordshire, Uppark, West Sussex, Sheffield Park, East Sussex, Cobham Hall, Kent, Dullingham, Cambridgeshire, Sheringham Hall, Norfolk, Burley-on-the-Hill, Leicestershire, Sezincote, Gloucestershire, Attingham Park, Shropshire, Stanage, Powys, Wentworth Woodhouse, South Yorkshire, and Mulgrave Castle, North Yorkshire. Sheringham, for which the Red Book of 1812 survives, is one of the most enchanting and well-maintained of all Repton's creations. He designed not only the park but, with his son, the simple classical villa for Abbot Upcher and his wife in open farmland near the sea. To emphasise the modest character of the property, he retained cornfields between the house and the wooded hills in a way that would have shocked Brown. He contrived the entrance to the property on the east side from Upper Sheringham in his favourite manner by swinging the drive round a wood and suddenly giving a beautifully composed distant vista of the house which, tantalisingly, disappears temporarily. He welcomed the proximity of the 'cheerful village' of Upper Sheringham since, as a Tory, he admired houses like Cirencester Park and Petworth which were built on the edge of towns and not isolated in the midst of proud and lonely parks. Repton himself chose to live in a modest cottage in the village street at Harestreet, Romford, Essex, of which he wrote: 'I have obtained a frame to my landscape; the frame is composed of flowering shrubs and evergreens; beyond which are seen, the cheerful village, the high road, and that constant moving scene, which I would not exchange for any of the lonely parks that I have improved for others'.[20]

Repton was more keenly aware than Brown had been that architecture was, as he put it, 'an inseparable and indispensible auxiliary' to landscape gardening. For about five years from 1796 he was in partnership with the architect John Nash, the fruits of which it will be more appropriate to investigate in the next chapter. Repton is also notable for reinstating the flower garden near the house. This meant breaking up the sweeping harmonious unity which had been the mid-eighteenth-century aesthetic ambition as exemplified in the work of Brown. Repton, by contrast, developed after 1800 a type of eclectic, additive garden laid out for comfort and prettiness in a series of asymmetrical compartments. This was a process akin to the contemporary revolution in interior design in which the formal arrangements of Georgian furniture were dissolved in favour of scattered

Sheringham, Norfolk. View from Repton's Red Book of 1812 showing the site 'before' (*above*) and, with the flap raised, 'after' (*above right*) the proposed improvements. In his text Repton emphasises his avoidance of Brown's 'artificial smoothing' in favour of preserving the 'accidental character' of the hilly partly wooded site. He was anxious in forming the drive 'that its banks should be left steep and abrupt, and not smoothed and turfed over; since a road is an artificial object, and may be avowed, in such cases, as a work of art'. He also deliberately did not remove the gaunt trees on the side of the drive, bent sideways by the sea winds.

groups disposed in response to ideals of freedom and comfort. Indeed Repton himself, in his *Fragments on the Theory and Practice of Landscape Gardening* (1816) illustrated a 'View of the ancient cedar parlour' contrasted with the 'Modern living-room', opening into a conservatory. The explanatory poem printed beneath them begins:

> No more the *Cedar Parlour's* formal gloom
> With dulness chills, 'tis now the *Living-Room*;
> Where guests, to whim, or taste, or fancy true,
> Scatter'd in groups, their different plans pursue . . .
> Here, books of poetry, and books of prints,
> Furnish aspiring artists with new hints:
> Flow'rs, landscapes, figures, cram'd in one portfolio . . .[21]

Just at the moment when Repton's younger contemporaries like Crome, Cotman, Girtin, Turner and Constable were turning with quickened response to nature, Repton, as Pevsner tellingly put it, 'converts gardening into a department of furnishing'.[22] Typical is Repton's work at Woburn Abbey where his Red Book, unfortunately, is lost. He wrote in 1806 of:

The terrace and parterre near the house, the private garden, only used by the family, the rosary, or dressed flower garden, in front of the greenhouse, the American garden, for plants of that country only, the Chinese garden, surrounding a pool in front of the great Chinese pavilion to be decorated with plants from China, the botanic garden, for scientific classing of plants, the animated garden, or menagerie, and, lastly, the English garden, or shrubbery walk, connecting the whole; sometimes commanding views into each of these distinct objects, and sometimes into the park and distant country.[23]

Repton was probably prouder of his work at Ashridge, Hertfordshire, where between 1808 and 1820 James Wyatt and his nephew Jeffry created a spectacular

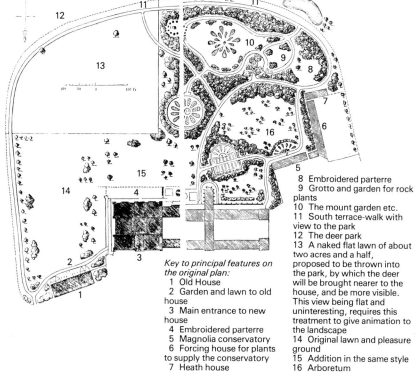

Key to principal features on the original plan:
1 Old House
2 Garden and lawn to old house
3 Main entrance to new house
4 Embroidered parterre
5 Magnolia conservatory
6 Forcing house for plants to supply the conservatory
7 Heath house
8 Embroidered parterre
9 Grotto and garden for rock plants
10 The mount garden etc.
11 South terrace-walk with view to the park
12 The deer park
13 A naked flat lawn of about two acres and a half, proposed to be thrown into the park, by which the deer will be brought nearer to the house, and be more visible. This view being flat and uninteresting, requires this treatment to give animation to the landscape
14 Original lawn and pleasure ground
15 Addition in the same style
16 Arboretum

Ashridge, Hertfordshire. Plan of the gardens proposed by Repton in c. 1813 for the Earl of Bridgewater. This eclectic inward-looking garden contains the seeds of Loudon's 'Gardenesque'. Repton claimed that 'Of all the subjects on which I have been consulted, few have excited so much interest in my mind as the plan for these gardens', explaining that in his declining years 'when no longer able to undertake the more extensive plans of *landscape*, I was glad to contract my views within the narrow circle of the *garden*, independent of its accompaniment of distant scenery'.

Gothic palace for the 7th Earl of Bridgewater, inspired by Fonthill Abbey. A few fragments survived of a mediaeval college on the site, so that Repton 'ventured boldly to go back to those ancient trim gardens, which formerly delighted the venerable inhabitants of this curious spot, as appears from the trim box hedges of the monks' garden, and some large yew-trees still growing in rows near the site of

83

the monastery'.[24] Repton's unusual proposals of 1813 included as many as fifteen different types of garden, including a rock garden, physic garden, winter garden, monks' garden, arboretum, paved terrace, embroidered parterre before the south front, and a rosary adorned with 'a conduit, or holy well', an elaborate Gothic structure eventually built of cast iron in 1820 from designs by Jeffry Wyatville. Repton explained in 1816 that:

> The novelty of this attempt to collect a number of gardens, differing from each other, may, perhaps, excite the critic's censure; but I will hope there is no more absurdity in collecting gardens of different styles, dates, characters, and dimensions, in the same inclosure, than in placing the works of a Raphael and a Teniers in the same cabinet, or books sacred and profane in the same library.[25]

It is doubtful whether picturesque eclecticism could be carried further. These small gardens were finally designed and constructed in 1814–20, but not under Repton's direction. Further alterations were made in the nineteenth and twentieth centuries, including a grotto and tunnel by Sir Matthew Digby Wyatt in 1851. The long period of growth and present style of maintenance of the Ashridge gardens heighten the proto-Victorian mood of Repton's original proposals.

It is entertaining to recall that the parks of Brown and Repton proved so popular that owners wanted them indoors as well. We should therefore not ignore the eminently picturesque tradition of the panoramic painted room. Gaspard Poussin himself had painted whole landscaped rooms in the seventeenth century, but at Standlynch (now Trafalgar) House, Wiltshire, Giovanni Battista Cipriani (1727–85) painted an interior in c.1766 which, according to Edward Croft-Murray, is a turning point in the history of the painted panoramic room in England because, 'perhaps for the first time, we find the architectural framing dispensed with, and the landscape treated as a real panorama running continuously round the walls'.[26] Standlynch represents a remarkable conjunction of antique and picturesque enthusiasm, for Nicholas Revett (1720–1804), who had made the measured drawings for the *Antiquities of Athens* with James Stuart, was altering the house externally and internally at the same moment that Cipriani was painting the walls of the parlour. The owner, Henry Dawkins, was a member of the Society of Dilettanti, while his brother James had visited Palmyra and Baalbek with Robert Wood and had helped finance Stuart and Revett's stay in Athens. On to the east entrance-front of the red-brick house, built in 1733, Revett clapped a complex neo-Greek portico of fourteen columns grouped in an un-Greek way but with fluting only at the top and bottom of the shafts – a device inspired by the Temple of Apollo on Delos.

Cipriani also came from a world we have met before. When he went to Rome in 1750 aged twenty-three he made the acquaintance of members of the English colony, two of whom, Sir William Chambers and Joseph Wilton, brought him to England in 1756. He was subsequently much employed as a decorative painter by Chambers and by Adam and was elected a Foundation Member of the Royal Academy in 1768. His parlour at Standlynch is a curious and original production in that the landscape changes on each of the four walls according to the character of the figures in it. Three female figures symbolising the arts are disposed in an Arcadian landscape containing a circular temple on the pattern of the mauseoleum at Castle Howard; the scene darkens on the chimney-piece wall

where Venus passes in her chariot; on the third wall a storm is in full swing overthrowing an obelisk and lashing the trees in front of which appears Shakespeare, prototype of the Romantic genius, seeking inspiration from the elements; finally, the fourth window wall returns to normality with a conversation-piece featuring pets and animals.

At Norbury Park, Surrey, for the connoisseur and artist William Lane, Cipriani collaborated with three other artists in c.1781 on the creation of an enchanting painted drawing-room resembling a bower commanding views of the Lake District. The house is beautifully placed on a hilltop with superb views, and the skilful way in which the bow window and the view from it are incorporated into the total effect of the room is a triumph of the Picturesque. These sunlit landscapes express the genuine love of nature which lies at the heart of the Picturesque movement. The design of the house has been attributed to the topographical artist and Deputy Ranger of Windsor Great Park, Thomas Sandby (1721–98).

Drakelow Hall, Derbyshire, The Painted Room, 1793, by Paul Sandby (destroyed save for one wall re-erected in the Victoria & Albert Museum and reproduced here). Sandby created the illusion of a clearing in a forest defined by wooden treillage and palings with a view of a river valley on one wall, and on another a grotto (in fact the chimney-piece), studded with real spars, ores and shells.

85

At Drakelowe Hall, Derbyshire, in 1793 Thomas Sandby's better-known brother Paul painted a room similar to that at Norbury Park. The chimney-piece is designed as a grotto, and branches of trees spread dramatically over the coved ceiling and frame painted views of Peak scenery. Drakelowe Hall was demolished in 1934 and the room partially reconstructed in the Victoria & Albert Museum where, without the benefit of the window wall which commanded fine views of real Peak District scenery, it naturally loses much of its poetic effect.

The enthusiasm for lake landscapes fringed with grottoes survived into the nineteenth century as can be seen, for example, at Busbridge Hall, Surrey, laid out by H. Hare Townshend in *c.*1810 with a chain of four lakes, a rockwork Hermit's Cave, grotto and temples. More exotic and thus closer in mood to Alton Towers and Biddulph Grange described in Chapter 2, are the gardens at Stancombe Park, Gloucestershire, created in the 1840s by the Rev. David Edwards. The gardens are in a secluded valley some distance from the house, a spot chosen, according to local legend, to enable him to meet his gipsy lady-friend without his wife's knowledge. They have been admirably described by Barbara Jones:

Stancombe is transitional. The choice of site for the house at the head of a pretty valley, the flowing, informal landscaping and planting, the use of cottages as part of the design, the building of exotic conceits, all belong to the romantic tradition. The enclosure of the lake in a tight belt of garden; the beds, theatres and pavilions for flowers; the chalet air of the cottages; the static tightness of the fountains; the gravel and elaborate herbaceous borders; the choice of Egyptian and prehistoric themes for the conceits instead of Chinese, all anticipate the second half of the nineteenth century; still beautiful and still romantic, but with a changed focus, the eye looking close instead of across the valley, not at a plantation but at a rose.[27]

The confusion of elements at Stancombe may be attributable in part to the influence of the indefatigable Scottish gardener and theorist, John Claudius Loudon (1783–1843). Loudon kept Repton's ideals alive well into the nineteenth century by reprinting all his landscape writings in one volume in 1840 under the title *The Landscape Gardening and Landscape Architecture of the late Humphry Repton, Esq.* His other publications, totalling four million words, included a *Treatise on Forming, Improving and Managing Country Residences* (1806), *Encyclopaedia of Gardening* (1822), *Encyclopaedia of Cottage, Farm and Villa Architecture and Furniture* (1833), and the *Suburban Gardener and Villa Companion* (1838) in which book he divided houses and gardens into categories according to the social status of their owners, so that we find chapters with unpromising titles like 'Third-Rate Gardens'. Loudon also founded and edited three journals which were the first of their kind, *The Gardener's Magazine* (1826–43), *The Magazine of Natural History* (1829–36) and *The Architectural Magazine* (1834–8) in which the young Ruskin published 'The Poetry of Architecture'.

Loudon was also interested in industrial design and was a pioneer in the promotion of iron and glass as constructional materials. However, his approach to architectural style was eclectic to a degree and his influence on Victorian domestic architecture widespread but not always beneficial. His aim as a gardener was to apply Reptonian techniques, devised for large parks, to the smaller grounds surrounding the residences of the middle classes, and to incorporate into these

Barnbarrow, Dumfries and Galloway Region, 'before' (*above*) and 'after' (*right*) the proposed alterations by J. C. Loudon as depicted in his *Treatise on Forming . . . Country Residences* (1806). This dramatic and somewhat dangerous scheme, which dates from the start of Loudon's career before he had invented the 'Gardenesque', shows him siding with Knight against Brown. Some of his alterations to the house (since called Barnbarroch) were carried out for Robert Agnew in *c.* 1806, but since both it and the park have been in a state of romantic decay since the 1940s, it is unclear how far Loudon's schemes for rocks and cascades were ever fulfilled.

(not always successfully) a colourful clutter of herbaceous borders, bedding plants in formal patterns, flowering shrubs and specimen trees. He called this the 'Gardenesque', a style 'calculated for displaying the art of the gardener'.

Echoes of Loudon's combination of the Eclectic and the Picturesque can be found in the fantastic garden at Friar Park, Henley-on-Thames, created from the 1890s by Frank Crisp (1843–1919), a successful London solicitor who was Vice-President of the Linnean Society, was knighted in 1907 and made a baronet six years later. Eight mediaeval gardens were laid out at Friar Park on the basis of illustrations in fifteenth-century manuscripts which were reproduced in the guidebook for the purposes of comparison. The 'Guide for the use of Visitors', an unusual production for Edwardian England, was necessary since the gardens were open to the public at sixpence per head from 2 p.m. to 6 p.m. on Wednesdays from May to September.[28] Indeed in 1919 Friar Park was claimed as 'a garden that has been visited perhaps more than any other in the British Isles'. It also boasted a reduced version of the Matterhorn which presided over an immense four-acre Alpine rock-garden, still being extended in 1913 and formed from 10,000 tons of millstone grit specially transported from Yorkshire. As *Country Life* explained in 1905, apparently without irony, 'It has been the object of Mr Crisp to reproduce, as far as possible, a portion of the Alps in miniature, and only those who have seen the huge natural rocks and boulders, and little crags and pathways winding here and there, can realise the stupendous work involved. The garden is still unfinished . . .'[29]

An improbable meeting of opposites took place in *c*.1902 when Lady Ottoline Morrell visited Friar Park and having inspected its grottoes with their gnomes, skeletons and stalactites was rowed by Mr Crisp through 'elaborate caves and underground lakes, lit up with electricity, and festooned with artifical grapes, spiders, and other monsters'. She records with droll amazement how 'He took his visitors round the caves and the garden (which was also filled with china hobgoblins and other surprises) dressed in a long frock-coat and top hat and with a large umbrella in his hands, as if he was walking to his Throgmorton Street office, his manner perfectly serious when warning one against the danger of a monstrous spider alighting on one's head'.[30] Alas, this description is as close as we can now hope to come to Friar Park, since it is not shown to the public under any circumstances: we can therefore only wonder whether even gnomes become picturesque in decay.

The Picturesque tradition ceased to dominate garden and landscape design after the early nineteenth century. It was replaced by a range of interests which included in the first place Loudon's 'Gardenesque' and, later in the century, the historical revival of Italianate and seventeenth-century English garden design. Though the 'Gardenesque' may not be essentially picturesque in character, it is important to realise that it was a revival and development of the tradition of the flower garden which, despite the grand parks of Brown and Repton, had flourished during the eighteenth century. Examples of this tradition, the survival of which is often overlooked today, include designs by Joseph Spence and Thomas Wright, and the gardens of Richard Bateman at Grove House, Old Windsor in the 1740s, of Hugh Hamersley at Woodside, Berkshire in the 1750s, and at Kew in the 1760s. If the Picturesque became less important in garden and landscape design in the Victorian period, it survived in architecture in various significant ways which we shall investigate in the following chapters.

The Picturesque House: Vanbrugh to Soane

As the Picturesque dissolved the traditional elements of garden design such as formal avenues, terraces, clipped hedges, stone steps and balustrades, so it gradually dethroned the symmetrical Palladian architecture which, in the beginning, it had accepted happily enough. By 1794, as we have seen in the illustrations to Payne Knight's *The Landscape*, a substantial mansion could be presented visually as though it were a clump of trees, and the architect advised to let his work 'be a mere component part of what you see' in the landscape as a whole. To trace this revolutionary approach to its origins is to return to that towering imaginative genius of eighteenth-century architecture, Sir John Vanbrugh (1664–1726).

In 1718, towards the end of his colourful career, Vanbrugh acquired a small estate near the top of Greenwich Hill between Greenwich Park and Blackheath, where he built Vanbrugh Castle for himself, as well as four other houses, gateways and outbuildings. Thus over the years he created for the benefit of the Vanbrugh family a private residential estate of an unprecedently picturesque character This romantic domain was approached through a twin-towered, arched gateway from which a sinuous drive led to a group of three machicolated houses for his sisters Victoria and Robina and his brother Philip. Nearby was 'Mince Pie' House, or 'Vanbrugh House', built for Vanbrugh's brother Charles and described by the architect in 1722 as 'a Tower of White Bricks, only one Room and a Closet on a floor'. A little way to the south he built his own house, Vanbrugh Castle, on the edge of the hill commanding magnificent views northwards of Greenwich Hospital, the Thames and beyond. It was a peculiar building on a neo-Elizabethan plan with a spiral staircase in a tower projecting from the middle of the south front and, behind, a single large room with a semi-circular bow window taking advantage of the panoramic view. This little turreted villa was symmetrical, but when Vanbrugh extended it in *c.*1723, possibly in expectation of the birth of a son, he did so in a deliberately asymmetrical way with a wing extending eastwards. The whole group of semi-fortified mediaevalising buildings disposed irregularly among trees on a sloping terrain commanding fine distant views, is the perfect realisation of Vanbrugh's ambition in 1709 of preserving the ruins of Woodstock Manor in the park at Blenheim so as to recall 'One of the Most Agreable Objects that the best of Landskip Painters can invent'.

Sir Joshua Reynolds seems to have had Vanbrugh Castle in mind in his remarkable encomium of Vanbrugh in his 13th Discourse at the Royal Academy in 1786 when he spoke of the pleasure given by 'whatever building brings to our remembrance ancient customs and manners, such as the Castles of the Barons of ancient Chivalry . . . Hence it is that *towers and battlements* are so often selected by the Painter and Poet, to make a part of the composition of their Landskip; and it is from hence, in a great degree, that in the buildings of Vanbrugh, who was a Poet as

Vanbrugh Castle, Greenwich, built in 1718-19 by Sir John Vanbrugh for himself. View from the south by the antiquary William Stukeley in 1721 Stukeley shows that the effect of the mock fortifications and out-buildings, now largely demolished, was to make the whole appear asymmetrical even before the additions which Vanbrugh made to the Castle in *c*. 1723.

well as an Architect, there is a greater display of imagination, than we shall find perhaps in any other'.[1] Reynolds may have had in mind Vanbrugh's Seaton Delaval, Northumberland (1720–28) which, especially when viewed from the side, recalls the kind of scenic architecture in landscape paintings like Claude's *Landscape with Psyche and the Palace of Amor*. It was in his 'heroic' buildings such as Seaton Delaval, Eastbury and Blenheim that Vanbrugh achieved the ambition to which he referred in a letter of 1707 to the Earl of Manchester about the remodelling of Kimbolton Castle: 'As to the Outside, I thought 'twas absolutely best, to give it something of the Castle Air, tho' at the same time to make it regular . . . I'm sure this will make a very Noble and Masculine Shew'.[2] Other relevant aspects of Vanbrugh's work include the relation of garden buildings to each other and to the landscape at Castle Howard and Stowe, his irregular fortified walls and bastions at Castle Howard, and the Great Room which he added at Claremont in 1719–30 and which towered above the existing building in such an uncompromisingly asymmetrical way. In an album of his drawings preserved at Elton Hall there is even one sketch for a small deliberately asymmetrical house.

We have already noticed Alfred's Hall at Cirencester Park built in 1721 and extended asymmetrically eleven years later as the first of all castellated ruined follies. The next asymmetrical and castellated houses after Vanbrugh Castle were Horace Walpole's Strawberry Hill and Payne Knight's Downton Castle. Strawberry Hill was in some ways the most remarkable and the most picturesque house of the eighteenth century. The element of make-believe, never very far from the Picturesque, was central to Walpole's confection on the banks of the Thames at Twickenham. As early as 1747, in which year at the age of thirty he began to rent the property, he was writing to his friend Henry Conway of his 'little play-thing house . . . the prettiest bauble you ever saw. It is set in enamelled meadows, with filigree hedges . . . Pope's ghost is just now skimming under my window by a most poetical moonlight'.[3] To Sir Horace Mann he explained in 1748 that 'The prospect is as delightful as possible, commanding the river, the town and Richmond Park; and being situated on a hill descends to the Thames through two or three little meadows, where I have some Turkish sheep and two cows, all studied in their colours for becoming the view'.[4]

(*Left*) Seaton Delaval, North-umberland, 1720–8, by Sir John Vanbrugh for Admiral George Delaval. View from the west. Vanbrugh's powerful imagination creates a heroic grouping of towers and masses anticipatory of the kind of asymmetrical picturesque architecture produced later in the eighteenth and nineteenth centuries.

(*Below*) *Landscape with Psyche and the Palace of Amor* or *The Enchanted Castle* 1664, by Claude Lorrain. Based on a story in Apuleius's *Metamorphoses* which includes a 'royal palace . . . built by a divine artist', this painting, which was in an English collection by the 1770s, shows the seductively picturesque quality of Claude's architectural inventiveness.

Two years later he bought the modest house with its five acres and wrote to Mann, 'I am going to build a little Gothic castle'.[5] He justified his choice of style with an argument which was to be of great consequence in the future of the Picturesque: 'The Grecian is only proper for magnificent and public buildings . . . The variety is little, and admits no charming irregularities. I am almost as

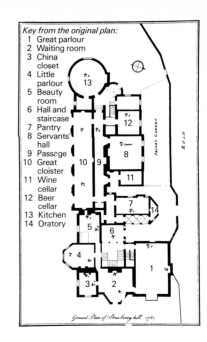

Key from the original plan:
1 Great parlour
2 Waiting room
3 China closet
4 Little parlour
5 Beauty room
6 Hall and staircase
7 Pantry
8 Servants' hall
9 Passage
10 Great cloister
11 Wine cellar
12 Beer cellar
13 Kitchen
14 Oratory

Strawberry Hill, Twickenham. Engraving of the north front (*above*) and plan of ground floor (*above right*) from *A Description of the Villa of Mr. Horace Walpole . . . at Strawberry Hill* (1784). On the right in the view is the castellated Round Tower built by Chute in *c.* 1760 (marked '13' on the plan); the conical roof next to it is that of the Beauclerk Tower, built from designs by James Essex in 1776. Beyond the clump of trees can be seen the one-storeyed bow-window of the Holbein Room (1758–9), while the rectangular building projecting on the extreme left is the library of 1753–4. The garden wall is inspired by an engraving in Dugdale's *Warwickshire* of the Jacobean Aston Hall, Birmingham. The combination of irregular buildings with trees at Strawberry Hill anticipates the ideals of Payne Knight.

(*Right*) The Round Drawing-Room, projected as a bedroom in the Round Tower in 1760 and decorated as a drawing-room by Robert Adam in *c.* 1766–9. Watercolour by John Carter, 1788, looking into the Long Gallery. Walpole confidently explains that 'The design of the chimney-piece is taken from the tomb of Edward the Confessor, improved by Mr Adam', while that of the ceiling was inspired by Dugdale's engraving of a rose window at Old St Paul's. The walls were hung with crimson Norwich damask and the chairs upholstered in white and green Aubusson tapestry with green and gold frames.

THE ROUND DRAWING-ROOM.

92

fond of the *Sharawaggi*, or Chinese want of symmetry, in buildings, as in grounds
or gardens'.[6] He took up this theme in another letter to Mann in 1753: 'You say,
"you suppose my garden is to be Gothic too". That can't be; Gothic is merely
architecture; and as one has a satisfaction in imprinting the gloomth of abbeys and
cathedrals on one's house, so one's garden on the contrary is to be nothing but
riant, and the gaiety of nature'.[7]

So it seems that Walpole hit on Gothic as a way of achieving charming
irregularity rather than deliberately choosing it as a desirable style in itself.
Moreover, just as a landscaped garden, being a living thing, grows and develops
with time as trees mature or are felled to open new vistas, and new garden
buildings are added, so Strawberry Hill itself was conceived as a building which
could grow and change over a period of forty years. Amongst Walpole's earliest
additions are the staircase, armoury and library of 1753–4 – 'my house is so
monastic', Walpole wrote to Mann as early as 1753 – followed by the Long
Gallery, Holbein Room and Tribune in 1758–63, the Round Tower in *c*. 1760–6,
the cloister in 1761, the chapel in the garden in 1771–3, the Great Bedchamber in
1772, the Beauclerk Tower with its extinguisher top in 1776, and the office wing in
1790. Walpole's pictorial and associational approach is evident in his comment in
1776 that the Beauclerk Tower has been 'carried up higher than the round one: it
has an exceedingly pretty effect, breaking the long line of the house picturesquely,
and looking very ancient'. Similarly he wrote in July 1759 in connection with the
design of the Tribune, that he intended to create 'a cabinet that is to have all the
air of a Catholic chapel – bar consecration!'[8]

He employed as many as ten different architects, including Robert Adam,
James Wyatt, James Essex and John Carter, though most of the designs are by his
friend John Chute of The Vyne, Hampshire, and Richard Bentley, son of the
Master of Trinity College, Cambridge. For the decoration of the interiors he
devised an unprecedentedly eclectic technique of copying mediaeval monuments,
especially those on a small scale like tombs, chapels and oratories. Thus the
chimney-piece in the library is inspired by John of Eltham's tomb at Westminster
Abbey, and that in the Holbein Chamber from Archbishop Wareham's tomb at
Canterbury. Bentley's fantastical screen in the Holbein Chamber echoes the gates
to the choir at Rouen Cathedral, while the design of Adam's ceiling of 1766 in the
Round Drawing Room is based on the rose window tracery at Old St Paul's.
Though these details are assembled in a playful rococo way, the serious
archaeological knowledge and enthusiasm which lie behind them mark a new
departure in the history of the Gothic Revival. The notion that there are correct
sources which ought to be correctly applied echoes the long-established vocabulary
of the orders in classical architecture as published in the great Renaissance
textbooks. Indeed, Walpole and his friends gained their information about
mediaeval design from the plates in recent antiquarian works of scholarship like
Dugdale's *Warwickshire* (1656) and *St Paul's* (1658), Dart's *Canterbury* (1726) and
Westminster (1742), Thomas's *Worcestershire* (1727) and Bentham's *Ely* (1771).

The house was thus assembled self-consciously like a literary work of art. In
1788 John Carter painted a series of watercolours of the interiors for Walpole, the
first such record of the interiors of any English country house. More importantly,
Walpole had already produced one of the first guidebooks to any country house as
early as 1774. In fact he had produced a catalogue of his collection in 1760, but in

1774 came *A Description of the Villa of Mr. Horace Walpole*, which was expanded ten years later with nearly thirty illustrations, including several plans and views of the grounds. The house was open to the public from noon to 3 p.m. between 1 May and 1 October to those who had applied in advance for tickets. The notion that a house is to be admired, illustrated and discussed like a work of art may not be exclusively the product of the Picturesque movement, but is nonetheless eminently characteristic of it. Walpole's extensive and catholic collection of works of art with which every interior was profusely littered, was especially strong in classical antiquities, English coins and enamels, and English prints. But these were interspersed with any number of amusing baubles, curiosities, snuff-boxes, all of which vastly entertained visitors and were lovingly described in the catalogue: 'Two tall chocolate cups and saucers, beautifully painted with holyoaks, of Seve china; presents from lady Ailesbury', 'A red and white rose, executed in feather, by Werman Cany'. The unmistakeably camp atmosphere, the silk cushions, tame canaries, tuberoses, bowls of pot-pourri, heliotrope, and pots of incense brought on after dinner by Swiss men-servants – all this underlined the Strawberry Hill make-believe as a picturesque retreat devoted entirely to pleasure and to the cultivation of all the senses. With anyone less brilliantly gifted than Walpole as its inspirer, this private paradise, tinselly, theatrical and flimsily constructed, might have estranged more people than it attracted. To William Beckford it was 'a species of gothic mousetrap – a reflection of Walpole's littleness ... He built everything upon family honours and gossip'.[9] However, in his *English Interiors, 1790–1848, the Quest for Comfort* (1978), John Cornforth argues that Strawberry Hill was especially influential as an example of the intimacy and comfort which were beginning to be sought after in the late eighteenth century. He also sees it as the origin of two important trends: the preoccupation by the connoisseur and amateur with his own surroundings, and the recording by professional antiquarian topographers of the interiors of modern houses and not merely of mediaeval churches.

Probably more influential in the long run than Strawberry Hill was Downton Castle, Herefordshire, even though it may initially have been inspired by Strawberry Hill. We have already touched on the significance of this romantic, asymmetrical castle built for himself from his own designs in 1772–8 by the independently-minded connoisseur Richard Payne Knight (1750–1824). We know from his *An Analytical Inquiry into the Principles of Taste* (1805) that in designing Downton he looked to the great landscape paintings of the seventeenth century, such as Claude's *Landscape with Psyche and the Palace of Amor*, as a model for the visual harmony between a building and its setting which he was so anxious to create. Pointing out that 'in the pictures of Claude and Gaspar, we perpetually see a mixture of Grecian and Gothic architecture employed with the happiest effect in the same building', he came to the conclusion that:

The best style of architecture for irregular and picturesque houses, which can now be adopted, is that mixed style, which characterises the buildings of Claude and the Poussins; for as it is taken from models, which were built piecemeal, during many successive ages; and by several different nations, it is distinguished by no particular manner of execution, or class of ornaments; but admits of all promiscuously from a plain wall or buttress, of the roughest masonry, to the most highly wrought Corinthian capital.[10]

(*Opposite*) Downton Castle, Herefordshire, 1772–8, built by Richard Payne Knight for himself. Despite the castellated asymmetry of Downton, its interiors are emphatically neo-antique. This eclecticism may be related to Knight's belief that the style of English mediaeval castles was derived from Roman architecture, and also to the heterogeneous buildings in the background of Claude's paintings which he took as one of his models. The porch and adjacent left-hand round tower in the photograph are Victorian additions.

Downton, therefore, is remarkable as perhaps the earliest building designed from the start to give the idea of growth. The south, originally the entrance front is dominated by a centrally-placed square keep flanked by asymmetrical wings terminating in towers. The western tower is octagonal and acts beautifully as a

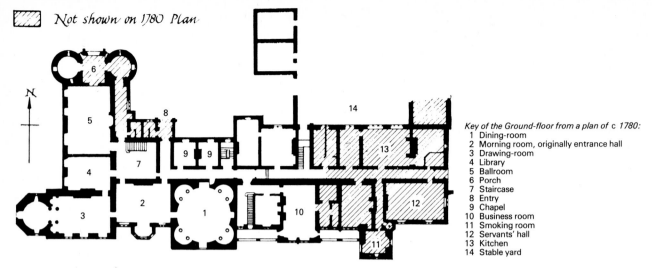

Key of the Ground-floor from a plan of c 1780:
1 Dining-room
2 Morning room, originally entrance hall
3 Drawing-room
4 Library
5 Ballroom
6 Porch
7 Staircase
8 Entry
9 Chapel
10 Business room
11 Smoking room
12 Servants' hall
13 Kitchen
14 Stable yard

Downton Castle plan

pivot for the whole composition at the point where the ground descends to the rocky limestone gorge containing the river Teme. Knight was helped in the earliest stages of design by the talented local architect Thomas Pritchard (1723–7), though some mediaeval details may have been collected for him by an antiquarian artist such as John Carter (1748–1817). However, Knight's intentions were not antiquarian but, as we know from his *Analytical Inquiry*, were coloured by an eclectic functionalism applied to the creation of a modern type of house planned irregularly for convenience, aspect and site. Considerations of practical convenience meant that the interiors, somewhat surprisingly, were not mediaevalising, like those of Strawberry Hill, but were in the up-to-date neo-classical style of Henry Holland or James Wyatt. Thus the central keep on the south front is entirely filled by a spectacular circular dining-room inspired by the Pantheon. This is startlingly polychromatic with its red scagliola columns imitating porphyry, its walls marbled in green and yellow panels with red borders, and its top-lit coffered dome painted in blue, red and gold. Between the columns in the niches are black 'basalt' figures, in fact of painted Coade stone. Several rooms contain decorative examples of genuine porphyry which Knight seems to have purchased in Italy. The handsome chimney-pieces, of which at least one was carved by Flaxman, include one in the drawing-room, which is flanked by Greek Doric columns. Knight justified his curious split-personality house in his *Analytical Inquiry* where he wrote:

It is now more than thirty years since the author of this inquiry ventured to build a house, ornamented with what are called Gothic towers and battlements without, and with Grecian ceilings, columns, and entablatures within; and though his example has not been much followed, he has every reason to congratulate himself upon the success of the experiment; he having at once, the advantage of a picturesque object, and of an elegant and convenient dwelling; though less perfect in both respects than if he had executed it at a maturer age. It has, however, the advantage of being capable of receiving alterations and additions in almost any direction, without injury to its genuine and original character.[11]

Knight did indeed make a number of additions to the house after 1780, including the formation of a north-west entrance which was elaborated in the mid-nineteenth century by the addition of a second circular tower and linking arch. Though the long terrace before the south front is not shown in an estate plan of *c*. 1780, it is so much in keeping with his proposals in the *Inquiry* that its formation is presumably due to him. He certainly added the isolated square tower at the east end of the terrace in which he retained rooms for himself after he made the castle over to his married brother Andrew in 1809. In 1808 he had moved from Downton to No.3, Soho Square where he installed his fine collection in an impressive domed library and museum designed and constructed for him in 1809 in fireproof cast-iron by a Mr Andrews. He bequeathed to the British Museum his extensive collection of gems, coins, bronze sculptures, marbles and 250 superb Claude drawings. His pictures, which he left to his brother who brought them back to Downton, included a Van Dyck, three Rembrandts, a fine portrait of himself by Lawrence, as well as works by those painters essential to the picturesque vision, Gaspard Poussin, Ruysdael, Salvator Rosa and Turner.

In the same decade that saw the birth of Downton, Robert Adam developed a markedly original castle-style of his own. By the 1770s he was no longer quite so much in the forefront of fashion as he had been ten and twenty years earlier, and for a group of major Scottish houses he worked out a novel style which is best appreciated at Culzean Castle (1778–81 and 1787–92) and Seton Castle (1789–91). With their bold geometrical forms, symmetry and lack of picturesque detail, such buildings are obviously not generated by a spirit of mediaeval romance, nor do they represent the first steps towards the Gothic Revival. They depend on a variety of sources including Roman military architecture, such as the fortifications at Spalatro which Adam had reconstructed for the plates in his *Palace of the Emperor Diocletian at Spalatro* (1764). Another very important source is surely Vanbrugh: one only has to compare Seton Castle, with its powerfully operatic forecourt, to Vanbrugh Castle to see the force of this comparison. Moreover, we know that Adam was a passionate admirer of Vanbrugh: 'Sir John Vanbrugh's genius', he wrote in the Preface to the *Works in Architecture of Robert and James Adam* (Vol. I, 1773), 'was of the first class; and, in point of movement, novelty and ingenuity, his works have not been exceeded by anything in modern times'. He went on to define what he meant by movement in a beautiful passage which has become justly famous:

Movement is meant to express, the rise and fall, the advance and recess, with other diversity of form, in the different parts of a building, so as to add greatly to the picturesque of the composition. For the rising and falling, advancing and receding, with the convexity and concavity, and other forms of the great parts, have the same effect in architecture, that hill and dale, fore-ground and distance, swelling and sinking have in landscape: That is, they serve to produce an agreeable and diversified contour, that groups and contrasts like a picture, and creates a variety of light and shade, which gives great spirit, beauty and effect to the composition.[12]

The bold massing and the variety of forms of Culzean Castle, dominated by its great round tower and brilliantly disposed on its narrow site sloping down to the sea, is a triumphant statement of Adam's 'movement', as well as a realisation of the many romantic drawings he made between 1777 and 1783 of scenic castellated buildings merging into rocky landscapes. His interest in triangular, D-shaped and V-shaped plans, as at Great Saxham Hall, Airthrey, Barnton and Cluny Castles and Walkinshaw House, is also an expression of a picturesque concern to achieve a visually stimulating liveliness and movement. The Temple or sham castle at Aske Hall, North Yorkshire, with its octagonal centre flanked by half-circular towers,

Aske Hall, North Yorkshire. Temple, probably built *c.* 1735 by Daniel Garrett for Sir Conyers D'Arcy from designs by William Kent. A forceful and complex mediaevalising pile in Kentian Gothick. Garrett may also have designed the Culloden Tower a mile or so away at Temple Lodge, Richmond, an assertive octagonal Gothick tower built in 1746 to commemorate the Jacobite defeat.

had come close to the effect Adam was aiming at. This brilliant composition was built some time between 1727 and 1758 by the architect Daniel Garrett from designs by William Kent. Adam was also able to draw on the long tradition of triangular prospect towers and houses, mainly in the Gothick style, which began with Shrub Hill Tower (later Fort Belvedere), built by Flitcroft in *c.*1750 at Virginia Water for the Duke of Cumberland in order to command views of Windsor Castle, the Hog's Back and St. Paul's Cathedral. The tradition of similar towers included, in the 1760s, Horton Tower, Dorset, Blaise Castle, Somerset, and Alfred's Tower at Stourhead; in the 1770s Racton Tower, Sussex, Midford Castle, Somerset, and the Belvederes at Powderham Castle and Haldon, both in Devon; in the 1780s Grimston Garth, Humberside, and Severndroog Castle, Shooter's Hill; and in the 1790s Hiorn's Tower at Arundel Castle park, Nash's house for Sir Uvedale Price at Aberystwyth, and Broadway Tower, Worcestershire.

The quality of movement so desirable to Adam could also be obtained by semi-circular and semi-octagonal bays, in fact by bay windows. Tudor architecture had derived part of its special colour from bay windows, but these were spurned by the austerer tastes of the neo-Palladians from Jones to Burlington and his successors. However, bays returned to favour in the late 1740s, when even Burlington provided a pair at Kirby Hall, North Yorkshire. Rococo Palladians like Isaac Ware and Thomas Wright quickly followed Burlington's example: the former at Wrotham Park, Barnet, and his own house, Westbourne House at Paddington; the latter at Dundalk House, Co. Louth, Horton House, Northamptonshire, Nuthall Temple, Nottinghamshire, Shugborough, Staffordshire, Stoke Gifford, Gloucestershire, and Tillymore, Co. Down. In his *The Villas of the Ancients Illustrated* (1728) Robert Castell had referred to the Roman admiration for rooms, presumably circular, oval or octagonal, planned to imitate the path the sun makes round the earth, and it was to be in villa design that the picturesque potentiality of the bay was to be most strikingly exploited.

Robert Morris in his *Rural Architecture* (1750) had led the way with his design for a 'Structure overlooking a valley'. This was a square building containing four octagonal rooms which project in the form of three-sided bay-windows on each of its four sides. James Paine's South Ormsby Hall, Lincolnshire (1751–6) has canted bays on three sides corresponding to three octagonal rooms, and the canted bay thereafter became a hallmark of his style and that of Carr of York. The most revolutionary and beautiful houses of this type are a group of villas by Sir Robert Taylor (1714–88). The first was Harleyford Manor, Buckinghamshire, designed in 1755 for Sir William, Clayton, Bart., a lawyer and M.P. in a setting attributed to Capability Brown. Its canted and semi-circular bows command views down the Thames and create façades as varied as the interiors. The development of the villa in the first half of the eighteenth century as an informal house for relaxation and parties helped to loosen the formal planning of earlier houses and so paved the way for the freedom, variety and movement associated with the Picturesque. At Harleyford there are no servants' rooms or bedrooms on the ground floor, which is given over entirely to a central staircase hall flanked by three differently shaped reception rooms: one for dancing, one for cards, and one for supper, as Mark Girouard has pointed out.[13] In *c*.1760 came Taylor's enchanting and ingenious Asgill House for Sir Charles Asgill, a rich city merchant. It was built on the banks of the Thames by Twickenham Bridge, a part of London long noted for its delectable villas. Indeed, Walpole boasted of Twickenham that from Strawberry Hill 'we have a glimmering of a *Venetian* prospect . . . [in which the Thames is] our Brenta . . . and villas as abundant as formerly at Tivoli and Baiae'.[14] At Asgill House the central octagonal saloon is carried up externally in a canted bow with something of the form of a tower rising above the lower side wings; with its broad Italianate eaves it thus has perhaps a touch of Nash's Cronkhill. More spectacular was Sharpham House in Devon designed by Taylor in *c*.1770 on a magnificent promontory above the River Dart. Marcus Binney has suggested[15] that Taylor's patron, Captain Philemon Pownoll, may have been influenced in his dramatic choice of site by Burke's *Enquiry into the Origin of our Ideas of the Sublime and the Beautiful* (1757). The exposed setting of Sharpham, above steep and richly wooded river-banks, provides all the solitude, emptiness, vastness and awe that Burke could have wished. Here is a house contrived with the pictorial purpose of looking at a view: there is thus no garden front and all the windows are at the front and sides.

Another and very different house with something of the Sublime was the hauntingly romantic but now demolished Hafod House, Dyfed. Hafod was built in the Gothic style in 1786–8 by the Bath architect Thomas Baldwin (1750–1820) for the gifted soldier, politician, publisher and picturesque patron, Colonel Thomas Johnes (1748–1816). Johnes, a friend of Uvedale Price, John Nash and Payne Knight who was his mother's cousin, was one of the most cultivated men of his age. He had been brought up in Herefordshire not far from Downton at Croft Castle, which his father had Gothicised in 1765 with Thomas Pritchard, Knight's architect at Downton, as designer. Johnes's second wife was his cousin Jane, daughter of John Johnes of Dolaucothi, Carmarthenshire, a house which was remodelled by John Nash in 1792–5.

Nash now begins to assume a central role in the story of the Picturesque. It seems that in 1794 Thomas Johnes employed John Nash to extend Hafod with a fanciful octaganal library capped with a Moorish domelet and connected to a conservatory. The house was burnt in 1807 and reconstructed by Baldwin, but as there are no views of the house between 1794 and 1807 we cannot be sure how far the library, as rebuilt after the fire, followed Nash's original designs. Johnes's aesthetic adviser was the connoisseur and author George Cumberland (1754–*c*.1844), with whom he collaborated on a book called *An Attempt to Describe Hafod* (1796). Johnes also translated and published at the Hafod Press Froissart's *Chronicles* and Monstralet's *Memoirs*, and commissioned fourteen bas-relief paintings by Thomas Stothard, based on subjects in these books, to adorn the hall and library at Hafod. He was an extensive patron of the sculptor Thomas Banks (1735–1805) whose group of *Thetis dipping Achilles in the River Styx* adorned the conservatory. Eclectic clutter filled the hall, where Malkin mentioned in 1807 seeing 'an antique bust of Isis, in red granite, and two tables of lava from Vesuvius; an antique statue of Ariadne . . . A fragment of the base of Pompey's column at Alexandria and a petrifaction found in the old bed of the Nile'.[16] The whole picturesque retreat was appropriately presided over by two portraits of Richard Payne Knight by Webber and Lawrence.

Outside, in the enchantingly remote mountainous valley of Ystwyth, the landscape designer's art was as little needed as at Downton. As Malkin explained: 'In laying out the grounds, art has been no further consulted, than to render nature more accessible . . . the system of planting is to be extended, on a still larger scale, till nothing breaks in upon the scenery, except some rock, whose picturesque effect exempts it from obedience to the cultivator'.[17] The system of planting was indeed comprehensive. From June 1796 to June 1797, 400,000 larches and 250,000 other trees were planted; from October 1797 to October 1798, 10,000 oaks; from October 1798 to April 1799, fifty-five acres were planted with acorns, while 25,000 ash-trees and another 400,000 larches were planted. This extensive planting was partly carried out with a view to providing employment for the poor. For their benefit Johnes also built numerous cottages, roads, bridges, two free schools and a church designed by James Wyatt in 1793, and provided a surgeon, an apothecary and a printing press as well. The care that he lavished on his tenants, many of whom were imported from distressed areas of Scotland, became legendary. In this Johnes was markedly different from the proprietors of other picturesque retreats: Walpole at Strawberry Hill, Payne Knight at Downton, Beckford at Fonthill, and Hope at The Deepdene. Nonetheless, Hafod – the name means 'summer dwelling' – occupies a central place in the history of the private picturesque paradise so that, appropriately, it was painted in idealised form by Turner. The circumstances in which Turner's highly architectural

watercolour was produced remain obscure, but it may have originated in discussions between Johnes, Nash and Turner at Hafod in 1798.

In 1810 a second guidebook appeared, *A Tour to Hafod* by J. E. Smith, but three years later Johnes's reduced financial circumstances forced him to attempt to sell the house. It was eventually bought in 1833 for £70,000 by the 4th Duke of Newcastle, from whom it was purchased for £94,000 thirteen years later by Henry Hoghton of the old Catholic family of Hoghton Tower, Lancashire. Hoghton unexpectedly employed Nash's pupil, Anthony Salvin, to extend the house with an Italianate wing sporting colonnades or loggias in both storeys, and terminating in an asymmetrically placed campanile. The solid local granite contrasted strangely with the brittle stucco of Baldwin's adjacent ranges, and the disturbing clash of styles puzzled George Borrow so much that his description of the house in 1854, though evoking the atmosphere correctly, is wholly wrong in detail:

A truly fairy palace it looked, beautiful but fantastic, in the building of which three styles of architecture seemed to have been employed. At the southern end was a Gothic tower; at the northern an Indian pagoda; the middle part had much the appearance of a Grecian villa. The walls were of resplendent whiteness, and the windows which were numerous shone with beautiful gilding.[18]

Salvin's wing, which had been left uncompleted inside, was a cavernous shell by the late 1930s, haunted by bats and rats, with small trees growing in the stonework of the campanile. It had become a classic example of Payne Knight's dictum in *The Landscape*:

> But harsh and cold the builder's work appears,
> Till soften'd down by long revolving years;
> Till time and weather have conjointly spread
> Their mouldering hues and mosses o'er its head.[19]

In its twentieth-century decay, the magical poetry of this isolated folly attracted the attention of the artist John Piper who added to our appreciation of its

Hafod, Dyfed. A photograph taken shortly before demolition showing the ruins of the Gothic house which Thomas Baldwin built in 1787-8 for Thomas Johnes. Nash's octagonal library of *c.* 1794 with its Moorish dome is hidden from sight. On the left are the remains of part of the long wing culminating in an Italianate tower which Salvin added in 1846-51

picturesque charms by his illustrated article, 'Decrepit Glory: a tour of Hafod', published in 1940.[20] Geoffrey Grigson followed in 1947 with 'Kubla Khan in Wales',[21] and three years later Elisabeth Inglis-Jones published her full-length study of Johnes and Hafod, *Peacocks in Paradise*. In 1958 what was left of the house was blown up with dynamite and the site is now a caravan park.

Hafod, remarkable though it was, pales almost to insignificance in comparison with the justly better-known Fonthill Abbey, that *locus classicus* of picturesque, not to say sublime, drama. William Beckford (1760–1844), author, collector, patron, builder, gardener, traveller, and bibliophile, was arguably the most gifted and certainly the most colourful of those Men of Taste who produced the age of Georgian connoisseurship. We can describe their activities as picturesque because they used their inherited wealth to make of their lives and surroundings a kind of pictorially contrived work of art with as little contact as possible with mundane reality. In the case of Beckford, 'the great Apostle of Paederasty' as Byron dubbed him, this air of romantic unreality or isolation was heightened by the social ostracism inflicted on him after his injudicious handling of his love-affair with the sixteen-year-old William Courtenay in 1784.

By 1796, when work on Fonthill began, Beckford's best works were already written: *Vathek* (1786), a picaresque novel with an Arabian setting which influenced the writings of Byron, Thomas Hope and Disraeli, and his brilliant travel books, *The Journal of William Beckford in Portugal and Spain* (written 1787–8, published 1954) and *Recollections of an Excursion to the Monasteries of Alcobaça and Batalha in 1794* (1835). The idea of Fonthill Abbey came only gradually. In 1790 he played with the idea of adorning with a few picturesque ruins the estate of Fonthill 'Splendens' which, with its vast Palladian mansion, he had inherited from his father aged only ten in 1770. He first discussed with James Wyatt proposals for erecting a tower and a ruined convent in 1793, and in the same year was so infuriated by a pack of hounds hunting in his grounds that he surrounded the inner domain with a twelve-foot-high wall seven miles long, known as the Barrier. Three years later he returned from his second sojourn to Portugal annoyed at having been rebuffed by William Pitt in the diplomatic mission with which he had been entrusted by the Regent of Portugal. 'Some people drink to forget their unhappiness', he wrote to his beloved friend Gregorio Franchi, a former choirboy, 'I do not drink, I build'.[22] His ambition was to build the most fantastic house in England and then to prevent the English, apart from a small chosen band of artists and friends, from ever seeing it. So, with the perimeter wall built and the estate increased by 1,700 acres, the stage was cleared and the construction of the scenery could begin.

Beckford's architect, James Wyatt (1746–1813), had made a name for himself as a stylistic weathercock prepared to work in any style demanded, but his speciality from the 1770s was a picturesque if somewhat thin Gothic, which was popular as an antidote to the increasingly familiar Adam style. An early work in this vein is his Sheffield Park, Sussex (c.1776–7) for Edward Gibbon's intimate friend John Baker Holroyd, 1st Earl of Sheffield. The north entrance front and the south front, which Wyatt altered in the 1780s, are symmetrical and unremarkable, and it is the strikingly asymmetrical east front, commanding a view over the park and lakes by Brown and Repton, which is especially memorable as a picturesque composition. It is dominated by a vast traceried Gothic window which, though

Fonthill Abbey, Wiltshire. *Perspective of Fonthill Abbey from the north-west, c. 1799*, by Charles Wild. A watercolour developed from a design by James Wyatt of 1798 at which stage it was proposed to crown the abbey with an octagonal tower and spire inspired by Salisbury Cathedral, which Wyatt had ruthlessly restored in 1789-92. Behind the tower can be seen the similarly unexecuted Revelation Chamber. A mausoleum enriched with paintings, this boasts octagonal turrets which may derive from the reconstruction of King Manuel's unfinished chapel in J. Murphy's *Plans . . . of Batalha* (1795).

giving a 'monastic' air, is structurally a total sham, having almost no lights in it at all. Wyatt's most important Gothic house before Fonthill also had spurious monastic associations. This was the now demolished Lee Priory, Kent, built in *c*.1785-90 for Thomas Barrett whose friend, Horace Walpole, described it as 'a child of Strawberry prettier than the parent'.[23] Lee Priory was asymmetrically grouped round an octagonal tower capped with a candle-snuffer spirelet apparently based on the Mausoleum of King Joao at Batalha in Portugal. Inside the tower was the octagonal library carrying a dome panelled with blind Gothic tracery and surmounted by a gallery and a lantern containing stained glass. Walpole was overcome with delight and wrote to Mary Berry in 1794: 'for to me it is the most perfect thing I ever saw, and has the most the air it was intended to have, that of an abbot's library, supposing it could have been so exquisitely finished three hundred years ago'.[24]

Beckford had visited the monastery at Batalha in 1794 and in the following year J. C. Murphy illustrated it in a celebrated and sumptuous volume of engravings. In October 1796 work began on the construction of Wyatt's 'convent' at Fonthill which had at its centre an octagonal tower with a spirelet just as at Batalha and Lee Priory. In the meantime, Beckford decided to enlarge this convent as his principal residence and to provide building materials by demolishing Fonthill 'Splendens'. Accordingly, Wyatt prepared designs in 1798 for a yet more extensive Fonthill, now called 'Abbey', with an extensive northern range in addition to the southern and western ranges of the earlier design, and a much taller octagonal tower crowned by an equally tall spire inspired by that at Salisbury, which is only about fifteen miles away. In the third and final plan of 1799, in connection with which a handsome model survives, the spire is replaced by a tall octagonal lantern owing something to that at Ely. Beckford now began to envisage Fonthill as a cathedral of the arts which would eventually contain his own tomb at the end of a long gallery, the revered resting-place of one who had encouraged the arts.

Work on the construction of this great shrine now continued in earnest, though it was arrested by a violent storm in May 1800 which brought down the central spire of timber faced with a patent compo-cement. According to one topographer, 'The fall was tremendous and sublime, and the only regret expressed by Mr. Beckford upon the occasion was that he had not witnessed its destruction'.[25] Although in December 1800 he entertained Nelson to a 'monastic fête' in the half-built abbey, lit by hooded figures holding torches, it was not ready for habitation until the summer of 1807, and was even then far from finished. Indeed, work continued on the construction of the huge eastern transept until 1818. The final building, cruciform but asymmetrical, was a combination of breathtaking contrasts, vertical and horizontal: the length from north to south being 312 feet, the same as Westminster Abbey, and the height of the tower 276 feet. In September 1808, Beckford was writing to Franchi:

I have no doubt that before the 30th of this month the tremendous spaces of the Octagon will be displayed in all their sublime majesty . . . It's really stupendous, the spectacle here at night – the number of people at work, lit up by lads; the innumerable torches suspended everywhere, the immense and endless spaces, the gulph below; above, the gigantic spider's web of scaffolding – especially when, standing under the finished and numberless arches of the galleries, I listen to the reverberating voices in the stillness of the night, and see immense buckets of plaster and water ascending, as if they were drawn up from the bowels of a mine, amid shouts from subterranean depths, oaths from Hell itself, and chanting from Pandemonium or the synagogue.[26]

Certainly no house in the world can ever have boasted anything like the drama of the three immense vistas to north, south and west which opened up to the visitor when he stood, amazed, at the foot of the central octagonal tower. The eight great arches, eighty feet high, that defined this space were hung with scarlet and blue curtains; three of them contained immense windows inspired by those in the monastery at Batalha and filled with stained glass in purple, crimson and yellow. The walls themselves were stone-coloured, but elsewhere in the abbey exotic damask wall hangings of scarlet, royal blue, purple and gold provided daring backgrounds for one of the most magnificent private collections of paintings and furniture ever assembled in this country. The hot colours and the glittering objects anticipated the effects which were created later by the Prince

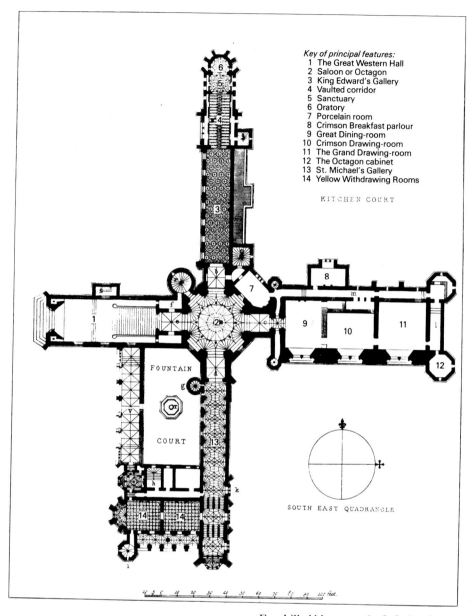

KITCHEN COURT

FOUNTAIN

COURT

SOUTH EAST QUADRANGLE

Fonthill Abbey, 1796–1818, by James Wyatt for William Beckford. Plan of the principal floor from *Delineations of Fonthill and its Abbey* (1823) by John Rutter.

Regent at Brighton. Beckford was a scholarly and discriminating collector. One of the first Englishmen to acquire works by the Italian Primitives, he was also unique among wealthy collectors in his appreciation of Blake, his exact contemporary. Among his magnificent French and English furniture, lacquer and precious metals there hung paintings by Van der Weyden, Bellini, Perugino, Memlinc, Elsheimer, Raphael, Sebastiano del Piombo, Rembrandt and Claude – twenty of his paintings are today in the National Gallery.[27]

The most dramatic internal vista was that running north from the octagonal saloon. The principal feature of this was King Edward's Gallery with its crimson carpet, crimson flower damask walls, purple and scarlet curtains, sumptuous rows of finely bound books and panelled oak ceiling. A great table from the Palazzo Borghese in Rome stood in the centre, with a top of *pietro commesse* containing the largest known piece of oriental onyx. In total contrast to King Edward's Gallery was the much darker and narrower corridor which connected it with the Sanctuary and Oratory at the far end. At the entrance to the Sanctuary, Beckford

Fonthill Abbey. St. Michael's Gallery, from Rutter's *Delineations of Fonthill and its Abbey*, looking north through the central octagon and on to the sanctuary at the end of King Edward's Gallery. St. Michael's Gallery was 127 feet long and fan-vaulted in stucco painted to resemble stone. The crimson carpet was woven with Hamilton cinquefoils in honour of Beckford's maternal ancestry, and above the Gothic dado the walls were washed pink. Both bookcases and windows were hung with double curtains, the inner purple and the outer scarlet.

would shout 'Open!' and, by stamping on a certain board in the floor, caused a folding door beneath a curtain to open and reveal the Oratory, lit by silver candelabra, glittering with jewelled reliquaries and monstrances, and dominated by an alabaster statue by J. C. F. Rossi of Beckford's favourite saint, Anthony of Padua. Here in a richly pious haze of incense and distant organ music Beckford, who believed in no religion, recaptured the sensations which had so much moved him when as a boy of eighteen he had visited the chapel of the Grande Chartreuse in Switzerland. One might thus interpret the abbey not merely as a gesture of defiance against society for ostracising him on account of his sexual deviation, but against God for not having given him the grace to become a Catholic.

It will have become clear from this description of a single part of the abbey that the guiding principles of Beckford and Wyatt in planning the whole must have been the contrast and surprise which dominated Picturesque theory from Pope to Price. Beckford was always anxious to stress the relation of the abbey to its grounds as a single work of art. Following Uvedale Price's precepts, as Payne Knight had done at Downton and Thomas Johnes at Hafod, he wanted to achieve the roughness, irregularity and sudden variation of natural scenery rather than the smoother, tamer landscapes which he associated with Brown and Repton. Indeed, he is supposed to have turned down a request from Repton to 'improve' Fonthill. Beckford brilliantly extended the architecture of the great entrance hall of the abbey into the landscape by creating, along the top of a wooded ridge, the Great Western Avenue. Turfed not gravelled, and 100 feet wide, this led up to the main entrance for three-quarters of a mile. Unlike previous avenues this did not consist of trees of a single variety, but of a great range of species mixed with shrubs and planted in dense clumps. In front of the abbey was a broader open area, 'broken by scattered native trees and wild bushes, as to leave no doubt in the mind of the spectator', wrote Loudon in 1835, 'of its having been cleared by the founders of the abbey from the native forest'. The land fell steeply away southwards from the plateau on which the abbey stood. Here Beckford planted exotic species of trees and shrubs that had been recently introduced into this country, but 'in secluded places only; and these he disposed in what may be called by-scenes in the woods, in such a manner as that a person who knew nothing of trees could never suspect that they were not natives. There was an American ground . . . consisting of many of the trees and shrubs of that country, disposed in groups and thickets, as if they had sprung up naturally . . . There was a rose-ground, a thornery, and a pinetum treated in the same manner'.[28] Thus the whole environment of the abbey, natural and artificial, became a single romantic landscape recalling the setting of 'monasteries in alpine countries'. In a natural hollow just south of the abbey Beckford created Bitham Lake, pronouncedly irregular in shape, with an island, herons and flocks of wildfowl. He explained to Franchi in 1811 that 'Here everything is gradually lapsing into antiquity – grass up to the very doors, etc. The lake looks as if God had made it, it is so natural, without the least trace of art . . . it spreads itself grandiosely and the swans look as if they are in Paradise. Am I not a poor Adam without an Eve?'.[29]

In 1822, heavily in debt, Beckford was forced to put the whole estate on the market. It was sold for £300,000 to John Farquhar, a septuagenarian, millionaire gunpowder merchant. Three years later Beckford was summoned to the death-bed of Wyatt's contractor at Fonthill who confessed that he had not laid proper foundations to the central tower which might therefore collapse at any moment. In fact it fell just before Christmas that year, destroying the octagon and the Great Western Hall.

Although only a tiny fragment of Fonthill – the Sanctuary and Oratory – stands today, it lives on almost as completely as though it had never been destroyed, in the coloured plates and engravings of the six books that were published about it between 1812 and 1836 by J. Storer, J. Rutter, J. Weale, G. and W. B. Whittaker, J. Britton and J. B. Nichols. No other English house has ever been exposed so fully to the searchlight of picturesque topographers. It was admired by Constable and Cobbett and was made the subject of at least seven watercolours by Turner, whilst John Martin, W. Finley, C. F. Porden, T. Higham, J. le Keux, J. P. Neale, G. Wild, G. Cattermole and J. Buckler also flocked to Wiltshire to paint or draw Beckford's sublime and legendary dream. Its architectural influence, on the early development of the Gothic Revival can be seen with especial force at Eaton Hall,

Lansdown Tower, Bath, 1824-7, by H. E. Goodridge for William Beckford. An Italo-Greek picturesque essay of uniquely original form, Beckford's compact but opulently furnished residence crouches at the foot of the Belvedere tower which is 154 feet high, as opposed to the 276 feet of the Fonthill tower.

Cheshire (1803–12 and 1820–6; demolished), by Porden and Gummow, and at Hadlow Castle tower, Kent (1838–40), by G. L. Taylor; while its cruciform plan may have inspired that of Barry's Houses of Parliament (1836–60). Other buildings influenced by Fonthill include Dance's Coleorton Hall, Hanbury-Tracy's Toddington Manor, Donthorn's Highcliffe Castle, Smirke's Eastnor and Lowther Castles, Elliot's Taymouth Castle, Wyatt's Ashridge, Wyatville's Windsor Castle and the unexecuted Gothic designs for the Fitzwilliam Museum, Cambridge, by Rickman and Hussey of 1834.

Having sold Fonthill, Beckford moved to Lansdown Terrace, Bath, where he began to lay out a picturesque garden running for a mile up Lansdown Hill. His aim was to avoid all traces of artificial cultivation, so that in the absence of any park-like or formal character the visitor would hardly know he was on private property at all. The estate was crowned by the inevitable tower built in 1824–7

from designs by a gifted local architect, Henry Edmund Goodridge (1797–1864). Incorporating Athenian references to the Choragic Monument of Lysicrates, it was a design of marked originality and competence, handled with a suave asymmetry. Its richly coloured interiors were recorded in the customary handsome illustrated folio, *Views of Lansdown Tower, Bath*, prepared under Beckford's supervision but published just after his death in 1844. The text was by E. F. English who had supplied furnishings for the Tower, and the strongly coloured lithographs were by the young local artist Willes Maddox.

Frederick Harvey, Bishop of Derry and 4th Earl of Bristol, was a builder and collector with something of the impressive eccentricity of Beckford. His bizarre mansion of Ickworth in Suffolk with its powerful central rotunda has more than a touch of the Sublime. Begun in 1796 by the Irish architect Francis Sandys on the basis of a design by Mario Asprucci, it was intended to be a temple of art like Beckford's Fonthill. Alas, it never filled this role. The Earl Bishop's collections were confiscated by the French in Rome in 1798, and he died five years later near Albano in the outhouse of a cottage which a peasant, charging him with heresy, would not allow him to enter. Ickworth was the architectural fulfilment of Ballyscullion, a mansion in Ireland which the Bishop had begun in 1787 but never completed. At its centre was a vast Pantheon-like rotunda inspired, according to a letter from the Bishop to his daughter, by Belle Isle on an island in Lake Windermere. Approachable only by boat, the cylindrical Belle Isle was built in 1774–5 by John Plaw (*c.* 1745–1820) for Thomas English in a romantic spot in the Lake District towards which William Gilpin was already beginning to draw

Belle Isle, Lake Windermere, Cumbria, 1774–5, by John Plaw for Thomas English. The Roman Pantheon, adopted earlier as a garden building for Burlington at Chiswick and Hoare at Stourhead, here forms the basis for the design of an entire house in an incomparably romantic natural setting.

A-la-Ronde, Exmouth, Devon, 1795. Detail of the gallery in the central hall. Decorated with shells and birds modelled in feathers, it has been described by Barbara Jones as 'a grotto in the air with no feeling of the tomb'.

attention. With its views towards Bowness and Windermere, Belle Isle was the first house in the Lake District generated by the new enthusiasm for the Picturesque.

Another pictorially freakish house is A-La-Ronde near Exmouth in Devon, built in 1795 for two lesbian cousins, the Misses Jane and Mary Parminter. It is a sixteen-sided structure supposedly inspired by San Vitale in Ravenna, centrally planned round an octagonal hall sixty feet high with a gallery mosaiced in shells and feathers. This is surmounted by a lantern surrounded outside by another gallery commanding good views towards the sea. On a hill above the house they built an institution known as Point-in-View, comprising a chapel, alms-houses and schoolroom.

The use of circular planning in order to create scenic surprise was also adopted by the architect Michael Searles (1750–1813) at Clare House, East Malling, Kent, which was built in 1793 for John Larking, a banker, timber merchant and paper-mill owner. This is an extraordinarily fetching composition with circular, oval and octagonal rooms centred on a circular staircase hall surmounted by a dome which is visible from outside. Before this is a circular library projecting outside in a bow,

(*Above*) Clare House, East Malling, Kent, 1793, by Michael Searles for John Larking. The perfect Regency villa which is a more animated version of Taylor's pioneering Harleyford of nearly forty years earlier. The canted bay on the right lights the dining-room which is balanced by a similiar bay in the drawing-room on the west front. The first-floor verandah over the semi-circular colonnade in front of the library is a later addition.

(*Left*) Dukinfield Lodge, Cheshire, *c*. 1780. A little-known house, now demolished, perhaps built for the portrait painter John Astley. It represents an attempt to produce a building with curvaceous forms which will blend more harmoniously than Palladian architecture with a Brownian landscape.

capped with a conical roof and encircled on the ground floor by a broad colonnade. This recalls Searle's contemporary Paragon at Blackheath, a crescent of semi-detached houses linked by colonnades. It is also stylistically close to the now demolished Dukinfield Lodge, Cheshire, which may have been built for himself by the painter John Astley (*c*. 1730–87).

Inventive planning was a characteristic of the prolific and colourful architect John Nash (1752–1835), who made it his business to purvey the Picturesque on a wide scale and in manageable form. We have already met him at Hafod where, through Thomas Johnes, he met Uvedale Price and almost certainly Payne Knight. Nash had withdrawn to Carmarthenshire in 1783 following his divorce and bankruptcy. Five years later Uvedale Price, probably on Johnes's recommendation, was made a burgess of Aberystwyth and given a plot of land on the sea front near the castle whose ruins Johnes owned. Here some time in the early 1790s Nash designed Castle House for Price, a curious triangular villa with octagonal towers set at the corners and round-headed openings in a faintly Norman style. In his description of Aberystwyth Castle in his *Journey into South Wales: . . . in the year 1799* (1802), G. Lipscomb recounts how 'a gravel walk has been made among the ruins by *Uvedale Price*, Esq. the proprietor of a whimsical castellated mansion near the spot'.[30] Another early and whimsical work of Nash's is the enchantingly scenic Gothick folly of Clytha Castle, Gwent, which he built in 1790 for William Jones of Clytha House. Serving as a hill-top eye-catcher in the romantic parkland created by Jones, 'it was undertaken', so an inscription on it records, 'to relieve a mind sincerely afflicted by the loss of a most excellent wife'. Its square and round towers linked by festive gables of concave outline are asymmetrically grouped on an L-plan. It shows Nash as a master of the Picturesque at the outset of his career.

It may have been in Johnes's circle at Hafod that Nash met Humphry Repton, who had certainly visited both Price and Knight before 1795. When Nash felt able to return to London in 1796 he formed a partnership with Repton which proved highly profitable to both. An early product of their short-lived association is Sundridge Park, Bromley, Greater London, for which Repton had produced a Red Book by 1795. A new owner in 1796 retained Repton's services, and Nash exhibited designs for the house in 1799. Set in a steep isolated valley below Elmstead Wood, the house stands on a narrow shelf specially cut out of the hillside by Repton. In order to command views up and down the valley, the house is an eccentric half-hexagon in plan with a circular bow sprouting at the apex. Samuel Wyatt, who completed the house in *c*.1800, may have had a hand in the extraordinarily dynamic design of the interior planning with its circular, hexagonal, oval and octagonal spaces revolving round a central cylindrical staircase.

Sundridge is a classical house encased within a rather coarse Corinthian order. The contemporary Luscombe Castle, Devon, for which the banker Charles Hoare asked Repton to provide one of his Red Books in 1799, is a happier composition. The house which Nash provided is in some ways the model house of the whole Picturesque movement. Compact yet asymmetrical, with its verandah and big sunny windows, this charming irregular villa is exquisitely related to its setting in the fold of a secluded valley near the sea. Certainly no other country at this date in Europe could boast a domestic architecture of comparable freedom, variety and subtlety. Repton and Nash were well aware of the revolution they were effecting. A flap over a watercolour in the Red Book contrasts a view of the unimproved setting, containing a neat villa in the modern 'Grecian' style, with a view showing the hills clothed with trees so as to provide a contrasting dark background to the lighter colours of Nash's irregular 'castle'. The architectural source is, of course,

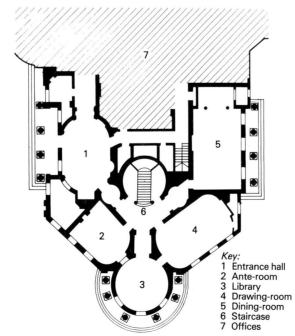

(*Above*) Clytha Castle, Gwent, 1790, by John Nash for William Jones. Nash's theatrical flair for creating strikingly pictorial images is well exemplified in this hill-top folly. However, in 1806 J. C. Loudon, who was improving the grounds at nearby Llanarth Court, condemned Clytha Castle as 'gaudy and affectedly common' in his *Treatise on . . . Country Residences.*

(*Left*) Sundridge Park, Bromley, Greater London, *c.* 1795–*c.* 1800, by J. Nash and S. Wyatt in a setting by Repton. Ground-floor plan. The novel geometrical plan produces an exterior composition which appears irregular when viewed from most directions.

Key:
1 Entrance hall
2 Ante-room
3 Library
4 Drawing-room
5 Dining-room
6 Staircase
7 Offices

113

(*Above*) Luscombe Castle, Devon, 1799, by John Nash with a setting by Humphry Repton for Charles Hoare. Luscombe is one of the comparatively few houses where Repton worked which was not the replacement or remodelling of an existing building. Its siting thus shows his ideals to perfection. In this distant view of the east front against a backdrop of Repton's cedars, we see from right to left the projecting block of the entrance hall, then the dining-room wing followed by the one-storeyed conservatory which leads into the service wing; the chapel was added by Scott in the 1850s.

(*Right*) Luscombe. Ground-floor plan. All the ground-floor windows come down to floor level. Repton claimed that 'Its very irregularity will give it consequence, while the offices and mere walls which, in a modern building, it would be necessary to conceal, by partaking of the Character of the Castle will extend the Site and make it an apparently considerable pile of building'.

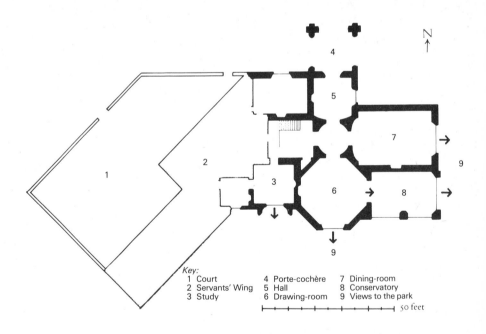

Key:
1 Court
2 Servants' Wing
3 Study
4 Porte-cochère
5 Hall
6 Drawing-room
7 Dining-room
8 Conservatory
9 Views to the park

50 feet

Payne Knight's Downton Castle, from which Nash borrows not only his asymmetry but his octagonal machicolated tower and the contrast between Gothic exteriors and classic interiors. The variety and intricacy of the house and its setting are equally inspired by Price's *An Essay on the Picturesque* of 1794.

Nash and his numerous clients up and down the country were happy for this formula to be repeated over and over again. Nash himself used it in his own extravagant house on the Isle of Wight, East Cowes Castle, at Garnstone, Herefordshire, Childwall, Merseyside, Caerhays, Cornwall, Ravensworth, Co. Durham, Knepp Castle and West Grinstead Park, West Sussex, and at Lough Cutra, Shane's Castle, Shanbally Castle, Kilwaughter Castle and Killymoon Castle in Ireland. In plan these houses exploit the picturesque principle of lively contrast, so that at Ravensworth and East Cowes Castle, for example, long galleries are juxtaposed with round or octagonal rooms.

At a number of villas at Dulwich, Kingston, Southgate and Surbiton, Nash and Repton provided influential exercises in suburban illusion where city merchants and solicitors could play at being squires on their miniature estates near London. Nash worked out an asymmetrical picturesque villa-type in a stuccoed Italianate style which, unfortunately, proved less popular than his castle style. The three widely separated surviving examples, all built between 1802 and 1807, are Cronkhill, Shropshire, Sandridge Park, Devon, and Lissan Rectory, Co. Londonderry. Their irregular grouping, pivoting on a round tower with a shallow conical roof, seems to be directly based on the Italianate vernacular buildings in the background of a number of paintings by Claude, for example his *Pastoral*

Caerhays Castle, Cornwall, *c.* 1808, by John Nash for John Trevanion, a cousin and acquaintance of Byron. One of the best preserved of Nash's castles, this is a perfect example of his episodic, scenic composition. It has a typical Nash plan pivoting on a long, wide, balconied gallery which is two-storeyed and top-lit. At one end of this is the staircase and at the other a circular closet, library and circular drawing-room.

(*Above*) Cronkhill, Shropshire, *c.* 1802, by John Nash for the steward to the 2nd Lord Berwick at nearby Attingham Park. Lord Berwick had acquired a large collection of paintings on his Grand Tour, including some by Claude. Cronkhill resembles a detail from a Claude painting brought to life. The shape of the round tower is decorative not functional since it does not contain a circular room.

(*Above right*) *Pastoral Landscape with the Ponte Molle* by Claude Lorrain, 1645. This painting, which was in England by 1753, is one of a number which Nash may have used as a source for buildings like Cronkhill. The way Claude relates buildings to trees and landscapes has influenced the way we see and photograph buildings, as can be seen in the photograph of Cronkhill.

Landscape with the Ponte Molle. Once again, Payne Knight, who as we have seen eventually owned about 250 of Claude's drawings, may have acted as an inspiration. Curiously, an Italianate house like Cronkhill and a castle-style house like West Grinstead Castle have virtually identical plans.

For evidence of the extent to which the Claudian image dominated the way in which people looked at architecture well into the nineteenth century, we can turn to the by now celebrated account in the diary of the architect C. R. Cockerell (1788–1863) of his visits to Grange Park, Hampshire, in 1823. Grange Park, built in 1809 from the designs of William Wilkins (1778–1839) is one of the most uncompromising Greek-temple houses in Europe. Yet it seemed to Cockerell so picturesque that 'there is nothing like it on this side of Arcadia'. He describes how he 'strolled about in the garden, a steady sunshine upon the building, as clear a sky the lights & shades & reflections as in Greece, the rooks & jackdaws in the lime tree avenue sailing & cawing in the air brought home the recollections of the acropolis, the buzzing of the blue flies & the flowers something of the aromatic scent of thyme'. His principal impression was that when 'viewed from ground opposite to

(*Below*) Grange park, Hampshire, *c.* 1809, by William Wilkins for the banker Henry Drummond. Grange Park is a skilful piece of stylistic illusion since it encases in stucco a red-brick seventeenth-century house which is largely intact beneath. This remarkable monument of the Greek Revival, superbly placed overlooking a lake in an earlier landscaped park, survives today as a maintained ruin.

Millichope Park, Shropshire, 1835–40,
by Edward Haycock for the Rev. Robert
Pemberton. The picturesque setting
with its winding lake and gem-like
temple combines with the Greek Revival mansion to produce a perfect
Arcadian image. In the house as originally built, the main entrance was
dramatically contrived at basement
level below the portico. This was a
picturesque surprise, echoing Ledoux's
Hotel Thélusson, by which the visitor
ascended from a low lobby into the
middle of the vast and lofty hall.

river, nothing can be finer, more classical or like the finest Poussins, it realises the
most fanciful representations of the painters pencil or the poets description'.[31] A
similarly Arcadian scene was created at Millichope Park, Shropshire, a massive
Greek Revival mansion built in 1835–40 from designs by Edward Haycock
(1790–1870), a pupil of Wyatville. The park already contained a circular Ionic
temple designed in 1770 by George Steuart. Haycock formed a lake by excavating
the rock below the temple which now stands on top of a small cliff. He also cut into
the hill on which the temple stands to form a rocky gorge through which the drive
passes on its circuitous way to the house. We have already seen a similarly
picturesque exploitation of quarries, perhaps inspired by the ideas of Payne
Knight, at Belsay Castle and Scotney Castle.

Nash naturally had many imitators. Amongst these were Robert Lugar
(c.1773–1855) who in 1806 was already providing a not very successful version of
Cronkhill at Gold Hill (now Dunstall Priory), Shoreham, Kent, and in 1808–9
introduced Nash's castle style to Scotland, much more successfully, at
Tullichewan Castle and Balloch (now Ardoch) Castle, both in Strathclyde
Region. Lugar is perhaps best known for his four attractive books of picturesque
designs, beginning with *Architectural Sketches for Cottages, Rural Dwellings and
Villas* (1805), and ending with *Villa Architecture* (1828). A more impressive
architect than Lugar was Jeffry Wyatville (1766–1840). Wyatville received his
architectural training successively from his two distinguished uncles, Samuel and
James Wyatt, and though lacking real imaginative brilliance or personal
refinement, he became one of the half dozen leading architects in the country by
the 1820s. Among his earlier works was Endsleigh, Devon, an extensive *cottage
orné* designed for the 6th Duke of Bedford in 1810, in which year Repton had been
invited to prepare one of his Reports. Thus Wyatville came to work here with
Repton in the same satisfactory way that Nash had at Luscombe. Repton waxed
enthusiastic about the romantic wooded site in the upper Tamar valley in his
Report, arguing that 'without the aid of art, the most romantic or picturesque
scenery in nature is a desert, and only fitted to the habitation of wild beasts. The

first question that obviously occurred was, what style of house will best accord with this landscape?' According to Repton, the existing 'irregular farm-house, little better than a cottage, backed by a hill and beautiful group of trees, presented an object so picturesque that it was impossible to wish it removed and replaced by any other style of building . . . viz. a castle, or an abbey, or a palace, not one of which could have been convenient and so applicable to the scenery as this cottage, or, rather, group of rural buildings'.[32]

Endsleigh, Devon, 1810-11, by Wyat-ville in a setting landscaped by Repton, for the 6th Duke of Bedford. (*Above*) Distant view. A lavish *cottage orné* blending effortlessly into its breathtaking setting in the Tamar valley. (*Below*) The west end of the scattered informal composition.

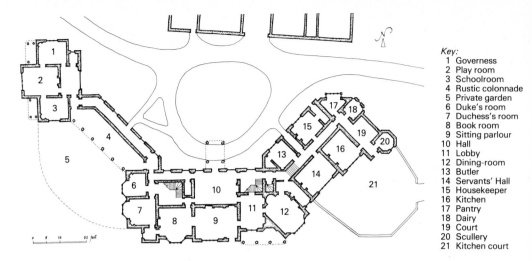

Key:
1 Governess
2 Play room
3 Schoolroom
4 Rustic colonnade
5 Private garden
6 Duke's room
7 Duchess's room
8 Book room
9 Sitting parlour
10 Hall
11 Lobby
12 Dining-room
13 Butler
14 Servants' Hall
15 Housekeeper
16 Kitchen
17 Pantry
18 Dairy
19 Court
20 Scullery
21 Kitchen court

Endsleigh. Ground-floor plan.

Wyatville brilliantly realised Repton's sentiments by subordinating a fairly substantial country house to the beauty of its natural setting, and by handling it as though it were an irregular group of traditional country buildings. In doing so he created a formula which was used for over a century by architects like Devey, Shaw and Lutyens. The highly original plan of Endsleigh, freely flowing in a zig-zag pattern, is echoed in two of Wyatville's houses of the 1820s, both in a neo-Elizabethan style: Lilleshall Hall, Shropshire, built for the immensely wealthy Lord Gower (later 2nd Duke of Sutherland), and Golden Grove, Dyfed, for Lord Cawdor. The same plan is also strikingly deployed in the extensive canted wings which he added in 1813–8 to his uncle James's already immense Ashridge Park, Hertfordshire. The rigidity of James Wyatt's main block is dynamited into action by Wyatville's imaginative strokes so that, as one looks at the house today from Repton's gardens, nothing could be more picturesque than the extensive, unfolding panorama. The juxtaposition between trees on a sloping site of turrets, conservatories, staircase tower and chapel spire – now renewed in a suitably sham material, fibre glass – is masterly indeed.

Wyatville's scenic talents were to be taxed to their utmost when in 1824 he won in a limited competition the prestigious commission for renovating and transforming Windsor Castle for George IV. With his towers and bays, machicolations and crenellations, Wyatville created the most magical skyline of any castle in the world, and if the top thirty feet of the celebrated Round Tower is just a hollow sham, Burke had, after all, proclaimed in 1757 that 'No work of art can be great, but as it deceives'. In terms of the Englishman's consciousness of the history, real or imaginary, of his country and his monarchy, Wyatville's achievement at Windsor is of unequalled significance. The King authorised Jeffry Wyatt to change his name to Wyatville on the day the foundation stone was laid in 1824, a curious but eminently picturesque move which prompted the publication in a daily newspaper of the following apt verses:

> Let George, whose restlessness leaves nothing quiet,
> Change if He must the good old name of Wyatt;
> But let us hope that their united skill
> Will not make of Windsor Castle *Wyatt Ville*.

The King's own reaction when Wyatt made the request is supposed to have been, 'Veal or mutton, call yourself what you like'.

Fort Belvedere, Windsor Great Park, 1827-30, by Wyatville for King George IV. View of the south-east front showing in the centre the triangular tower of c. 1750 by Flitcroft with the turret heightened by Wyatville. The brickwork of the whole building was faced with cement by Wyatville to give the appearance of stonework. The onestoreyed front range with the entrance and window each side dates from 1910. The interior was remodelled for the Duke of Windsor whose residence it was from 1930 until his abdication in 1936.

Wyatville's remodelling of Flitcroft's triangular Shrub Hill Tower of c.1750 at Virginia Water in Windsor Great Park was equally picturesque. The work was carried out in 1827-30 for George IV and the building emerged from its transformation into Fort Belvedere with a new octagonal dining-room and an arrestingly composed skyline punctuated by hexagonal towers of contrasting heights. These alterations followed the pattern established in castellated houses such as Grimston Garth, which was built in 1781 by Carr of York on the Holdernesse Coast in Yorkshire as an elaborate summer residence for Thomas Grimston. This remarkable asymmetrical composition consists of a triangular centre with circular towers at the corners and two parallel office and bedroom wings running north.

The dynamic plan and composition of the remodelled Fort Belvedere was paralleled by the vaster Penrhyn Castle, Gwynedd, built in c.1825-44 by Thomas Hopper (1776–1856) for George Hay Dawkins Pennant, a slate-quarry millionaire. Penrhyn, with its extensive views of the Menai Straits, is one of the most extravagant exercises in the art of designing architecture as scenery, admittedly by this date of the most massive kind. Effortlessly absorbing a mediaeval house already remodelled by Samuel Wyatt, its scattered dislocated plan with forecourts and gate-towers builds up to an immense keep, clearly modelled on those of the Norman castles of Hedingham and of Hopper's native town of Rochester. To pass directly from the deliberately modest entrance vestibule to the prodigious height of the Great Hall, remotely inspired by a section of Durham Cathedral, is to experience a thrill more sublime than picturesque. The customary pictorial record was made as soon as the castle was finished, and the brooding grey lithographs of c.1846 by George Hawkins (1810–52) are uncannily close to the actual building.

Gwrych Castle, Gwynedd, 1819 onwards, by L. B. Hesketh and others. Commanding the coastline near Abergele in an unforgettable, dramatic way, Gwrych is an explosive composition with a central core from which battlemented walls shoot out in different directions across the hillside.

Hopper was a star who emerged from the sparkling world in which the Prince Regent distributed his patronage and favours. His remodelling in *c.*1806 of a *cottage orné* at Fulham for Walsh Porter was much admired by the Prince. This led to a commission for Hopper to make alterations at Carlton House where his work included the famous cast-iron conservatory of 1807 with its fan vaults containing coloured glass though which light shone enticingly at night. In the numerous country houses which he subsequently designed in Greek, Norman, Tudor Gothic, Jacobean and Palladian styles, Hopper put into practice his own picturesque dictum, expressed in *Hopper versus Cust, on the subject of Rebuilding the Houses of Parliament* (1837): 'it is an architect's business to understand all styles and be in favour of none'.

The Welsh coastline was ideally suited to sprawling picturesque castles. Only a few miles from Penrhyn is the scarcely less dramatic Gwrych Castle, built from 1819 by Lloyd Bamford Hesketh largely from his own designs, but with assistance from several architects including the expert Goth Thomas Rickman (1776–1841) and Charles Busby (1788–1834) who was shortly to lay out much of Brighton. With its backdrop of steep wooded hills, Gwrych is more impressively sited than Penrhyn, while its mediaeval castellated style is more amenable to picturesquely massed irregularity than Hopper's four-square Norman.

From the strong meat of Hopper we turn to the more meagre diet afforded by William Atkinson (*c.*1773–1839). A pupil of James Wyatt, Atkinson specialised in picturesque if rather papery Gothic for a series of aristocratic patrons. At Scone Palace, Tayside Region, (1803–12) he introduced to Scotland what was known as the 'monastic' as opposed to the 'castle' style. It was the first revivalist building in Scotland in which every interior was Gothic, though his Rossie Priory, Tayside Region (1807–15) was much livelier. In 1807–20 he remodelled and completed Panshanger, Hertfordshire, a house begun in 1806 by Samuel Wyatt. Atkinson

Panshanger, Hertfordshire, from the south-east. (Demolished 1953.) Begun in 1806–7 for the 5th Earl Cowper by Samuel Wyatt on the basis of designs of 1800 by Humphry Repton, the house was continued after Wyatt's death in 1807 by W. Atkinson who also extended it to the west in 1819–20. The rambling and freely-grouped composition of brick coated with Atkinson's patent cement shifts stylistically from simplified Tudor Gothic to the 'church Gothic' of the east front shown on the right in this view. The chief glory of Panshanger was Repton's park where 110 workmen were busy in September 1799 widening the river Mimram so as to form a chain of three lakes.

created a low irregular façade, 350 feet long, drifting peaceably along like the contours of the exquisite Repton park which it so appropriately adorned until its demolition in 1953. His Ditton Park, Buckinghamshire (1813–17) was less extensive, but his most celebrated work was Abbotsford, Borders Region, built for Sir Walter Scott in 1816–23. This somewhat glum assymmetrical pile, which set the fashion for the Scots-Baronial style, was the product of Picturesque theory, for Scott was an enthusiastic reader of Uvedale Price. It was built during the years that Scott's Waverley Novels were appearing, and was a fitting residence for the author of those then enormously popular combinations of historical fact, archaeological detail and heady romance.

One of Atkinson's most interesting commissions came in c.1817 from the influential connoisseur, author, collector, patron and designer, Thomas Hope (1769–1831). Hope was one of the last in that line of Georgian men of taste which began with Lord Burlington. However, the certainties of the age of Burlington had by now been dissolved, both by the range of information about different cultures which the archaeological industry of the Neo-classicists had made available, and by the Picturesque movement with its essentially pictorial, synthetic and eclectic outlook. Hope represented the last moment at which it was possible to combine all these new romantic apprehensions within the guidelines of the classical tradition. The complex allusive web of sentiment and scholarship which surrounded his intensely aesthetic existence was replaced soon after his death by a new set of certainties based on absolute belief in Gothic.

The Deepdene, Surrey, watercolour by W. H. Bartlett, 1825, from John Britton's manuscript *History etc. of the Deepdene, Seat of Thos. Hope Esqr. 1821–6*. In the left foreground is the dairy crowned by what Cockerell described as 'a pergola a l'italienne', and to its right is the kitchen wing with its Italianate spirelet. In the background the loggia-topped Tuscan tower rises over the dining-room wing of the house itself. This scattering of a house and its offices through an umbrageous landscape is the classic statement of picturesque intricacy, irregularity and eclecticism but, like Sir John Soane's Museum which Britton also recorded, its expression here was too eccentric to find many direct imitators.

An opinionated and rather ugly little Dutchman of immense wealth inherited from the family bank, Hope and Co., he set off on a Grand Tour in 1787 at the end of which, in 1795, he settled in England as a result of Napoleon's invasion of Holland. He acquired a large Adam mansion in Duchess Street, off Portland Place in 1799. This he elaborately remodelled in the form of a colourful museum for his rich collection of Greek vases and sculpture; Old Masters; specially commissioned modern paintings, sculptures and silverware from artists like Benjamin West, Flaxman, Haydon, Westall, Thorvaldsen and Paul Storr; and sumptuous Empire style furniture made from his own designs by continental craftsmen. Following Horace Walpole's example, he opened it to the public by ticket in February 1804, and three years later was sufficiently vain to publish an illustrated book devoted to it, *Household Furniture and Interior Decoration executed from Designs by Thomas Hope* (1807). From this it is clear that highly coloured interiors like the Indian Room, the Egyptian Room and the Flaxman Room which were markedly novel in terms of late Georgian taste, were contemporary with, where they did not anticipate, Beckford's similar interiors at Fonthill.

The vivid colours of the Indian Room at Duchess Street, which was dominated by large topographical paintings of India commissioned from Thomas Daniell, were arranged so as to lighten from the skirting to the cornice. The ottomans round the edge of the room and the curtains were of crimson damask; the walls, hung with elaborate black and gold sconces, were sky blue; and the segmental coffered ceiling was a very pale blue punctuated with azure and sea-green ornaments. The senses were further delighted by 'incense urns, cassolettes, flower baskets and other vehicles of natural and artificial perfumes'. In the Flaxman Room, every detail of the colouring and iconography was selected so as to echo in a visual and literary way the theme of the sculptural group, *Aurora visiting Cephalus at dawn on Mount Ida*, which Hope had commissioned from Flaxman in Rome in 1791. Azure, black and pinky-orange satin curtains on three sides of the room were draped over looking-glasses edged with black velvet. The chimney-piece was of black marble flanked by owls and decorated with nine gilt-bronze stars, while the vaulted ceiling was an icy dawn-blue adorned with a rose-pink blush and more stars.

The 'Lararium', a small 'Closet or Boudoir fitted up for the reception of a few Egyptian, Hindoo, and Chinese idols and curiosities' was even more bizarre. Tasselled tent-like drapery, hanging from a ceiling formed by bamboo arches, framed a stepped chimney-piece set against a wall of looking glass. Emblems from the different religions of the world, including a large ivory crucifix, were united in terms of their romantic and artistic appeal. In the centre of the Egyptian or 'Black' Room was an Egyptian mummy in a glass case, so that if the house recalled Beckford's Fonthill it also recalled the London house of Sir John Soane in Lincoln's Inn Fields where the eery tomb-like Sculpture Museum, formed in 1808, eventually contained the magnificent sarcophagus for the mummy of Seti I which Soane acquired in 1824.

In 1807 Hope bought The Deepdene, a substantial late-eighteenth-century classical mansion dramatically placed on a narrow ledge half-way up the side of a broad steep valley. The hill immediately behind and above the house formed a U-shaped enclosure which had been laid out as a kind of 'amphitheatre garden' with stepped terraces, grottoes, vineyards and orange trees, in the mid-seventeenth century by the Hon. Charles Howard. This remarkable Italianate garden, set amidst the picturesque undulations of a spectacularly beautiful part of Surrey at the approaches to Leith Hill and Box Hill, seems to have made Hope especially receptive to the hints expressed by Price, Knight and Repton that a little Italianate formality near the house might in certain circumstances be welcomed. Thus in 1805 Knight claimed that 'the hanging terraces of the Italian gardens . . . if the house be placed upon an eminence, with sloping ground before it, may be employed with very good effect; as they not only enrich the foreground, but serve as a basement for the house to stand upon . . . Such decorations are indeed, now rather old-fashioned; but another revolution in taste, which is probably at no great distance, will make them new again'.[33]   Thomas Hope took up this theme in his essay 'On the Art of Gardening' which he published in 1808 and again in 1819 as the preface to Mrs Hofland's lavish publication on the Duke of Marlborough's house and gardens at White Knights, Berkshire. Hope admired

the suspended gardens within Genoa, and of the splendid villas about Rome . . . those striking oppositions of the rarest marbles to the richest verdure; those mixtures of statues, and vases, and balustrades, with cypresses, and pinasters, and bays; those distant hills seen through the converging lines of lengthened colonnades; those ranges of aloes and cactuses growing out of vases of granite and of porphyry scarce more symmetric by art than these plants are by nature.

Taking up Price's plea for variety and intricacy, Hope went on to argue that 'if we wish for variety, for contrast, and for brokennes of levels, we can only seek it in arcades and in terraces, in steps, balustrades, regular slopes, parapets . . . we cannot', he adds in a snub aimed at Payne Knight, 'find space for the rock and the precipice'.[34]

Hope described his ideal house and garden as one where 'the cluster of highly adorned and sheltered apartments that form the mansion . . . shoot out, as it were, into . . . ramifications of arcades, porticoes, terraces, parterres, treillages, avenues, and other such still splendid embellishments of art, calculated by their architectural and measured forms, at once to offer a striking and varied contrast with, and a dignified and comfortable transition to, the more undulating and rural features of the more extended, more distant, and more exposed boundaries'.

He began his alterations to The Deepdene in 1818 by adding on to the existing house an asymmetrical entrance front in a strange style of which C. R. Cockerell, who visited and admired the house in 1823, wrote: 'reminds me of the ancient villas of Pompeii.'[35] The house was dominated by Hope's asymmetrically placed loggia-topped tower of Tuscan origin, which was a landmark in the history of architectural taste in the nineteenth century. From Schinkel at Schloss Glienicke to Barry at Trentham and Cubitt at Osborne, architects enjoyed organising a scattered composition round the pivot of an Italianate tower. In the grouping of the kitchens and dairy among trees on a steep slope just before the entrance front of the house, Hope followed Uvedale Price who claimed that 'nothing contributes so much to give both variety and consequence to the principal building, as the accompaniment, and, as it were, the attendance of the inferior parts in their different gradations'.[36] Cockerell realised the significance of this aspect of The Deepdene, and wrote that by 'placing the offices in a low ground and showing the roofs of an agreeable form with occasional points & pinnacles, the genius loci is remarkably recalled. In the descent a dairy is contrived & above it as a pediment to conceal the roof, is a pergola a l'italienne with vines & flowers. This immediately opposite the entrance is the happiest thought turning a deformity into a beauty, for the roof could not but have been a deformity'.[37]

No less unusual were the conservatory, sculpture gallery and orangery which Hope added in 1823 at the other end of the house in a wing projecting at an angle of 45 degrees. Here again, he was following the advice of Price and Knight as well as the practice of Wyatville at Endsleigh. Not only did the building project at a diagonal, but Hope exploited with steps, terraces, balustrades and urns the fact that the ground fell sharply away. Division between exterior and interior was broken down: there were pots and sculpture outdoors, plants indoors, a fountain and a statue by Thorvaldsen in the conservatory. How far the varied architecture at this end of the house was due to Hope and how far to Atkinson is not clear, but at the corner it most unexpectedly turns Gothic in a style that is recognisably Atkinsonian.

Although The Deepdene has been demolished, there exist two handsome illustrated volumes called *The Union of the Picturesque in Scenery and Architecture with Domestic Beauties* by the prolific topographer John Britton which describe the house and its contents. Not intended for publication, the book was, unfortunately, never quite completed. However, it contains nearly seventy illustrations, many of which are brightly coloured watercolours painted for Hope under Britton's direction in 1821–6 by two talented topographical artists, W. H. Bartlett (1809–54) and Penry Williams (c.1800–85), a pupil of Fuseli, who settled in Rome in 1827.

In the very year that Britton was preparing his volumes on The Deepdene, he was also compiling with W. H. Leeds a companion volume on Sir John Soane's

Sir John Soane's Museum. *The interior of the Museum as arranged in 1813* by Joseph Gandy. This shows the Dome built by Soane at the back of 12, Lincoln's Inn Fields in 1808–09; the earliest part of the present museum. An evocative medley, like a three-dimensional realisation of a Piranesi engraving, it incorporates antique fragments and casts, cinerary vases and busts, and works by Chantrey and Flaxman.

astonishing house-cum-museum in Lincoln's Inn Fields. It is surely fitting that the two most original collectors of the day should have had their houses recorded by the same man.

Like Walpole half a century before, Soane himself also published an illustrated guide to his house, *Description of the . . . Residence of John Soane* (1830), a book which was enlarged in subsequent editions. Soane's house had grown, as a picturesque building should, between 1792 and 1824, though the most important work was carried out in 1812 and 1824. Parts of three houses in Lincoln's Inn Fields, Nos 12, 13 and 14, eventually formed a complex rabbit-warren of interlocking spaces exploiting their different levels and heights, some of them domed or top-lit or making entertaining use of mirrors. The principles of design were consciously picturesque so that, as Soane explained of the north drawing-room, for example, 'The ceiling of this room is partly groined and partly flat; a mode of decoration calculated to give variety and movement to the composition'.[38] Embedded in this poetical maze was Soane's heterogeneous collection of antique architectural fragments, sculpture, vases and cinerary urns, English eighteenth- and early-nineteenth-century paintings and watercolours, architectural drawings, models and engravings, as well as a magnificent architectural library. For once, a watercolour by Gandy, *The Interior of the Museum as arranged in 1813*, is not the fantasy it might seem but sober fact.

It could be maintained that no contemporary architect was as close in artistic vision to Soane as the painter J. M. W. Turner (1778–1851). The preoccupation with light is central to both, as it had also been to Soane's hero Dance. Soane's dissolution of conventional architectural forms into a series of poetically-lit hollowed-out spaces is surely a parallel to Turner's late style. We have already noted in the Preface the significance of Turner's role in the development of a pictorial representation of architecture by means of seductive watercolours. The plates in Soane's *Sketches in Architecture . . . of Cottages, Villas and other useful buildings, with Characteristic Scenery* (1793), especially the foliage and vegetation, are close to the work of Turner and Malton. Soane complained to the Royal Academy in 1807 that no lectures on perspective had been delivered for many years. In February 1807 his assistant Gandy offered to deliver the lectures but in December that year Turner was appointed Professor of Perspective. He was not ready to deliver his first lecture until January 1811, having prepared nearly two hundred large drawings and diagrams to demonstrate his preoccupation with coloured light and reflections. Ruskin wrote admiringly of these how 'elaborate attention is always paid to the disposition of shadows and (especially) reflected lights. Huge perspectives and elevations of the Dome of St. Paul's lie in this portfolio side by side with studies of the reflections on glass balls; and measured gleams of moonlight on the pillar of Trajan, with dispositions of chiaroscuro cast by the gaoler's lantern on the passages of Newgate'.[39] Ruskin's words were prompted by Turner's coloured studies of reflection and refraction based, for example, on the juxtaposition of glass balls, some empty and some half-filled with water. Is it too romantic for us to find a parallel here to Soane's late interiors with their diaphanous lighting effects, mirrors and coloured glass?

In 1810–12 Turner built a little Italianate house for himself at Sandycombe Lodge, Twickenham, the kind of picturesquely sited chalet which Ruskin was later to admire in his 'The Poetry of Architecture; or the Architecture of the Nations of Europe considered in its Association with natural Scenery and national Character' (1837–8). At the same time, the building has a certain Soanean flavour both inside and out, especially in the detailing of the entrance hall with its tall thin arches. At 47, Queen Anne Street West, Turner built a second picture gallery for himself in 1819–21 which he seems to have discussed with Soane from as early as

1815. Opened in 1822, it was a long narrow room, top-lit with octagonal skylights and walls covered with dull red drapery. It thus had something in common with Harrison's gallery of *c*.1810 for Turner's patron Sir John Leicester at Tabley House, Cheshire. It was closer, however, to Soane's Gallery at Dulwich, the British Institution Gallery and the Grande Galerie of the Louvre which Turner had drawn on a visit in 1819, following its remodelling with top-lights. Turner's preoccupation with light in painting was thus appropriately accompanied by a concern for the proper display of pictures, which he also shared with Soane. In 1832 he even considered turning his own house into a permanent Turner Museum along similar lines to those which Soane was adopting at that moment.

In Soane's eighth lecture at the Royal Academy, first delivered in 1815, he remarked that 'In Galleries . . . light is often introduced very advantageously above the Cornice, so that the window is not seen from below: by this contrivance a pleasing kind of demi-tint is thrown over the whole surface of the Ceiling',[40] a point he illustrated with a section of Dance's gallery of 1788–91 at Lansdowne House. In praising in this lecture what he described as the 'lumière mystérieuse' practised by architects in eighteenth-century France, he also revealed his debt to a French romantic tradition to which we shall return briefly in Chapter VI.

Visiting the Soane Museum in 1877 in preparation for his great work, *Ancient Marbles in Great Britain* (Cambridge, 1882), the solemn German scholar Adolf Michaelis was not amused by the qualities we have described as Turneresque. He complained that:

A number of very narrow passages, very dark corners, and the like, impedes a steady investigation equally with the overcrowding of the rooms and incredibly inconvenient mode in which a great part of the contents are arranged . . . It is not too much to say that some of the better specimens can only be seen from the back. Then again the impressions conveyed by so wild a confusion of promiscuous fragments is necessarily bewildering and fatiguing to the visitor.[41]

Britton, it is interesting to note, had prefaced his book on Soane's house with an appropriate quotation from Pope which indicates a more sympathetic point of view:

> Let not each beauty ev'rywhere be spy'd
> When half the skill is decently to hide.
> He gains all points who pleasingly confounds,
> Surprizes, varies and conceals the Bounds.

The 1820s and 1830s saw not only books on the houses of Hope and Soane, but a whole spate of illustrated publications which reflect a renewed interest in the pictorial approach to architecture as promulgated by Price and Knight. The illustrated narrative was a form which greatly appealed to the picturesque sensibility. The guides of houses from Strawberry Hill to Fonthill Abbey, The Deepdene, and Soane's Museum indicate an enthusiasm for visual representation which has become deeply engrained in the English mentality. It might be worth drawing a parallel between the plethora of illustrated architectural books of the 1820s and the repetition of this phenomenon in the 1980s. The eclectic architect P. F. Robinson, for example, published *Rural Architecture* (1823), *Designs for Ornamental Villas* (1827), and *Village Architecture, being a Series of Designs . . . illustrative of the Observations contained in the Essay on the Picturesque, by Sir Uvedale Price* (1830).

Shrubland Park, Suffolk, 1849-54, by Sir Charles Barry for Sir W. F. Middleton, Bt. The fantasy of recreating the gardens of the Villa d'Este in the heart of Suffolk may be regarded as picturesque in origin, though the thoroughgoing revivalism of the way in which it is executed seems characteristically Victorian.

Italian domestic architecture, as employed by Nash, Hope and Goodridge, was promoted as a vehicle for the Picturesque in influential publications by T. F. Hunt (*c.*1791–1831), G. L. Meason and Charles Parker (1799–1881), a pupil of Wyatville. Hunt, whose personal preference was for the Picturesque Tudor style, nonetheless published *Architettura Campestre, displayed in Lodges, Gardeners' Houses, etc. in the Modern or Italian Style* (1827) with a text suitably adorned with poetic quotations from Shenstone, Mason and Cowper. His plea for the adoption of campaniles and of Italian tiles as aids to the Picturesque was taken up by Charles Barry at Walton House and elsewhere. In some ways more remarkable was Meason's book, *On the Landscape Architecture of the Great Painters of Italy* (1827) which, though limited to 150 copies, was one of the central documents of the whole Picturesque period. Meason assembled sixty drawings of buildings in Italian painted landscapes as an aid to architects in the design of irregular compositions. Inspired directly by Payne Knight, he assumed that these painted buildings were based on real buildings which had been gradually altered from ancient Roman times up to the Renaissance. Charles Parker, a Roman Catholic who had spent several years in Italy, published *Villa Rustica* in monthly parts from 1823–41 (2nd. ed. 1848), containing nearly a hundred lithographs of compositions 'selected from Buildings and Scenes in the Vicinity of Rome and Florence, and arranged for Lodges and Domestic Dwellings', which exercised considerable influence on the Early Victorian Italianate Revival.

However, apart from the asymmetrical Italianate style adopted by Sir Charles Barry in the 1830s and 1840s at Walton House, Surrey, Trentham Hall, Staffordshire, and Shrubland Park, Suffolk, and also, reluctantly, by Sir Gilbert Scott at the Foreign Office in the 1850s, the future of the Picturesque lay not with classically-inspired buildings like The Deepdene, Dunglass or Lansdown Tower, but with the Gothic Revival and, eventually, the Domestic Revival.

The Picturesque House:
Salvin to Lutyens

THE 1830s saw a powerful re-action against the modern world in favour of what were regarded as the finer, more poetic, more beautiful, and more Christian values of the Middle Ages. To take one small example, few of those apparently historic English family names which include 'de', 'De' or 'd'' date back earlier than that decade.

A transitional house, in which the picturesque variety and intricacy of the late eighteenth century is combined with the new archaeology of the nineteenth century, is Highcliffe Castle, Hampshire, built in 1830–4 for Lord Stuart de Rothesay by W. J. Donthorn (1799–1859). A pupil of Wyatville from 1817–20, Donthorn was clearly inspired by his master's diagonal planning in his creation at Highcliffe of an amazingly asymmetrical composition with spreading diagonal wings of different heights punctuated with towers and bay windows. The sublime entrance porch and staircase directly echo Fonthill, as Lord Stuart's daughter realised when she complained that Donthorn had 'a silly desire to build a house that would emulate Fonthill or Ashridge'. Donthorn's patron was Charles Stuart, British Ambassador to France during the Bourbon restoration from 1815–24 and 1828–30, who took the mediaevalising title Lord Stuart de Rothesay in 1828 and left Paris in 1830 bringing with him his eclectic collection of French mediaeval stonework, carvings and stained glass, as well as Louis XV *boiseries* and Empire furniture. It was Donthorn's bizarre task to incorporate these objects into a visually appropriate setting. His dynamic plan does indeed generate sufficient energy to digest features like the sumptuous Flamboyant Gothic oriel window from the Grande Manoir des Andelys in Normandy, the fragments from Jumièges Abbey, the Jesse window from St. Vigor, Rouen, and the rococo panelling. It is attractive to think of Donthorn turning for help in truly picturesque fashion to the illustrations in J. S. Cotman's *Architectural Antiquities of Normandy* (2 vols., 1820–2) which included Les Andelys before demolition. However, in Lady Stuart's opinion, Donthorn was 'totally unfit to plan a house . . . I wish the whole thing had fallen over the cliff'.[1]

The onslaught on Georgian taste which gathered force from the 1830s, and was implicit in Lord Stuart's devotion to mediaeval French architecture, might have involved – as it did in the case of Pugin – an onslaught on the Picturesque. However, the technique of informal pictorial massing pioneered by the Picturesque had by now become so deeply embedded that it coloured most architectural practice for the remainder of the century. There is thus a sense in which a vast quantity of Victorian architecture is incidentally picturesque, but since picturesque values were not the primary concern of the architects, it would be inappropriate to discuss it at length in the present book. Moreover, the mediaeval and vernacular styles which Pugin and his followers were now recommending as the embodiment of all truth were, ironically, precisely the styles

Highcliffe Castle, Hampshire, 1830-4, by J. Donthorn for Lord Stuart de Rothesay. A neo-Flamboyant château on a cliff-top site incorporating an eclectic assembly of internal and external features of different periods brought from France. This view shows the irregular garden front with the porch from Les Andelys in the centre. The whole building is now ruinous.

in which it had been found easiest to design picturesquely. This confusion meant that Pugin's ideal of 'truthful' architecture, as expressed in books like his *Contrasts* (1836), with its emphasis on the primacy of the plan rather than on contrived visual effects, and its belief in 'honesty' of structure and materials, did not deal the mortal blow to the Picturesque which might have been expected. Indeed, the emphasis which picturesque theorists from the time of Vanbrugh had placed on the associational and evocative qualities of architectural style had doubtless helped to create a number of heightened expectations about what architecture might be expected to achieve. It is these expectations which go some way to accounting for the popular reception given to Pugin's identification of Gothic style with religious truth.

Pugin evidently considered picturesque theory very carefully before condemning it. In *The True Principles of Pointed or Christian Architecture* (1841) he argued that:

The picturesque effect of the ancient buildings results from the ingenious methods by which the old builders overcame local and constructive difficulties. An edifice which is arranged with the principal view of looking picturesque is sure to resemble an artificial waterfall or a made-up rock, which are generally so *unnaturally natural* as to appear ridiculous.

An architect should exhibit his skill by turning the difficulties which occur in raising an elevation from a convenient plan into so many *picturesque* beauties . . . But all these [modern] inconsistencies have arisen from this great error, – *the plans of buildings are designed to suit the elevation, instead of the elevation being made subservient to the plan.*[2]

Thus, though Pugin's major domestic buildings like Scarisbrick Hall and Alton Castle of the 1830s and 1840s are markedly irregular, their asymmetry is not really any more picturesque in intention than is that of Modern Movement buildings. The different elements of a Pugin house – hall, chapel, clock tower and so on – are

Aloupka, Crimea, 1837–40, by Edward Blore for Prince Michael Woronzow. The Picturesque is here strained to breaking point in this unsuccessful attempt to digest such different styles as Tudor for the dining-room wing on the left, and Moorish for the entrance archway in the centre.

assembled in disparate staccato compositions which are far from the smoothly flowing pictorial groupings of the Picturesque.

The world into which Pugin irrupted with his passionate, uncomfortable views was dominated, so far as country house design was concerned, by five architects who were considerably older than him, Edward Blore (1787–1879), John Dobson (1787–1865), William Burn (1789–1870), Charles Barry (1795–1860) and Anthony Salvin (1799–1881). Blore, an antiquarian and a gifted topographical draughtsman, was taken up by Sir Walter Scott for whom he prepared designs for Abbotsford and published *The Provincial Antiquities and Picturesque Scenery of Scotland* (2 vols., 1826). Sir Samuel Rush Meyrick was another characteristic patron of Blore's. Meyrick, a leading authority on armour and costume, arranged the royal armour at Windsor Castle for George IV, advised Drury Lane on costume for historical plays, and commissioned Goodrich Court from Blore in 1828, a castle-style house on the banks of the Wye, a mile or so from the ruins of the mediaeval Goodrich Castle. Goodrich has been demolished but a later house, Merevale Hall, Warwickshire (1838–44), survives as an impressive example of the Elizabethan revival, a style which Blore helped popularise. Though the main front is symmetrical, there are two asymmetrically placed towers of different sizes, as well as a mass of chimneys, turrets and gables which ensures that the house forms a picturesque group from a distance. One of Blore's largest and most impressive houses is Great Moreton Hall, Cheshire, built in 1841–3. Here, George Holland Ackers, a Manchester cotton manufacturer, could play at being squire beneath the hammerbeam roof of his Great Hall, lit by tall traceried windows in the Decorated style. This totally asymmetrical house is dominated by a tall castellated staircase tower designed to look like the keep of an earlier house on the site.

The most picturesque of Blore's creations was undoubtedly the strange palace of Aloupka in the Crimea overlooking the Black Sea, built for Prince Michael Woronzow in 1837–40. The anglophile prince wanted to be reminded of the years he had spent in England when his father was Ambassador, but also felt that a

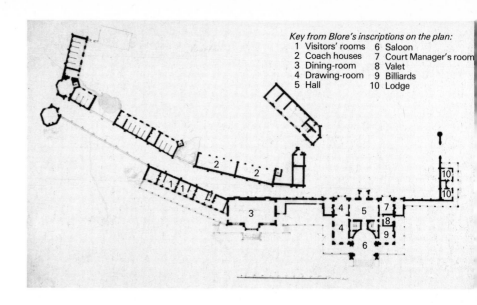

Key from Blore's inscriptions on the plan:
1 Visitors' rooms 6 Saloon
2 Coach houses 7 Court Manager's room
3 Dining-room 8 Valet
4 Drawing-room 9 Billiards
5 Hall 10 Lodge

Aloupka plan.

certain Moorish touch would be appropriate to the building's romantic setting. Blore provided a schizophrenic half Tudor, half Moghul design assembled, as *The Builder* explained in 1850, 'with such an admixture of the two styles as was necessary not to render their combination and necessarily close approximation too violent for good taste'.[3] The informal and widely scattered plan of Aloupka was also strikingly picturesque.

An architect abler than Blore was John Dobson of Newcastle, whose enormous practice was confined to the north of England. In 1820 he went to London in order to be taught by the watercolourist John Varley. He also made lasting friendships at this time with William Hunt, Mulready, West and Turner. Two mansions begun by Dobson in 1837 are close to Blore's style, though with better skylines than Blore was capable of achieving. The first, Holme Eden Hall, Cumbria, was built in an Early Tudor style for Peter Dixon, a cotton manufacturer. The second, Beaufront Castle, Northumberland, built for William Cuthbert, a Tyneside shipowner, is a spectacular exercise in what Dobson called 'the domestic castellated, or House Gothic of the 15th century'.[4] The marvellously varied grouping of this brilliant building shows how well Dobson had learnt his lessons in romantic landscape painting. It may also suggest that his early commission for alterations at Vanbrugh's Seaton Delaval had taught him how to handle masses in the manner of Vanbrugh, an architect whom he is known to have especially admired for his 'light and shade'.[5] At the same time, Dobson brought to the art of picturesque design a new archaeological knowledge which, in the hands of a less gifted architect, might have stifled the Picturesque. However, the elements borrowed at Beaufront from Haddon Hall, Wressel Castle, South Wingfield Manor and the Vicar's Close at Wells, are effortlessly incorporated into a dynamic and original composition. At the centre of the plan is an aisled and vaulted Gothic Hall with a remarkable canted clerestory. Round two sides of this is an L-shape are the four principal living-rooms, commanding panoramic views to south and east over the Tyne valley, now sadly marred by a motorway in the middle distance.

One of the most influential, though not necessarily the most gifted, of this group of architects was William Burn. He was prepared to design façades in a great range of styles, classical, Elizabethan or Scottish Baronial, but his chief

importance is as the pioneer of a new kind of plan which was asymmetrical for practical rather than picturesque reasons. He sensed that country house owners would welcome privacy from the increasing numbers of their guests and servants. Thus Burn planned houses in four sections, basically separate but interlocking at key points, consisting of private family rooms, public rooms, guest rooms and servants' rooms. The sections were generally themselves subdivided into, for example, a bachelors' wing, nurseries and separate servants' areas presided over by the butler, housekeeper and cook, each with their own corridors and staircases. It was naturally much easier to dispose such a complex network on an asymmetrical than a symmetrical plan, though the resultant asymmetry was often exploited visually according to picturesque precepts. A characteristic example was Milton Lockhart, Strathclyde Region, built in 1829 on a site in the Clyde valley selected by Sir Walter Scott. This now demolished house was a pioneer in the Scottish Baronial style which Burn's pupil David Bryce (1803–76) made especially his own in a series of boldly inventive mansions of the 1850s and 1860s, such as Ballikinrain Castle, Central Region, Castlemilk, Dumfries and Galloway Region, Craigends, Renfrewshire (demolished), Langton House, Borders Region (demolished), and Kinnaird Castle, Tayside Region. His complex plans are built up on the same principles as those of Burn and therefore tend to include a multiplicity of passages and small rooms, However, in the astonishingly vigorous massing of his elevations he reveals himself as a true child of the Picturesque. According to his obituary in *The Builder*, he worked like a painter at a canvas, rubbing out and altering his compositions until the grouping was perfect.[6]

Anthony Salvin (1799–1881) who, as a pupil of Nash, had been well trained in picturesque methods is more relevant to our story than either Blore, Burn, Dobson or Bryce. It is appropriate that one of his earliest commissions was for a house near Nash's Luscombe, just below the Haldon Hills north of Dawlish.

Castlemilk, Dumfries and Galloway Region, 1863-4, by D. Bryce for Sir Robert Jardine, Bt. An enormous Scottish-Baronial mansion which is the High Victorian answer to Nash's Caerhays of 1808. The private wing is on the left at the south-east end of the entrance front, while the west front contains a symmetrical suite of rooms. The service wing is to the north.

Bayons Manor, Lincolnshire, 1836-42, by C. Tennyson d'Eyncourt and W. A. Nicholson (demolished 1965). A dream of mediaeval England created by the uncle of the poet Tennyson. Its fetchingly picturesque romance belongs rather to the world of Sir Walter Scott and Bulwer Lytton than to the Arthurian solemnity of the Poet Laureate.

Salvin designed and built Mamhead in a handsome Tudor Gothic style in 1827–33 for Sir Robert Newman, Bart., at whose instance the plan of the main body of the house was regular and symmetrical. However, Salvin imparted a strikingly picturesque character to the whole in two unusual ways. He extended the east garden-front southwards with a cloister-cum-greenhouse terminating in a tall pinnacled pavilion, a Gothic echo of the Indian conservatory at Sezincote. He also grouped the brewhouse and stables on a slope above the entrance front in the form of a remarkably convincing castle inspired by Belsay in his native Northumberland. Salvin was a talented artist and a number of his watercolours survive to show the evolution of this theatrical composition. To add to the fiction, he built this 'castle' of local red sandstone suggestive of a mellow antiquity, which is in sharp contrast to the hard grey Bath stone of the house itself.

At Scotney in Kent in 1835, as we have already seen, Salvin found a real mediaeval castle which, suitably improved, became a romantic landscaped feature to be admired from the windows of the new house built on a hill above it in 1837–43. The asymmetrical grouping of Salvin's new house, like that of Pugin's houses, is not primarily picturesque in intention but is related to the practical planning within, as well as echoing the simplicity, directness and naturalness of many sixteenth-century manor houses. Exactly contemporary with Scotney is the yet more romantic Bayons Manor, Lincolnshire, where Salvin was consulted over the design of the library by Charles Tennyson, uncle of Alfred Tennyson, who added d'Eyncourt to his surname in 1835. As Mark Girouard has pointed out, Bayons Manor 'was not only built for romantic reasons; it was to be a demonstration of the social status of the Tennyson family, concealing behind its haze of battlements and turrets the truth of their comparatively recent rise to fortune'.[7] Bayons grew gradually according to no fixed plan in true picturesque fashion between 1836 and 1842 from designs by Charles Tennyson d'Eyncourt himself and a local architect called W. A. Nicholson. In 1836 they added two wings on to a modest existing house, one containing a large free-standing Great Hall, and the other a fine library. A tower was added as a pivot for the composition

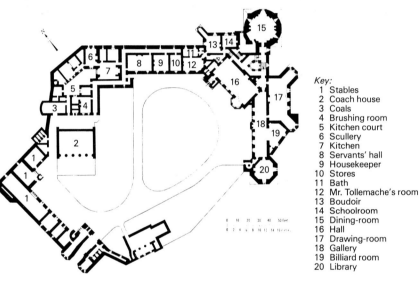

Key:
1 Stables
2 Coach house
3 Coals
4 Brushing room
5 Kitchen court
6 Scullery
7 Kitchen
8 Servants' hall
9 Housekeeper
10 Stores
11 Bath
12 Mr. Tollemache's room
13 Boudoir
14 Schoolroom
15 Dining-room
16 Hall
17 Drawing-room
18 Gallery
19 Billiard room
20 Library

(*Above*) Peckforton Castle, Cheshire, 1844-50 by Anthony Salvin for Lord Tollemache. Of the two castles in this view the more distant is the ruined thirteenth-century Beeston Castle. It is outdone in picturesque effect by Salvin's Peckforton with a straggling skyline which, from the distance, suggests falsely that the building is ruinous.

(*Left*) Peckforton Castle. Ground-floor plan. The brilliant planning combines picturesque effect with an understanding of the way in which mediaeval castles were constructed round the idea of the defensive wall. However, it can scarcely be claimed that the small windows and exposed stone walls make for comfortable interiors.

n the next year, and in 1839 the stable and kitchen court was encircled by a great castellated wall with bastions and gateways, while a second wall with gatehouse, moat and drawbridge ran round the house itself. Finally, an impressive ruined keep was built in 1842 on a mound inside the inner wall. Though solidly built of stone with many accurately designed mediaeval features, the spirit of Bayons was as picturesque as the manner of its composition. It was in the visual painterly tradition which had produced the sham castles of the Georgian landscaped parks. By the early 1960s the house, now alas demolished, was in a state of total decay, a magical island of towers, trees and undergrowth, rising from a sea of waving grass. How delighted Payne Knight would have been with it!

At Peckforton, Cheshire, Lionel (later 1st Lord) Tollemache gave Salvin an opportunity to go one better than Bayons and build a bigger castle on a finer site, not piecemeal like Bayons but according to a single coherent plan. There was no need to lend appropriate 'tone' by fabricating a mediaeval building nearby as had been done at Mamhead and Bayons, because, as at Scotney, a genuine mediaeval ruin, Beeston Castle, was conveniently to hand on a neighbouring eminence: a

Harlaxton Manor. Lincolnshire, 1831-
c.55, by Anthony Salvin and W. Burn
for G. de Ligne Gregory. View looking
through the baroque forecourt gates
along the avenue to the Tudor Gothic
gatehouse and beyond. The house is
built on the side of a hill so that the first-
floor apartments open directly on to the
garden at the back and side of the
building.

picturesque object to be viewed from the carefully-placed windows of the new
castle. The diagonal emphasis and the seemingly random grouping of contrasting
forms at Peckforton Castle, designed and built in 1844–50, are the result of careful
visual experiment which is recorded, as at Mamhead, in a series of beautiful
watercolours by Salvin. Certain elements of the extraordinary plan echo Nash's
Luscombe Castle, while the spatial sequence from the circular dining room
through a long gallery to the octagonal library is also a classic Nash device. To this
familiar picturesque technique Salvin brought a detailed knowledge of mediaeval
military architecture which lends its own justification to the scattered plan, free
grouping and comparatively low skyline. Indeed, the success of Peckforton led to
Salvin's employment as a 'restorer' at a chain of important castles including
Warwick, Rockingham, Dunster, Alnwick, Longford, Muncaster and the Tower
of London. The idea of Peckforton as a great feudal castle came from Lord
Tollemache who evidently subscribed to the ideas of Disraeli's and Lord John
Manners's 'Young England' movement with its emphasis on the rights and
coresponding duties of great landowners. Girouard quotes Tollemache as saying
that 'the only real and lasting pleasure to be derived from the possession of a
landed estate is to witness the improvement in the social condition of those
residing on it'.[8] Certainly his provision of cottages, farmhouses and land for all
who worked for him was remarkably generous by the standards of any age.

Although Mamhead, Scotney, Bayons and Peckforton could be interpreted in
differing degrees as belonging to a Late Georgian Picturesque tradition, Salvin
had already designed a very different house as early as 1831 for George de Ligne
Gregory, a Lincolnshire landowner. Harlaxton Manor, begun in 1831 from

Harlaxton Manor. Staircase. Harlaxton picturesquely combines Elizabethan and Jacobean allusions with the Baroque. The extravagant staircase is probably by William Burn of *c.* 1840.

Salvin's designs and continued by William Burn from 1838 to *c.*1855, is the spectacular climax of the Elizabethan Revival which was foreshadowed in the engraving of a house based on Wollaton in Payne Knight's *The Landscape* (1794). The Elizabethan Revival was at its height in the 1830s when the Gothic or Elizabethan styles were chosen for the new Houses of Parliament competition on associational and patriotic grounds. At the same time Joseph Nash had begun publishing the nostalgically alluring lithographs of his *Mansions of England in the Olden Time*. The 'orchestration' of the approach to Harlaxton is brilliantly dramatic. It is achieved by means of a series of crescendi extending through a valley, over a bridge, past the Baroque Revival walls of the kitchen gardens, through the detached Baronial-style gatehouse, and so eventually to the baroque gates and screen of the forecourt and the almost overwhelming climax of the entrance façade. Inside, the most celebrated *tour de force* is Burn's Cedar Staircase of *c.*1840, a continental baroque extravaganza with coupled caryatids engulfed in billowing drapery, shells and swags, all in the finest stuccowork.

139

Humewood Castle, County Wicklow, 1866–70, by William White for H. Dick. The stableyard from the east. The inventive jagged skyline of massive granite blocks is an adaptation of the picturesque to the High Victorian muscular style.

True to his training under Nash, Salvin remained obstinately pre-Puginian in his stylistic range. Despite Harlaxton and Peckforton, he was quite happy to design in an Italianate style with asymmetrical campaniles in the Barry fashion. His work in this vein at Burwarton House, Shropshire, and Hafod, Dyfed, has been destroyed, but Penoyre, Powys, built in 1846–8 for Colonel Lloyd Vaughan Watkins with magnificent views of the Brecon Beacons, survives as an admittedly rather joyless example of the type. Salvin's work in the next decade introduces us to a brief consideration of how far picturesque themes survived into the High Victorian period from 1850–70. His vast 'super-Jacobean' Keele Hall, Staffordshire (1856–61) has a predominantly U-shaped entrance front, four-storeyed with emphatically random fenestration and consisting of a series of immense gabled masses of different heights and widths. Further variety is introduced in the angle of the whole composition by the great staircase tower, capped with a tall clerestory. Though such a powerfully irregular concatenation of forms could scarcely have been designed without the revolution that the Picturesque had effected, it is surely easier to see it as aggressive and confused rather than picturesque. The same is true of Bear Wood, Berkshire, the unbelievably grandiose pile built in 1865–74 for John Walter, the proprietor of *The Times*, by Robert Kerr (1823–1904), author of the popular book, *The English Gentleman's House* (1864).

This High Victorian muscularity is nowhere better expressed than at William White's Humewood Castle, Co. Wicklow, built in 1866–70 for Hume Dick, an Irish landowner and Conservative M.P. With irregular chunks of granite, White built up a tense composition of pyramids and triangles, jagged as German Expressionism, and, indeed, as the skyline of the nearby Wicklow mountains. White wrote that 'For exterior effect our attention must be directed to the sky outline before expending it upon minutiae; and this is of the greatest consequence in an undulating and picturesque country'.[9] However, one of the things which separates Georgian Picturesque from architecture of this date is precisely the new preoccupation with skylines which have an almost independent life of their own, as at Pearson's Quar Wood, Teulon's Tortworth Court, Godwin's Dromore Castle and Clutton's Minley Manor.

The 1860s saw the birth of a movement which coloured much English domestic architecture in various ways until at least the time of the Great War. Beginning with Shaw and ending with Lutyens, it had a variety of names and phases such as the 'Old English' style, the 'Queen Anne' Movement, the Domestic Revival and the Free School. Whereas the favoured building type of the Gothic Revival from the 1830s was the church, the new movement shared with the Picturesque a preoccupation with domestic architecture. The great Victorian expansion of urban and industrial architecture and technology, created an understandable reaction in favour of vernacular buildings and the rural scene – in fact, in favour of everything that Nash, for entirely picturesque reasons, had so brilliantly recreated in his idyllic Blaise Hamlet of 1810. In this reaction against the new commercial and industrial England of the nineteenth century, the writings of John Ruskin (1819–1900) were such a powerful influence that it is time we discussed his contribution to the Picturesque movement. He is so much associated with the Gothic Revival that we should not forget that this vigorous advocate of Turner also promoted the Picturesque in architecture. Thus his earlier writings on architecture, published in Loudon's *Architectural Magazine* in 1837–8, had the wholly picturesque title, 'The Poetry of Architecture; or the Architecture of the Nations of Europe considered in its Association with natural Scenery and national Character'. Here he considered two building types, the cottage and the villa, in relation to the feelings, manners, scenery and skies of the different countries of Europe, emphasising that he would 'be more interested in buildings raised by feeling, than in those corrected by rule'.[10] He was as hostile here as he was to be throughout his life to contemporary English architecture, though his aesthetic categories and assumptions are still fundamentally those of Price and Knight. For example, when he writes 'Only one general rule can be given, and that we must repeat. The house must NOT be a noun substantive, it must not stand by itself, it must be part and parcel of a proportioned whole: it must not even be seen all at once',[11] he is simply repeating Knight's command of 1794 that 'mix'd and blended, ever let it be/A mere component part of what you see'.

Ruskin's especial interest in the cottage was given further expression in his lecture on domestic architecture delivered at Edinburgh in 1853. The sweeping roof of even quite modest vernacular houses came to have a deep moral significance for him: 'The very soul of the cottage – the essence and meaning of it – are in its roof; it is that, mainly, wherein consists its shelter . . . It is in its thick impenetrable coverlid of close thatch that its whole heart and hospitality are concentrated. Consider the difference, in sound, of the expression "beneath my roof" and "within my walls"'.[12] After the roof came the bay window as a visually pleasing expression of human generosity: 'You surely must all of you feel and admit the delightfulness of a bow-window; I can hardly fancy a room can be perfect without one'.[13]

In the course of his discussion of the lamp of memory in *The Seven Lamps of Architecture* (1849), Ruskin attempted, like Price before him, to define the term 'picturesque': 'It is of some importance to our general purpose', he explained, 'to determine the true meaning of this expression, as it is now generally used . . . Probably no word in the language, (exclusive of theological expressions,) has been the subject of so frequent or so prolonged dispute; yet none more vague in their acceptance'. Ruskin's solution was to coin the unattractive phrase, 'Parasitical Sublimity', by which he meant 'a sublimity dependent on the accidents, or on the least essential characters, of the objects to which it belongs'. He claimed that 'whatever characters of line or shade or expression are productive of sublimity, will become productive of picturesqueness . . . [e.g.] angular and broken lines, vigorous oppositions of light and shadow, and grave, deep, or boldly contrasted colour; and all these are in a still higher degree effective, when, by resemblance or association, they remind us of objects on which a true and essential sublimity exists, as of rocks or mountains, or stormy clouds or waves'.[14]

Ruskin was acutely conscious of the difficulty of achieving the true Picturesque in architecture. 'It so happens', he explained, 'that in architecture, the superinduced and accidental beauty is most commonly inconsistent with the preservation of original character, and the picturesque is therefore sought in ruin, and supposed to consist in decay'. However, he believed that inasmuch as 'it can be rendered consistent with the inherent character, the picturesque or extraneous sublimity of architecture has just this of nobler function in it than that of any other object whatsoever, that it is an exponent of age'. From this awareness springs Ruskin's remarkable conviction that 'a building cannot be considered as in its prime until four or five centuries have passed over it; and that the entire choice and arrangement of its details should have reference to their appearance after that period'.[15]

Even more striking, in some ways, is his conclusion in the last volume (1853) of *The Stones of Venice* that the work of his beloved Turner is just a substitute for the picturesque architecture which came to an end with the victory of the Renaissance over the Gothic:

The picturesque school of art rose up to address those capacities of enjoyment for which, in sculpture, architecture, or the higher walks of painting, there was employment no more; and the shadows of Rembrandt, and savageness of Salvator, arrested the admiration which was no longer permitted to be rendered to the gloom or the grotesqueness of the Gothic aisle. And thus the English school of landscape, culminating in Turner, is in reality nothing else than a healthy effort to fill the void which the destruction of Gothic architecture has left.

Ruskin did not, of course, find this state of affairs satisfactory: 'the void cannot thus be completely filled . . . The art of landscape-painting will never become thoroughly interesting or sufficing to the minds of men engaged in active life, or concerned principally with practical subjects'. Architecture alone, he believed, could fill that vital role, and he looked forward at the end of *The Stones of Venice* 'to the revival of a healthy school of architecture in England'.[16]

Thus, at the moment in the nineteenth century when one might suppose that the Picturesque would be on the way to becoming a spent force, it was given quickened impetus between the 1830s and 1850s by the most widely-read author of the day on art and architecture. Ruskin emphatically endorsed the importance

of relating buildings closely to their natural setting; he emphasised as a building type the vernacular tradition of the country cottage with its steep roofs and bay windows; and, interpreting architecture as 'an exponent of age', he wanted to be able to read the history of a building in its changed forms and weathered surfaces. Finally, he was influential as a writer concerned with painting – especially Turner – who then transferred this painterly vision to architecture, where he called for a new way of building that would rival the picturesque qualities of Turner's landscape paintings. Although Ruskin himself undoubtedly envisaged this new architectural awakening in terms of the Gothic Revival, his sentiments were echoed by architects like George Devey (1820–86) and Richard Norman Shaw (1831–1912) who came to be associated especially with the Domestic Revival. Ruskin would surely have approved of Devey's training which included apprenticeship to the great watercolourist John Sell Cotman (1782–1842) and also a period under J. D. Harding, a lithographer who specialised in views of old manor houses and picturesquely decayed cottages. By 1850 Devey was translating such images into reality in the form of a group of cottages by the churchyard at Penshurst which he designed sensitively in the Kentish vernacular tradition. At Betteshanger, also in Kent, he built a rambling house in 1856–61 and 1882 for Sir Walter James (later 1st Lord Northbourne) who, like Devey himself, had studied under J. D. Harding. Betteshanger could have been designed to demonstrate Ruskin's view of architecture as 'an exponent of age', since it is contrived to give

Betteshanger, Kent, 1856–61 and 1882, by George Devey for Sir Walter James, Bt., 1st Lord Northbourne from 1885. A modest neo-Tudor villa of the 1820s by R. Lugar, on the right in this view, was aggrandised and completely rebuilt by Devey over a period of twenty-six years in local vernacular styles and materials intended to bind the house into its setting and to suggest growth during several centuries. On the left is Devey's tower and a new wing of 1856–8 with, peeping above the latter, the attractive cupola of the Ellison tower which he added at the end of the north-east entrance front in 1882. The house continued to grow after Devey's death, a stable-court, dining hall and studio being added in the 1890s for the 2nd Lord Northbourne.

the impression of a late mediaeval house with various additions and alterations in the seventeenth and eighteenth centuries. The composition as well as the blend of styles is picturesque. A main block is linked to a lower wing ending in a tower, a form which became a favourite of Devey's in later houses. Another plan he particularly liked was the bent form with a wing sticking out at an obtuse angle, derived from Wyatville and Thomas Hope and subsequently developed by Shaw in the 1870s. An early Devey house with this plan is Coombe Warren, Surrey (*c*.1865). At Betteshanger and at St. Alban's Court, Kent, of 1875–8, Devey used stone in some of the lower parts of the exterior walls, which he separated by a ragged line from the upper parts of brick, thereby implying the re-use of an earlier house on the site. It must, however, be confessed that in execution the rather aggressive colour and texture of the building materials tend to militate against this impression.

More brilliant and even more prolific than Devey was Richard Norman Shaw, whose early ambitions we can interpret as an attempt to unite Pugin and the Picturesque. A pupil of William Burn from 1849–54, he attended Pugin's funeral at Ramsgate in 1852, aged twenty-one, with the young architect William Eden Nesfield. He and Nesfield were both working in Salvin's office in 1856–8, but by 1859 Shaw had become the principal assistant of the strident Ruskinian leader of the Gothic Revival, the High Church architect George Edmund Street (1824–81). In 1862 Shaw was sketching Devey's work at Penshurst. Early in the following year he and Nesfield set up office together, and in 1866–8 he designed his first two major houses, both in East Sussex: Glen Andred, for the Royal Academician E. W. Cooke, marine painter and former draughtsman to A. C. Pugin, and Leyswood, for Shaw's cousin, James Temple of the Shaw Savill shipping line. Leyswood, now largely demolished, was a flamboyant *tour de force* in the 'Old English' manorial style. It is a fantasy of high chimneys, sweeping tiled roofs, long bands of mullioned windows contrasting with steeply-arched Gothic doorways, freely grouped round a courtyard and approached dramatically through a tall gate-tower. If the tower owed something to the city gateways of Nuremberg, which Shaw had visited in 1856 and published in his *Architectural Sketches from the Continent* (1858), the manorial garth looked back to the type of mediaeval house which had been illustrated in Joseph Nash's *Mansions of England in the Olden Time* like Ightham Mote, Kent, and Haddon Hall, Derbyshire. Nesfield's stable tower and yard at Cloverley Hall, Shropshire, of 1864 must also be considered as a likely influence on Leyswood. Shaw exhibited two clever pen-and-ink perspective drawings of Leyswood at the Royal Academy in 1870. These set the pattern for the dramatic high- and low-level bird's-eye views which he was to exhibit for over a decade. Essentially scenic views, they can surely be interpreted only in terms of a revitalisation of the Picturesque tradition.

At houses such as Grims Dyke, Harrow Weald (1870–2), for Frederick Goodall, R.A., and Merrist Wood, Surrey (1875–7), Shaw adopted the 'offset' plan, with one wing picturesquely canted in the manner inherited from Wyatville and Devey. Grims Dyke is one of Shaw's most picturesque compositions. Its agglutinative plan was, surprisingly, admired by Viollet-le-Duc in 1875 because it suggested that the building had grown with time.[17] The variety and intricacy, to borrow Price's terms, continued indoors with a 'split-level' plan and a staircase drifting through the house so as to create an extended spatial entertainment.

Key:
1 Bedroom
2 Dressing-room
3 Bathroom
4 Studio
5 Breakfast room
6 Drawing-room
7 Hall
8 Dining-room
9 Butler's pantry
10 Store
11 Servants' hall
12 Kitchen
13 Yard

FIRST FLOOR

GROUND FLOOR

Feet 10 0 10 20 30
Metres 3 0 3 6 9

(*Above*) Leyswood, East Sussex, 1866–9, by Richard Norman Shaw for James Temple (largely demolished 1955 save for the entrance tower). Set high on a rocky outcrop Leyswood is an early work, but one in which Shaw's 'Old English' domestic style is already mature. The dynamics of its composition are captivatingly displayed in this bird's-eye drawing by Shaw which he exhibited at the Royal Academy in 1870.

(*Left*) Grims Dyke, Harrow Weald, London, 1870–2, by Richard Norman Shaw for F. Goodall, R.A. First-floor and ground-floor plans. Grims Dyke has been described as a split-level house with one wing starting from the half-landing stage. This carefully contrived complexity in plan and elevation was designed for a painter whose lofty studio, with its north-south lighting, is marked '4' on the plan.

Sir William (later 1st Lord) Armstrong (1810–1900), the Northumbrian inventor, hydraulics engineer and armaments manufacturer who commissioned Shaw to extend his Northumbrian shooting lodge at Cragside, Rothbury, in 1869, was a collector of paintings by Cooke, Shaw's patron at Glen Andred. We know that in 1867, when Glen Andred was rising, Shaw and Cooke heard Ruskin lecture, and the climax of the phase in Shaw's career, which we might describe as 'Ruskinian Picturesque', came with the gradual development of Cragside between 1869 and 1885. The end product of this additive process is perhaps the most pictorially conceived house in England, both in elevation and plan. In his masterly biography of Shaw, Andrew Saint describes the picturesque, processional way nearly 175 feet in length, along which the visitor must pass from the drawing-room to the dining-room via the picture gallery, down no less than six flights of stairs and along a narrow corridor which forms the spine of the original lodge.

In his interiors Shaw manipulated space in an increasingly complex way, using concealed iron girders to liberate planning and create new experiences in domestic architecture. Stairs could thus arrive at very different points on the plan from that implied by their starting places, and corridors could run across halls below them. Reception rooms of contrasting heights and positions involved a subtle interlocking of floor levels which Shaw exploited to achieve a dramatic spatial play unequalled till the work of Lutyens. Shaw developed this technique particularly effectively behind the comparatively sober façades of his town houses, such as 185, Queen's Gate of 1889–91.

Little Moreton Hall, a rambling Tudor manor house in Cheshire, had an irresistible appeal for the Victorians as a source for half-timbering carried to excess. It was the model for Grayson and Ould's superbly detailed Bidston Court, Cheshire, built round three sides of an open irregular court in 1891–2 for the soap manufacturer Robert Hudson. As early as 1894 the *British Architect* could write: 'what must strike everyone who sees Bidston Court is the extraordinary appearance of age which it has managed to put on in its short life of two years'.[18] Ould himself stated that 'No style of building will harmonise so quickly and so completely with its surroundings', and in perverse fulfilment of this claim the house was dismantled and re-erected in 1929–31 as Hill Bark, Frankby, a few miles south of its original site.

In Shaw's country houses the half-timbering was always decorative not functional, and was often fastened to a brick wall, to a separate load-bearing timber frame, or even to iron girders. He was well aware of the fictive picturesque game he was playing, as we can see from a letter he wrote to Sedding in 1882 in which he referred to his suspicion '1st that old work is *real* and 2nd that ours is not real, but only like real'.[19] In fact, he had come to feel that his neo-vernacular architecture was a fake, and so he turned to the classical tradition for reality. In the meantime, he had remodelled Flete, Devon, in 1877–87 for the banker H. B. Mildmay, the richest of all his clients. Shaw was obliged to incorporate much of the original structure and planning of Flete, for it was a mediaeval house extensively remodelled in successive centuries and especially in 1835. He was even more hampered than he had been at Cragside and the result, though determinedly picturesque, is less successful. He made characteristically skilful use of the sloping site by exploiting the change of levels with flights of stairs, particularly in the long

gallery. Outside, though the powerful asymmetry may lack final coherence, the long north-west service wing is an especially happy souvenir of the gallery wing at Haddon Hall.

It is impossible to look at Flete without thinking of Lutyen's more sophisticated solution of a similar problem at Castle Drogo (1911 onwards), also in South Devon. Lutyens was the last and perhaps the greatest exponent of the Picturesque. Whether he would have immediately recognised himself in that description is unclear, but there can be no doubt that his sensitivity to local materials, his love of irregular massing, and his concern to relate the plan and the form of a house to its setting both natural and man-made, were deeply part of everything we have described as picturesque. He and his mentor or 'fairy godmother', Gertrude Jekyll, were also profoundly coloured by the ever-increasing nostalgia for old country ways and rural crafts which came to a climax with the foundation of the National Trust for Places of Historic Interest or Natural Beauty in 1893 and of *Country Life* four years later. The borders of Surrey, Sussex and Hampshire were suddenly found to have preserved in their quiet lanes a rich assembly of cottages in varied local materials, together with a range of associated country crafts. Watercolourists like Myles Birkett Foster (1825–99) who settled in Surrey in 1863, and Mrs William Allingham (1848–1926) produced landscape and rustic scenes dotted with picturesque gabled cottages and farmhouses which were much admired by Ruskin. The work

Flete, Devon, 1877-87, by Richard Norman Shaw for H. B. Mildmay. On the left is the north-west service-wing inspired by the Jacobean Long Gallery wing at Haddon Hall with, reading from left to right, the huge window lighting the scullery, then the kitchen window followed by the semi-circular oriel of the dining-room. The lower gables on the right belong to the original mansion which, not entirely felicitously, Shaw incorporated into a composition in which the Picturesque seems to be getting out of hand.

of Mrs Allingham and Kate Greenaway (1846–1901) is mentioned at the head of Ruskin's lecture on 'Fairy Land', while Randolph Caldecott (1846–86), who worked in a similar vein, used to visit Lutyens's parents at Thursley in Surrey. Indeed Lutyens claimed that it was Caldecott's drawings that had first directed his attention to architecture. Certainly Lutyens's chief pastime as a boy was travelling on foot and by bicycle round the villages of his native Surrey sketching the cottages and their many-textured materials: ironstone, brick, Bargate stone, cob, thatch, tile, brick-nogging and half-timbering. In 1885, at the age of sixteen, he went to the South Kensington School of Art to study architecture, and towards the end of the following year entered the office of Ernest George and Peto. In the design of houses like Rousden and Stoodleigh Court, both in Devon, Batsford Park, Gloucestershire, and Motcombe House, Dorset, Ernest George (1839–1922) had shown himself as perhaps the most talented and prolific populariser of the Nesfield–Shaw style. Thus the magic of Shaw's pictorial genius was transmitted direct to the young Lutyens, whose subsequent career shows that he never forgot these lessons.

Lutyens's first significant commission, which came in 1889, was for a modest house at Crooksbury near Farnham in Surrey for Mr (later Sir) Arthur Chapman. In 1890 Lutyens described his not very able exercise in the Shaw or Ernest George manner as 'built of red brick with old tiles on the roof and for the tile hanging . . . planned following the natural levels of the site'.[20] In an appropriately picturesque way Lutyens was twice invited to extend and remodel his house in 1898 and again, by a new owner, in 1914. It was through Mrs Robert Webb, who had almost played the role of a second mother to Lutyens as a boy, that he first met Arthur Chapman. More importantly, Chapman was a friend of Gertrude Jekyll (1843–1932) whom he introduced to Lutyens, so helping to create a partnership which was to transform Lutyens's career. In 1895 Miss Jekyll invited Lutyens to build her dream-house at Munstead Wood, Surrey, in the woodland garden she had been creating amongst the ferns and silver birches from the early 1880s. Large, mannish, appallingly short-sighted and surrounded by cats, Miss Jekyll was a familiar type of English gentlewoman. She was also, in Christopher Hussey's words 'Perhaps the greatest *artist* in horticulture and garden-planting that England has produced . . . one whose influence on garden design has been as widespread as Capability Brown's in the eighteenth century'.[21]

Gertrude Jekyll, with William Robinson (1838–1919), led the English away from the various Early Victorian kinds of formality and 'artificiality' in garden design and, above all, from the practice of 'carpet-bedding' or 'bedding-out' – a technique relying on the temporary placing of greenhouse plants out of doors in the spring and summer months. They replaced all this with woodland gardens, 'wild' gardens, cottage gardens, flower gardens, fruit gardens, rock gardens and, especially, herbaceous borders, combined to create an atmosphere of sweet simplicity and indigenous 'Englishry'. How far can this approach be described as picturesque? Both Miss Jekyll and William Robinson were profoundly influenced by Ruskin, while she was also a passionate admirer of Turner. If we read the two books in which she lovingly traced the results of her collaboration with Lutyens at Munstead Wood, *Wood and Garden* (1899) and *Home and Garden* (1900), it becomes increasingly clear that her approach would have been impossible without the visual expectations which had been established during well over a century of

Munstead Wood, Surrey, 1895–97, by Edwin Lutyens for Gertrude Jekyll. Miss Jekyll was consulted on the design of about 350 gardens, over 100 of them in collaboration with Lutyens. Her Surrey home, viewed here from its woodland garden, represents the perfect convergence of picturesque and Arts and Crafts ideals. It was constructed of local bargate stone, brick, tiles and oak. The oak beams were coated for fifteen minutes with hot lime which was then scraped off to produce an effect of surfaces silvered with antiquity.

picturesque theory and practice. She thus writes, as Price himself might have done, 'Planting ground is painting a landscape with living things; and as I hold that good gardening takes rank within the bounds of the fine arts, so I hold that to plant well needs an artist of no mean capacity'. Thanks to the influence of Ruskin and the Arts and Crafts movement, the intimate relationship between a house and its setting, which was so central to picturesque practice, had become charged with a kind of moral urgency. House and setting were no longer to be merely pictorially related to each other, but the house was to have deep roots in the English soil, both physically and emotionally.

Miss Jekyll conveys the intense poetry of this new dimension to picturesque taste when she writes in her painterly romantic way about the house Lutyens had built for her at Munstead Wood:

there is the actual living interest of knowing where the trees one's house is built of really grew. The three great beams, ten inches square, that stretch across the ceiling of the sitting-room, and do other work besides, and bear up a good part of the bedroom space above (they are twenty-eight feet long), were growing fifteen years ago a mile and a half away, on the outer edge of a fir wood just above a hazel-fringed hollow lane, whose steep and sandy sides, here and there level enough to bear a patch of vegetation, grew tall Bracken and great Foxgloves, and the finest wild Canterbury Bells I ever saw . . . Often driving up the lane from early childhood I used to see these great grey trees, in twilight looming almost ghostly against the darkly-mysterious background of the sombre firs . . . . I am glad to know that my beams are these same old friends, and that the pleasure I had in

(*Above*) Orchards, Surrey, 1898-9, by
Sir Edwin Lutyens for Sir William
Chance. A subtle kind of instant history
is achieved in this rambling vernacular
house, sophisticatedly composed round
a courtyard like Shaw's Leyswood.
Local Bargate stone, oak and tiles create
the impression of an old Surrey manor
farmhouse, though what appears to be
the oriel of the great hall on the right of
the entrance archway is, in fact, Lady
Chance's studio.

(*Right*) Orchards. Ground-floor plan.

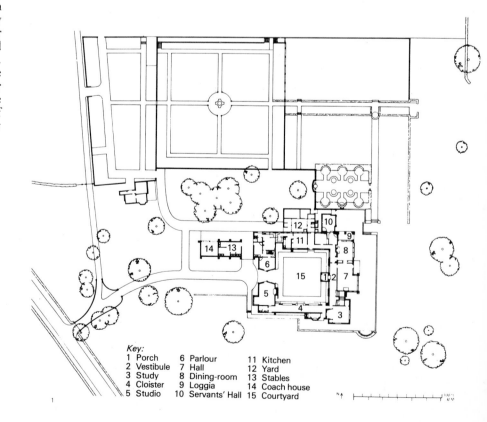

Key:
1 Porch	6 Parlour	11 Kitchen
2 Vestibule	7 Hall	12 Yard
3 Study	8 Dining-room	13 Stables
4 Cloister	9 Loggia	14 Coach house
5 Studio	10 Servants' Hall	15 Courtyard

watching them green and growing is not destroyed but only changed as I see them stretching above me as grand beams of solid English oak.[22]

The walls of Munstead Wood were, of course, also built of local materials, and in her eulogy of them Miss Jekyll unexpectedly but perceptively uses the work of the architect George Dance (1741–1825) to illustrate one of the principal tenets of picturesque theory:

The architect [of Munstead Wood] has a thorough knowledge of the local ways of using the sandstone that grows in our hills, and that for many centuries has been the building material of the district, and of all the lesser incidental methods of adapting means to ends that mark the well-defined way of building of the country, so that what he builds seems to grow naturally out of the ground. I always think it a pity to use in any one place the distinctive methods of another . . . For I hold as a convincing canon in architecture that every building should look like what it is. How well that fine old architect George Dance understood this when he designed the prison of Newgate![23]

To lead the 'simple life' it was necessary, in fact, to be extremely well off. Within two years of Gertrude Jekyll's death, Lutyens was complaining in a letter to his wife that without the eleven gardeners who were 'essential' at Munstead Wood, the gardens had already 'collapsed'.[24] By 1900 Munstead Wood had become a second home to Lutyens in which he designed many of his most important early houses. The friendship with Miss Jekyll survived until her death in 1932, by which time she had collaborated with him on the design of most of his gardens: Deanery Garden, Hestercombe and Lambay being amongst the most successful combinations of his genius for large architectural composition and her sense of appropriate detail and colour. For Sir William and Lady Chance, who had admired Munstead Wood, he built Orchards in 1898–9 only a mile or so away. Here Lutyens played the picturesque game of grouping the house round a courtyard, though as always with his own exquisitely controlled spatial ingenuity. As Hussey observed, 'Orchards is essentially a symphony of local materials, conducted by an artist, for artists'.[25]

An even more sophisticated exercise on similar themes was Deanery Garden, Berkshire (1897) for Edward Hudson (1854–1936) who founded *Country Life* in the same year. It would be impossible to exaggerate the influence of this journal in propagating through beautifully illustrated articles the work of Lutyens and Miss Jekyll, and in giving renewed impetus to attitudes which had originally been part of the Georgian Picturesque movement. These attitudes included a sensitivity to natural scenery and to the apparently natural English countryside, and the consequent ambition to learn how to design buildings which would fit harmoniously and 'naturally' into their setting. In his *History of Gothic Art in England* (1900) and *The Cathedral Builders in England* (1905), the Arts and Crafts architect E. S. Prior (1852–1932) could argue that not only was English mediaeval architecture 'picturesque' but that we find 'reflected therein the qualities of English landscape'.[26]

In 1902 Hudson sold Deanery Garden and purchased the ruins of a small sixteenth-century fort on Lindisfarne, the incomparably romantic Holy Island which had been the heart of the Northumbrian Christianity established by St. Aidan in the seventh century. Treating it as a painter would, Lutyens created a piece of solid scenery beautifully defined by a series of winding passages and stairs hewn out of the rock. He was fortunate enough to receive from the Hon. Cecil

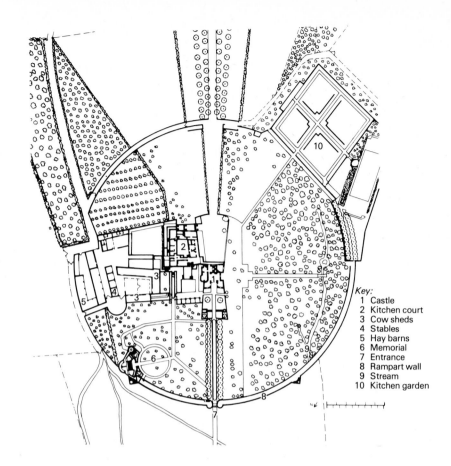

Lambay Castle, County Dublin, 1905-20, by Sir Edwin Lutyens for the Hon. C. Baring, Lord Revelstoke. At the heart of the plan lies the sixteenth-century fort which Lutyens restored and reconstructed. Sprouting from its top left-hand corner is the kitchen court which Lutyens half-sunk into the sloping ground so as not to dominate the old house. Lambay was conceived as a self-contained earthly paradise in which the house, gardens, farm-buildings and plantations are united by a symbolic circular wall, 700 feet in diameter.

Key:
1 Castle
2 Kitchen court
3 Cow sheds
4 Stables
5 Hay barns
6 Memorial
7 Entrance
8 Rampart wall
9 Stream
10 Kitchen garden

Baring (1864-1934), later 3rd Lord Revelstoke, a similar commission to remodel an island fortress at Lambay off the coast of Co. Dublin in 1905. Here, thanks to a family banking fortune, the picturesque Arcadian dream which had haunted the English imagination for two hundred years found one of its loveliest and strangest realisations. Whilst work on the castle was proceeding Cecil Baring and his young French wife moved to a shepherd's cottage higher up the hill where, since he had taught her to read Greek, they read Homer to each other to the accompaniment of gulls and guillemots, looking out across the Irish Sea to the distant Wicklow Mountains.

Sealed off by a wall and rampart, entirely circular in plan, the core of Lambay Castle is the modest harled house with crow-stepped gables, fifteenth-century in origin, which Lutyens repaired and extended. He added a four-sided office courtyard built of the island stone, a blue-green porphyry shot with feldspar crystals, to the east side. This courtyard deliberately resembles farm-buildings in appearance, and is partly sunk into the hillside so as not to dominate the house itself. Thus on one side the pantiled roofs come down almost to ground level, a device curiously recalling Thomas Hope's office wing at The Deepdene. Indeed The Deepdene is recalled by the whole play of shifting levels, terraces and steps so that, as Lutyens's pupil A. S. G. Butler wrote of Lambay:

Probably there is no other domestic work by him in which the house and its setting are so closely united. On a fine day in summer the difference between being in or out-of-doors can be hardly noticeable. Stone landings and terraces merge into one another. Garden steps and staircases in the house perform a mutual function in much the same material; and small neat lawns are kept mown in walled enclosures like rugs in rooms.[27]

(*Above*) Castle Drogo, Devon, 1911-30, by Sir Edwin Lutyens for Julius Drewe. The last of the fairy-tale re-creations of mediaeval castles. Lutyens originally designed a building three times the size. Built throughout of solid local granite, which has given rise to considerable problems of water penetration, Drogo blends harmoniously but magnificently into its setting above the gorge of the river Teign.

(*Left*) Castle Drogo. Private Staircase. This is at the point of junction between the two-storeyed south wing containing the principal reception rooms, and the three-storeyed north wing containing the family and servants' rooms. Lutyens dramatically exploits the shift in axis between the two wings as well as the contrast in floor levels. The grim stone-domed staircase has always been praised for recalling the mood of Piranesi's *Carceri* engravings.

The third and last in the sequence of Lutyens's picturesque castles is Castle Drogo, Devon, commissioned in 1910 by Julius Drewe, founder and chairman of the Home and Colonial Stores. The huge, irregular pile of local granite, which grew gradually during the next twenty years, is an unresolved fragment representing only about a third of the original scheme on which work was begun in 1911. Its curiously truncated and not immediately comprehensible form is suggestive of the dramatic changes of fortune in distant times to which castles are especially prone, and which always appealed to the picturesque mentality. The castle stands magnificently on the edge of a promontory above a ravine, so that the principal reception rooms are on a lower level than the main forecourt entrance. By means of dramatic staircases and galleries Lutyens naturally exploited these changing levels with all the variety and intricacy of which he was master.

Lutyens fully shared the picturesque pleasure at seeing the representation of growth and change in a building: for example, in his work at Ashby St. Ledgers, Lambay and Clifford Manor. He also particularly enjoyed making additions in different styles to buildings he had constructed earlier in his career, as at Crooksbury and Folly Farm. A special and markedly influential case is represented by his work of 1910 at Great Dixter, East Sussex, which was built for Nathanial Lloyd. Lloyd, incidentally, later published an impressive monograph on the *History of English Brickwork* with a foreword by Lutyens. At Great Dixter, Lutyens restored a magnificent but neglected timber-framed manorial hall of the fifteenth century on to which he added a similar, but slightly more modest, hall house of similar date brought by Lloyd from Benenden in Kent. Lutyens linked the two in a masterly way with a substantial modern wing, which is subtly designed yet unobtrusive in effect. Since the ground sloped to the south, the house brought from Benenden had to be raised on a considerable brick substructure, allowing Lutyens to create one of his characteristic gardens with a fine play of terraces and stairs. All the other farm-buildings were retained and restored, though they now found new uses dedicated not to labour but to pleasure: the cattle-hovel became a garden shelter; another hovel the fruit house; a thatched hovel in the former ox-yard became the children's playhouse; while the great thatched barn became a garage and electricity generating station. The element of scene painting in this whole process at Great Dixter is especially striking. Moreover, the pictorial approach to architecture encouraged by the Picturesque had by now made it possible for buildings to be seen as stage scenery to be moved about the country at will.

Lutyens, the most consistently brilliant architect at work between the 1890s and the 1930s, had many gifted contemporaries and followers who helped maintain the tradition of domestic architecture related to its setting which, as we have seen, reached back through Shaw, Salvin and Nash to the Georgian Picturesque. The 1850s and 1860s saw the birth of an astonishing number of exceptionally sensitive domestic architects whose work, viewed collectively rather than individually, can in some ways be seen as the climax of the whole Picturesque movement: Ernest Newton, Sir Mervyn Macartney, H. Thackeray Turner, E. S. Prior, Sir Guy Dawber, Sir Robert Lorimer, H. M. Baillie Scott, Ernest Gimson, Detmar Blow, Ernest Barnsley, C. R. Ashbee, Gerald Horsley, C. E. Mallows, George Crawley, and many others. One of the most influential and prolific was Ernest Newton (1856–1922), a pupil of Norman Shaw and a founder member of the Art Workers' Guild. One of his most attractive buildings is Oldcastle at Dallington in East Sussex, where in 1910 he imaginatively enlarged a modest cottage into a courtyard house for the distinguished judge Sir Henry Buckley (1845–1935), later 1st Lord Wrenbury. Buckley was a man of some visual discernment who also owned a house in Melbury Road, Kensington, the grandest artists' quarter in London. Like Devey, only more sympathetically, Newton used irregular courses of local stone in the lower parts of Oldcastle, brick and tile hanging in the upper parts. The result bears out well his son's observation that though his work 'is less exciting and dramatic very often than is the work of Shaw or Lutyens, you will less often say, on seeing one, "This is a Newton house"; but perhaps more often, "This is the house for this position"'.[28]

Towards the end of the nineteenth century the Cotswolds were rediscovered as the perfect expression of that harmony between building and setting that was supposedly based on those unselfconscious traditions of rural craftsmanship long applauded by Ruskin and Morris. In 1902 C. R. Ashbee (1863–1942) moved his Guild of Handicraft and 150 of its members from the East End of London to Chipping Camden, and eight years earlier Ernest Gimson (1864–1920) and the two Barnsley brothers had moved to Pinbury Park, Gloucestershire. They established a craftsworkshop both here and at Daneway House, Sapperton, nearby. Dawber, Lutyens, Ashbee, Blow, J. L. Ball, Oswald Milne, Gimson and Ernest Barnsley all designed houses and cottages in the Cotswolds, often producing work virtually indistinguishable from original vernacular buildings. Perhaps the finest of these was Rodmarton Manor, near the Wiltshire border of Gloucestershire, built by Ernest Barnsley (1863–1926) in 1909–26 for the Hon. Claud Biddulph, a banker and landowner. The entrance front is flanked by asymmetrical canted wings, a disposition which goes back to Wyatville, while in true Arts and Crafts fashion the stone was quarried from the estate. In fact, the place swiftly became a centre for the revival of vanishing Cotswold crafts.

Ernest Gimson, a passionate admirer of William Morris, was closely involved in the design of furniture and fittings for Rodmarton. With the help of Detmar Blow (1867–1939) he had already built five cottages between 1897 and 1908 near Markwood on the edge of Charnwood Forest in Leicestershire, mostly for members of his own family. The most interesting of them is probably Stoneywell Cottage built in 1898–9 for Sydney Gimson. It is placed on a rising outcrop of the local rock which determined its Z-shaped plan and largely replaced conventional foundations. The massive chimney merges imperceptibly into the rocks already existing on the site, while thatched roofs hug the immensely thick walls also built of the local stone. It unites themes from Nash's Blaise Hamlet and from Ruskin's emotional attachment to the symbolism of roof and chimney as expressed in his Edinburgh lectures of 1853. Indeed, to Sir Lawrence Weaver, describing it in *Small Country Houses of Today* (1919), it explicitly recalled Sir Joshua Reynolds's views on the role of association of ideas in architecture, painting and poetry. In 1915 Gimson built a pair of estate cottages for William Morris's daughter May at Kelmscott, Oxfordshire. They fit perfectly and unobtrusively into the rural scene to which Morris had retired in 1871.

Surrey, as we have already seen in the context of Shaw, Lutyens and Miss Jekyll, was also rediscovered in the later nineteenth century as a picturesque rural retreat. Whereas the Cotswolds were additionally attractive for their excellent

Stoneywell Cottage, Leicestershire, 1898-9, by Ernest Gimson for S. Gimson, drawn by F. L. Griggs. A late realisation of the picturesque dream of architecture growing out of the soil. Griggs claimed rather naively that 'All his work, indeed, through being done simply and without any pretence of stylism, became like old work itself'.

sporting facilities, Surrey was handy for London. Close in spirit to Gimson's Leicestershire cottages is Long Copse at Ewhurst, Surrey, built in 1897 by the mysterious Alfred Powell of the Art Workers' Guild for Mrs Mudie-Cook. With its Gimson woodwork inside, its complete absence of paper and paint, and its curious bent plan, it is a primitive idyll of yellow local sandstone, roofed partly with thatch and partly with Horsham stone tiles. To the painter G. F. Watts it was simply the most beautiful building in Surrey, while Weaver wrote of it: 'There is a tenderness about the way the moss and willow weed grow on this stone roof, that seems Nature's benediction of the use of local things . . . Long Copse does not give the feeling of having been devised. It seems rather to have happened'.[29] Mrs Mudie-Cook was not, of course, quite the rustic cottage-woman that her setting was intended to suggest, and the simple life she pursued was made a good deal more comfortable by her servants who were carefully though picturesquely concealed in a thatched cottage nearby. The little village of Ewhurst, incidentally, is remarkable in having in its immediate neighbourhood examples of picturesque domestic architecture between the 1880s and the 1920s by half a dozen architects of quality, as well as some gardens by Gertrude Jekyll. Here, for example, are Woolpit of 1885 by Ernest George and Peto; Coneyhurst of 1886 by Philip Webb, one of his best houses, subtly related in plan and elevation to its sloping site; Long

Copse by Powell; Hurtwood of 1910 by Arthur Bolton, an unusual Tuscan villa with an asymmetrically placed tower like The Deepdene; Lukyns of 1911 by Ernest Newton; and Maryland of 1929 by Oliver Hill, a kind of Lutyens-cum-Spanish-Colonial-Style dream house with green pantiles and yellow sandstone walls.

The Great War curtailed, but by no means ended, the realisation of the romantic dreams of men like Julius Drewe at Castle Drogo, William Waldorf Astor at Hever Castle, Edward Hudson at Lindisfarne Castle, and the architects, craftsmen and gardeners who served them. George Abraham Crawley (1864–1926) is a forgotten figure from this luxurious world which somehow just survived into the 'twenties. After Eton and Trinity College, Cambridge, he idled his time agreeably away in bric-à-brac shops acquiring a smattering of architectural knowledge. Following his marriage to May Brotherhood he acquired the lease of Crowhurst Place, Surrey, in about 1907, a modest and decayed timber-frame tile-hung hall house of the early fifteenth century surrounded by a moat. It amused him to pick up friends in London and take them back to Crowhurst in a taxi. He began to restore it but was able to do so on a truly

Crowhurst Place, Surrey, by George Crawley for himself in *c.* 1907 and for Consuelo, Duchess of Marlborough, in 1912 and 1918-19. A yeoman's hall-house of the 1420s lies buried beneath the romantic twentieth-century accretions. The result is a picturesque illusion, neither mediaeval nor modern.

157

fantastic scale from *c*.1912 when he transferred the lease to the Duchess of Marlborough, the former Consuelo Vanderbilt, whose stormy marriage had ended in 1906. Crawley transformed the house and its setting for her in 1912 and 1918–9 with additional wings, oriels, carved chimneys, an unbelievable wealth of half-timbering, circular dovecot, barns, gatehouse, water-garden, pergolas and bridges: the fifteenth century seen through rose-tinted spectacles. As the Duchess herself said: 'it had the charm of an engraving. It was, I thought, a dream come true . . . Coming down from London after a long week's work I would find a tea-table laden with scones, cakes and jams, and when my maid, Hatherly, brought in the golden tea and the fire flared in welcoming spirals I could, in a deep contentment, forget the worries of committees. And how lovely to wake to the smell of honeysuckle and roses and to doze to the lap of waters, while swans sailed their rounds . . . I used often to sit in the herb garden where the splash of the fountain tinkling near-by and the lowing of the cows in their fields were the only sounds to be heard'.[30] Despite the solemn earnestness of the Modern Movement, this lovely escapist idyll has been one of the most consistent characteristics of twentieth-century domestic architecture, so that no account of the Picturesque would be complete without at least a mention of the richly planted estates of romantic houses for business men and pop stars at places like St George's Hill, Weybridge, and the Wentworth Estate, Virginia Water.

From 1912 until his death George Crawley designed interiors in a range of historical styles for several great liners particularly of the Canadian Pacific Ocean Services. He provided fantasy of a different kind in 1922 when he waved his fairy wand over Old Surrey Hall, a fifteenth-century half-timbered house near the Sussex border of Surrey to which he added two wings so as to turn it into a U-shaped courtyard house. Crawley and his clients at Crowhurst and Old Surrey Hall must presumably have been inspired by Lutyens's transformation of the half-timbered Great Dixter, East Sussex, in 1910. As Ian Nairn observed of Old Surrey Hall, 'The total effect is like a rhapsody on Ightham Mote, and in fact oddly like the rhapsodies of early twentieth-century English composers on Tudor and folksong themes'.[31] The work was carried out for the Hon. Mrs George Napier, widow of the second son of the 1st Lord Napier of Magdala, but in 1937 extensions were made for new owners by Walter Godfrey, who had recently restored Hurstmonceux Castle, East Sussex. He was able to reopen the quarry of local stone which Crawley had used fifteen years earlier, and to acquire the precious Horsham stone slabs for the roof from a recently demolished house in the neighbourhood. He closed the courtyard on the fourth or entrance side with a half-timbered covered way through which motor cars, having crossed the bridge over the moat, could drive up to the front door. Afterwards, the chauffeur would return the motor to a rambling old barn which had been cleverly adapted as a garage and chauffeur's cottage.

This picturesque game of make-believe was widely played between the wars in the form of the often extremely skilful and sympathetic adaptation for modern domestic purposes of countless old cottages, decayed farmhouses and barns. Of the numerous architects who carried out such commissions we might single out in passing the partnership of G. Blair Imrie and T. G. Angell who built, for example, Hammels at Boars Hill, Oxford, in 1921 for Sir Frederick Keeble, Professor of Horticulture at Oxford. Superbly situated on a sloping site, it

Plumpton Place, East Sussex, 1927-8, by Sir Edwin Lutyens for Edward Hudson, proprietor of *Country Life*. This view shows the music room, with its giant corner windows, added by Lutyens at the north-east corner of the existing manor house on the edge of the first of three lakes.

effortlessly incorporated a handsome sixteenth-century barn brought from Burghope in Hertfordshire. A more prestigious and unusual commission came in 1930 from the Hon. Colonel Walter and Lady Evelyn Guinness who created at Bailiffscourt, West Sussex, an irregular quadrangular manor-house surrounded by cottages, gatehouse and chapel, assembled almost entirely from dismantled mediaeval buildings brought from Sussex, Hampshire, Hertfordshire and Somerset. Colonel Guinness, who was Minister of Agriculture, later 1st Lord Moyne and tragically assassinated in Cairo in 1944, used as his architect a craftsman and interior designer from Hitchin called Amyas Phillips. A T-shaped guest-wing was connected with the main house by an underground passage; nearby was a sixteenth-century sandstone and thatched cottage brought from Bignor to be given an unexpected new lease of life as a home for the electricity generating plant. Even the trees at Bailiffscourt are not what they seem but are part of the picturesque game. The estate, close to the sea, was rather bare of trees when Walter Guinness bought it in 1927, so he transported hundreds of oaks and elms, some a quarter of a century old, from Rewell Wood and Dale Park on the Downs.

The result is a totally convincing mediaeval village group. It posed deep moral problems for the topographer Ian Nairn who had been brought up to believe that rejection of the great truths of the Modern Movement was a kind of blasphemy. In the *Buildings of England* volume on *Sussex* (1965) he wrote of Amyas Phillips's 'flair for asymmetrical and eclectic designs', that 'twenty years later it could well have led him into designing some of England's best schools'.[32] The Guinnesses, however, even bought the spirit of mediaeval romance to their immense London town house at 10–11, Grosvenor Place where the dark rooms were lined with rough blackened wood, lit by imitation tallow candles, and were decorated not with flowers but with weeds and grasses. Guests were made to eat off pewter dishes made in his garage by the head chauffeur who had given up driving. In a tiny mediaeval yard contrived outside the dining-room window was a gnarled tree which had been transported there by crane.

Perhaps Lutyens should have the last word for he, of course, played this game more sensibly and more beautifully. At Plumpton Place, East Sussex, in 1927–8 he produced one of his loveliest compositions for Edward Hudson, for whom he had already provided Deanery Garden and Lindisfarne Castle twenty-five years earlier. At Plumpton, Lutyens enlarged and restored, though not as thoroughly as he would have liked, a derelict, moated, Jacobean manor-house on an island. He also added a gatehouse flanked by weather-boarded cottages, so as to form a three-sided courtyard leading to a timber footbridge over the moat by which the main house is approached. He cleared the chain of three lakes which had silted up, connecting them with ingenious cascades, and remodelled the Mill House at the far end as a residence of almost Quaker simplicity for the seventy-three-year-old Edward Hudson. Hudson lived here in preference to the manor house itself, because, in true picturesque fashion, he could thus look at the scene he had created. Against the sheltering backdrop of the South Downs, the contrived vistas across pools and through bird-haunted thickets made Plumpton one of the last picturesque 'circuit gardens' of which Shenstone's at the Leasowes had been the first, though, as Hussey pointed out, the incidental features were now supplied by colour and flowers rather than by temples and urns.

7

English
Influence Abroad

PATRONS and designers on the
Continent were naturally much intrigued by the picturesque gardens, buildings
and theory which were so characteristic a feature of England from the early
eighteenth century and the different countries of Europe developed their own
brands of what they called the *jardin anglais*, the *englischer Garten*, the *giardino
inglese*, and so on. English impact was especially striking in France since it
conflicted with the rationalist trend of architectural theory which survived from
the late seventeenth into the early twentieth century. The treatises of Perrault
(1673 and 1683), Frémin (1702), Cordemoy (1706) and Laugier (1753), and the
architecture of leading Neo-classicists like Peyre, Soufflot and Gondoin,
celebrated a rationalist approach which replaced unnecessary ornament like the
decorative pilaster with emphasis on the free-standing load-bearing column so as
to create a commanding architecture of shining intellectual coherence and grave
antique sobriety. Even while these buildings were being constructed in the mid-
eighteenth century, the more frivolous and pictorial approach of the English was
already being felt, so that a French translation of Whately's *Observations on
Modern Gardening* of 1770 appeared in 1771, and three years later the financier
Claude-Henri Watelet (1718–86) published his *Essai sur les jardins*. Though
Watelet was much influenced by Whately, his tone is coloured by Rousseau
rather than by Burke and he also felt obliged to criticise what he saw as the obvious
artificiality of some English gardens. He especially emphasised the charms of the
ferme ornée, which he illustrated with reference to the one he had created from
1754 on an island in the Seine near Versailles known as Moulin-Joli. The garden
at Moulin-Joli contained a cow barn and dairy, a restored mill, a menagerie and
Watelet's own modest house designed for him by the painter François Boucher.
There were also numerous poetic and sentimental inscriptions carved on to the
trunks of trees, a device which may possibly have been inspired by Shenstone's
Leasowes.

In 1777 the Marquis de Girardin, friend and last patron of Rousseau, published
his *De la composition des paysages* in which, like Watelet, he adopted a tone hostile
to the artificiality of the *jardin anglo-chinois*. His book was based on his own
celebrated garden at Ermenonville near Paris which he had laid out in a painterly
way with help from J.-M. Morel and Hubert Robert from the 1760s in four parts:
woods, forest, meadow and farm, so as to accord with the use and topography
of the land. Girardin's picturesque approach and his emphasis on the power of
landscape to appeal to the senses and to the soul, is derived from his reading of
Burke, Rousseau and, doubtless, William Shenstone's 'Unconnected Thoughts
on Gardening' (1764). He seems to have visited the Leasowes early in the 1760s,
and his treatise was the only eighteenth-century French treatise on picturesque
gardening to be translated into English: it appeared in 1783 in a translation by D.

Ermenonville, near Paris, laid out by the Marquis de Girardin from 1764–78. The Rousseau Island. Rousseau had lived at Ermenonville at Girardin's invitation and following his death in 1778 the painter Hubert Robert adorned one of the islands with the neo-antique tomb-shrine of the philosopher of the nature-cult. This still survives though Rousseau's remains have been transferred to the Panthéon in Paris. Ermenonville still supports Girardin's claim that 'In a situation of picturesque beauty, where nature unconfined displays all her graces', we can recall 'the scene of man's first happiness . . . and create anew by the hand of taste, an ideal setting, protected by natural ramparts of hills and mountains . . . the last asylum of peace and liberty'.

Malthus as *An Essay on Landscape; or, on the means of improving and embellishing the country round our habitations*. Girardin's treatise was, of course, old-fashioned by the time it was written, for English gardeners such as Capability Brown were designing gardens with purely visual effects in mind and had abandoned the interest in evoking philosophical reflection.

The garden south of the chateau at Ermenonville, dominated by a large irregular lake, was intended to recall an Italian landscape as painted by Claude Lorrain. In the foreground was a cascade and grotto, while the lake contained two poplar-planted islands, one of which contained the celebrated tomb of Rousseau added after his death in 1778 from designs by the painter Hubert Robert. The flatter ground north of the chateau was laid out in a more pastoral and rural fashion with a meandering stream, a rustic mill and ruined tower. The more important southern garden survives today in something like its original form, though shorn of many of its buildings. It is separated from the chateau by one of the main traffic routes leading in to Paris. This somehow serves to emphasize the character of the garden as an artificial plaything and is in contrast to the grand patrician parks of Capability Brown which contrived to eliminate signs of toil and activity from the rural scene. In England at this date the road would probably have been diverted, but at Ermenonville the Marquis de Girardin pulled down the walls separating the chateau and park from the road so as to heighten the animation of the scene. The adjacent village was similarly dressed up to recall the kind of North Italian vernacular architecture in the background of landscape paintings. A sequence of contrived pictorial vistas in the park, heightened by the introduction of artificial rocks, was intended to suggest the works of different

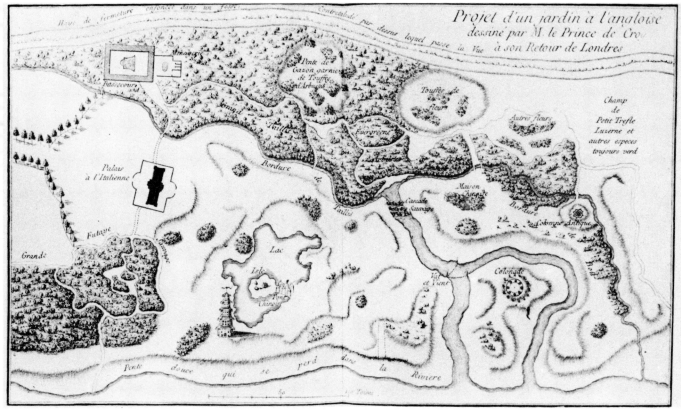

landscape painters such as Hubert Robert, Salvator Rosa and Jacob van Ruysdael. Sentimental, moral and pastoral reflections were aroused by monuments such as the Temple of Modern Philosophy, inspired by the Temple of the Sybil at Tivoli, the Altar of Reverie, and the Hermitage, and by numerous literary references and inscriptions, including a stone inscribed to William Shenstone. The Rustic Temple and the Monuments of Old Loves in the Wilderness were inspired by Clarence, the estate described in Rousseau's *Julie, ou la nouvelle Héloise*. Further essays in Rousseauesque sentiment included a series of primitive huts inspired by Laugier's theories and by Chambers's illustration of Vitruvius's idea of the origins of architecture.

The other type of garden found in eighteenth-century France was the *jardin anglo-chinois*. We have already noted in Chapter 1 how the writings of Jesuit missionaries had helped create a legend of the Chinese garden which was to be adopted and elaborated as a model for irregularity by numerous writers from Temple to Chambers. Especially characteristic of this phase were the English gardens of the 1740s and 1750s as depicted by Thomas Robins. The gardener singled out for praise in French publications of this period is William Kent who was regarded as having introduced the Chinese garden into England. Between 1776 and 1788, G.-L. Le Rouge brought out a series of twenty illustrated *cahiers* devoted to garden design of which half appeared under the title, *Jardins anglo-chinois à la mode*. The first *cahier* contained a plan of Lord Burlington's estate at Chiswick as well as an engraving inscribed, '*Projet d'un jardin à l'angloise dessiné par M.le Prince de Croÿ à son Retour de Londres*'. The Prince's plan crowds into a small space half-rococo elements from English gardens such as Richmond, Kew, Painshill and Stowe.

Plan for an English Garden, by the Prince de Croÿ, published by Le Rouge in 1776. According to the prince's journal for 1774, the Peace of 1763 encouraged the French to start erecting garden buildings. His plan includes numerous English elements such as a pagoda and Chinese house derived from Kew, and an antique column and a circular temple from Stowe.

Stanislaus Leszcynski, exiled King of Poland and father-in-law of Louis XV, had created a series of rococo gardens adorned with entertaining buildings which belonged in part to the sixteenth-century Mannerist tradition of garden artifice, but were yet an influence on some later eighteenth-century French gardens. Stanislaus's gardens at Chanteheux, Jolivet, Einville, Malgrange, Commercy and, most importantly, Lunéville, were designed between 1737 and 1747. At Lunéville the half-Turkish half-Chinese Kiosk of 1737 is one of the earliest exotic buildings in Europe. Five years later Stanislaus added Le Rocher, a weird automated village on the edge of an artificial rock in which picturesquely contrived groups of mechanically operated peasants gratified the exiled monarch's notions of romantic feudalism. In the 1750s, with the help of the architect Emmanuel Héré de Corny, he turned his attention to replanning the town of Nancy. Here, again, rococo and proto-picturesque elements combined to produce a series of visual surprises between the three interlocking and differently-shaped town squares.

Two of the most important early *jardins anglo-chinois* were created in the flat ground on the then outskirts of Paris: Tivoli, completed by 1771 for the financier Charles-Robert Boutin, and the Duc de Chartres's Parc Monceau begun in *c.*1773. Horace Walpole, who visited Tivoli in 1771, wrote witheringly of its small-scale whimsy that Boutin had 'tacked a piece of what he calls an English garden to a set of stone terraces with steps of turf. There are three or four very high hills, almost as high as, and exactly in the shape of, a tansy pudding. You squeeze between these and a river, that is conducted at obtuse angles in a stone channel, and supplied by a pump; and when walnuts come in, I suppose it will be navigable'.[1]

Monceau was one of the most celebrated and influential gardens of its day in France and its appearance can be reconstructed from the illustrated account of it published in 1779 by its designer, Carmontelle, and from L.-V. Thiéry's *Guide des amateurs et des étrangers voyageurs aux environs de Paris* (1788). Carmontelle, a dilettante playwright whose real name was Louis de Carrogis, was opposed both to the spirit of pensive melancholy which he believed English gardens were intended to induce, and also to the recent French emphasis on the supposed charms of rustic life which he felt was false to the fundamentally urban and social character of the French. Thus for his profoundly anglophile patron, the Duc de Chartres (Duc d'Orléans from 1785 and later Philippe Egalité), Carmontelle created a bizarre and lively garden which, though inevitably drawing on English precedent, was nevertheless as Carmontelle put it, 'not a *Jardin Anglois . . .* but precisely what has been said in criticism of it, [an attempt] to reunite in one garden all times and all places'. The garden was in fact a kind of outdoor drawing-room crowded with amusing objects and curiosities juxtaposed so as to act as a constant stimulus to conversation and sociability. Passing through the Chinese entrance gate near which stood a Gothic chemical laboratory, the visitor entered a pavilion lined with mirrors one of which, when pressed, revealed the entry to the *jardin d'hiver* with its waterfall, grotto and artificial trees. Nearby was a rustic farm with vernacular buildings artificially contrived to conceal the exterior walls of the park. The numerous attractions included a Turkish minaret, a Dutch mill, the Wood of the Tombs, the Naumachia, which was a ruined Corinthian peristyle on the edge of a pool, the island of rocks, a Chinese bridge, two Turkish tents, a ruined castle and a circular classical temple of marble now rebuilt on the Ile de la Grande Jatte at

Neuilly. Dora Wiebenson has recently shown that there are numerous French sources for the features and vistas of Monceau in earlier garden buildings, stage designs and engravings inspired by Piranesi, and that the interest in a synthesis of exotic or historical styles may have been stimulated by the Comte de Caylus's *Recueil d'antiquités égyptiennes, étrusques, grecques et romaines* (1752–67) and by Fischer von Erlach's *Entwurff einer historischen Architectur* published in German and French in 1721 and in English in 1730. None the less, Monceau was certainly regarded in eighteenth-century France as an English garden, for example by Alexandre de Laborde in his sumptuous *Description des nouveaux jardins de la France* (1808–15), and was, indeed, often compared with Stowe. In its present state the park is largely the work of Adolphe Alphand in the nineteenth century, though Carmontelle's Naumachia survives intact.

Perhaps the most remarkable of all *jardins anglo-chinois* was the Désert de Retz near Chambourcy on part of the royal forest of Marly. This property was acquired in 1774 and developed during the next decade by the chevalier François Racine de Monville, a colourfully eccentric friend of the Duc de Chartres. With François Barbier as his adviser, Monville created a wiggly rococo garden containing an elaborate *maison chinois* for his own habitation and another astonishing dwelling in the form of a shattered Doric column some eighty feet high, comprising four storeys of four rooms on each floor grouped round a central spiral staircase. Sometimes interpreted as a symbol of frustrated sexual ambition, it is arguably the most picturesque building in Europe and its present state of partially arrested decay hemmed in by trees and undergrowth seems not entirely inappropriate. In better condition is the contemporary pagoda at Chanteloup built from designs by L.-D. Le Camus in 1773–8 and distantly inspired by Chambers's at Kew.

The painter Hubert Robert (1733–1808) may have had a hand in the design of the Désert de Retz as well as of Moulin-Joli and Monceau. He certainly worked on the gardens at Versailles and the Petit Trianon, at Betz, Rambouillet and, most spectacularly, at Méréville from 1786. His formative years were spent in Italy

(*Above left*) Parc Monceau, Paris, laid out from 1773 by Carmontelle for the Duc de Chartres. The Circus or Naumachia. This ruined Corinthian peristyle in the northern corner of the garden is the only substantial surviving fragment of Carmontelle's work. Stylistically it recalls J. H. Mansart's colonnade at Versailles of 1686. Monceau, as Carmontelle explained, was a 'Garden of Illusion', a theatre for the creation of an imaginary world to which the spectator was transported through time and space. As in England, such gardens were to be enjoyed through the medium of engravings as much as through actual visits.

(*Above right*) Désert de Retz, near Paris. Woodland laid out for F. de Monville from 1774-84. The Column House. The theatrical nature of the French garden of illusion was nowhere better experienced than at Retz. Entered through a grotto guarded by torch-bearing satyrs, the garden contained a Chinese House, Gothic Chapel, pyramid, Temple of Pan, and an open-air theatre where real trees looked like stage scenery and the column house (virtually the only building to survive) served as a permanent backdrop.

Méréville, near Paris, begun 1784 by Belanger for the Duc de Laborde and continued by Robert in 1786. When the cult of the colossal arrived at Méréville, hills were formed, the river re-routed and enlarged, thunderous cascades and daring bridges constructed. Robert's Temple of Love, shown on the right in this engraving, was modelled on the Temple of Vesta at Tivoli. Like Robert's elaborate Dairy it was removed to the nearby château of Jeurre in the late nineteenth century.

from 1754–65 where he learnt the art of ruin painting from Piranesi and Panini. His dominant role in the creation of so many important French gardens lends support to the argument that French picturesque gardens were an indigenous development which was less dependent on English precedent than has sometimes been supposed. However, the park at Méréville where Robert worked from 1786 for the banker Jean-Joseph, Duc de Laborde, had been begun in 1784 by the leading architect François-Joseph Belanger (1744–1818) who had studied English garden design on more than one tour of England. Belanger's surviving sketchbook includes most of the important early gardens such as Stowe, Oatlands, Ilam, Stourhead, Wanstead, the Leasowes, Claremont, Painshill and Hagley. However, the grand cascade at Méréville with its precipitous rocks and dramatically frail bridge has a touch of Alpine picturesqueness far removed from English sources.

While Belanger visited England, a number of British gardeners worked in France. Indeed, at the Duc d'Orléans's estate at Raincy there were so many imported English gardeners, farmers, gamekeepers and huntsmen that Thomas Blaikie described it in 1786 as 'allmost an English colony'.[2] The Scotch gardener and botanist Thomas Blaikie (1750–1838) enjoyed the unusual distinction of working for the feckless and extravagantly eccentric Comte de Lauragais (later Duc de Brancas), an anglophile Liberal, the Comte d'Artois (the future Charles X), and the Duc de Chartres (later Duc d'Orléans). In this remarkably interesting diary, Blaikie shows us how far he thought the French had understood the principles of the English landscaped garden. For example, in September 1778 he was invited by the Comte d'Artois to the celebrated chateau of Maisons near Paris where, he complained:

they only showed a peice of ground about 4 or 5 acres which they said they wanted to make an English garden of. I told them that was not what was meant by English gardens, that

Hotel de Thélusson, Paris, 1778-83 (demolished 1824), by Ledoux for Mme. de Thélusson. View from the mouth of the primitivist grotto looking along the sunken garden with its exotic trees to the triumphal entrance arch. In one of the great theatrical set-pieces of French neo-classicism, the entrance arch serves as a proscenium arch both for passers-by to look into the garden and for inhabitants of the house to look out to the street. By a romantic conceit, the shape of the triumphal arch, serving also as porter's lodge, water tank and garden ornament, echoes that of the grotto below the semi-circular portico of the saloon.

the whole ground round the house ought to correspond else they never could think of having anything beautifull but this they had no ideas of. Mr Belanger who had been in England understood beter than the others but he told me to have patience and to do as well as we could untill they saw something and that there intention was to send me to England to buy trees in a few days.[3]

Blaikie also made the original design in 1778 for the layout of the grounds at the Bagatelle, the elegant pavilion which Belanger designed to enable the Comte d'Artois to fulfil a celebrated wager with Queen Marie-Antoinette. Belanger made a number of alterations to Blaikie's design and each claimed the garden as his own. However, in 1783 the Duc de Chartres employed Blaikie to 'improve' the Parc Monceau which had so recently been laid out by Carmontelle. Blaikie objected that on his arrival:

the whole was a Small confusion of many things joined together without any great natural Plan, the walks Serpenting and turning without reason which is the fault of most of those gardens done without taste or reason; after I changed most of those Gardins and destroyed most of those walks which I thought unessary or unaturel . . . those changes wrought a great effect upon those Gardins and upon the Mind of the Duke who began to see the difference from the changes I made in following the nature of the Ground and drawing perspectifs upon the different objects already placed, that is in making the walks to pass at those places where the different objects and parts of the Gardins are seen to the greatest advantage; in this I have succeeded as the first in this country . . .[4]

Paris was the compelling focus of French cultural life so that, as we have just seen with the Parc Monceau, the picturesque garden inevitably found its way there. Architects like De Wailly, Boullée and Ledoux designed complex houses linked to gardens and grottoes in a way which in England would be found not in London but in the country. The most striking of these was undoubtedly Ledoux's Hôtel de Thélusson built in the late 1770s for Mme de Thélusson, the widow of a wealthy Swiss banker, who died from a smallpox inoculation before her house was completed. The main entrance drive led through a great arch, like a half-buried building in the Roman Forum, to a *jardin anglais* and then disappeared through

Petit Trianon, Versailles. The mill of *c*. 1783 at the Normandy farm at the Hameau by R. Mique of 1778-82. Independently of English influence, the French developed a sentimental interest in the indigenous vernacular style of their cottage and farm buildings. This was experienced first in the form of paintings by Boucher, then in stage scenery and the theories of Rousseau, and eventually, as at the Hameau, in picturesquely grouped reconstructions.

the mouth of a rocky grotto to continue underground beneath the main body of the house. This extravagant palace caused such a stir that, like the Parc Monceau, it was opened to the public by ticket.

In their ideal abstract projects for megalomaniac public buildings in the 1780s and 1790s Boullée and Ledoux developed their picturesque style even further than in their executed designs. Their grandiose manipulation of light and shade to produce mysterious effects and their preference for buildings of aggressive scale were already adumbrated by the architect Le Camus de Mézières in his treatise of 1780, *Le génie de l'architecture, ou l'analogie de cet art avec nos sensations*. The creation of an architecture of mood and sensation, envisaged also by Boullée in his treatise *Architecture, Essai sur l'Art*, written in the 1780s and 1790s, can only properly be understood as the long-term influence of ideals originally formulated in the picturesque garden.

An especially characteristic feature of French garden architecture was the *hameau* of which the first example seems to have been that at Chantilly for the Prince de Condé, where a circle of seven thatched cottages including a mill and dairy was begun in 1775 from designs by J.-F. Le Roy. This picturesque interest in rustic life and vernacular architecture is an extension of the descriptions and illustrations of the rural scene from the 1740s onwards of men like Boucher, Watelet and Robert. Similar *hameaux* appear at Betz, Malmaison and Raincy, though the best-known is that in the grounds of the Petit Trianon at Versailles for which Richard Mique provided a plan in 1780 based on an idea by Hubert Robert. In true painterly fashion, models of the various buildings were set up to enable Queen Marie-Antoinette and Mique to judge their visual effect before carrying them into execution. Such buildings in Normandy or Swiss styles, often half-timbered with wooden galleries, were significant in foreshadowing the characteristic type of French nineteenth-century domestic architecture. In England they may have had some influence on John Nash, especially his Blaise Hamlet of 1810. The remarkable village of Clisson in the Vendée was laid out in 1805–20 as an artistic Italianate community in a kind of Claudian vernacular style.

It has much in common with the simplified rustic Italianate style of Nash at Cronkhill and Sandridge Park, or of Schinkel at Schloss Glienicke and the garden buildings at Schloss Charlottenhof. The chateau of Castille at Argilliers in Languedoc is another even stranger example of post-revolutionary fervour for Italianate sources, even to the extent of incorporating references to Bernini's colonnade at St. Peter's.

The *jardin anglo-chinois* with its *fermes ornées* and pastoral farms was largely brought to an end by the Revolution of 1789, though Brongniart's Père Lachaise cemetery of 1804 might perhaps be seen as a late example of the type. What the modern Englishman may well think of as a characteristic landscaped park – that is the green undulations of Brown or Repton – scarcely arrived in France before the nineteenth century. Something of the Brownian repertoire was carried into nineteenth-century France by Haussmann's gardener Adolphe Alphand (1817–91), an engineer from the Ponts et Chaussées. In the early 1850s Louis Napoléon employed Varé to turn the Bois de Boulogne in Paris into something resembling a park by Capability Brown. Haussmann soon replaced Varé with Alphand who completed the Bois de Boulogne, remodelled the Bois de Vincennes, smoothed away the oddities of the Parc Monceau, and created the new Parc des Buttes Chaumont in 1864 with a temple perched perilously on an improbably tall and rocky outcrop. In North America, which is outside the scope of the present book, Repton's influence was strongly felt in the work of Andrew Jackson Downing (1815–52), author of *A Treatise on the Theory and Practice of Landscape Gardening* (1841) and many other books, and of Frederick Law Olmsted (1822–1903) whose best known work is Central Park in New York (1857).

As we have noted, Fischer von Erlach (1656–1723) had set the stage for a picturesque drama in Germany as early as 1721 with his astonishingly eclectic *Entwurff einer historischen Architectur*. His initiative was not taken up by German architects, though a late hint of his exoticism can perhaps be found in the mosque at Schwetzingen near Mannheim built from designs by Nicolas de Pigage (1723–96) in 1778–95. Pigage, the leading architect in the Palatinate, was one of the many French architects who dominated eighteenth-century German architecture. Three phases of development can be traced in the Elector Palatine's famous gardens at Schwetzingen. The first was the formal layout of the 1750s by Johann Ludwig Petri, which was followed by the addition of neo-classical garden buildings by Pigage in the 1760s, including the Temples of Apollo, Minerva and Mercury, a Botanical Temple and a ruined aqueduct, and finally the planting of belts to create the atmosphere of an English park by Friedrich Ludwig Sckell in 1778–1804.

The first and in some ways the most impressive of all *jardins anglais* in Germany is at Schloss Wörlitz laid out from 1764 for Prince Leopold Friedrich Franz von Anhalt-Dessau (1740–1817) by Johann Friedrich Eyserbeck (1734–1818), Johann Leopold Schoch the elder (1728–93) and Neumark (1714–1811). The intensely anglophile prince and his talented architect Friedrich Wilhelm von Erdmannsdorff (1736–1800) spent most of the years from 1763–7 travelling in England, France and Italy where they studied architecture and design and made the acquaintance of leading connoisseurs and artists like Winckelmann, Cardinal Albani, Clérisseau and Sir William Hamilton.

(*Above left*) Parc des Buttes Chaumont, Paris, 1864-7, by J.-C.-A. Alphand and C.-J.-A. Davioud. An entertainingly picturesque extravaganza which derives its piquancy from being set in the heart of urban Paris, of which fine views are obtained from the belvedere temple. Like Carmontelle's Parc Monceau, it was thus conceived as part of the social life of Paris and not, like English parks, as an escape into the countryside.

(*Above right*) Schloss Wörlitz, near Dessau, 1769-73, by Erdmannsdorff for Prince Anhalt-Dessau in a setting landscaped by Eyserbeck from 1764. The arrival in Germany of the English Palladian villa and lake-landscape. With its numerous garden buildings built by Erdmannsdorff into the 1790s, Wörlitz is one of the most complete surviving ensembles of its kind in Europe.

Erdmannsdorff built a massive neo-Palladian schloss for the Prince on the edge of the village of Wörlitz in 1769–73. It is curiously close in general form to Claremont in Surrey, the house which Capability Brown and Henry Holland designed in 1770 for Clive of India. To the north and west of Schloss Wörlitz the Prince and Eyserbeck extended an existing lake to create a remarkable lake-landscape like that at Stourhead, but with greater intricacy and variety afforded by canals, streams, bridges and islands. Over twenty elaborate garden buildings survive today, each the focus of carefully composed views, so that Wörlitz, though little visited by anyone but East Germans, must be regarded as one of the most important of the remaining eighteenth-century parks in Europe. Perhaps the strangest building in the park is the Gothic House of which the first range was built in 1773–4 from designs by the Prince's valet Georg Christoph Hesekiel, based on the church of Sta. Maria dell'Orto in Venice of *c.* 1460. Following a visit to England, the Prince considerably extended the house in a faintly Tudor Gothic style in 1785–6 to form a residence for him and his mistress Leopoldine Luise Schoch, the gardener's daughter, who gave birth to three of his children. Meanwhile his wife, Princess Luise, was confined to the main schloss despite the fact that, like much of the park, it was open to the public. The Gothic House was also a place where the prince could meditate on a baronial past and enjoy his collection of sixteenth-century German paintings, antique weapons and Swiss stained glass. A first-floor room in the new wing is decorated with eight mural paintings including *vedute* of Westminster Abbey, Notre Dame, the cathedrals of York, Lincoln, Florence and Milan, and a ruined English church – a curious parallel to the interiors of the schloss which contained similar classical compositions by artists such as Clérisseau and Piranesi.

The Rousseau Island at Wörlitz is especially intriguing. It was created in 1782 in imitation of the one holding Rousseau's tomb at Ermenonville and was prompted by the prince's meeting Rousseau in 1775 on his way back from his third visit to England. Another curiosity is the construction in 1791 of the first cast-iron bridge on the Continent, a miniature version of the celebrated

Coalbrookdale bridge over the Severn by Wilkinson, Derby and Pritchard of 1777–9 which the prince may have seen on his fourth visit to England in 1785. Other buildings added to the park in the 1790s include the Temple of Venus, an open tholos of Greek Doric columns, the Pantheon, the Temple of Flora, and a Neapolitan corner with a reconstruction of Sir William Hamilton's villa and even of Vesuvius itself! Extensive areas of meadowland and cornfields, woodland and water, prevent the park from giving a crowded rococo impression despite its many buildings, statues and urns.

Scarcely less important than Wörlitz were the theoretical writings of the indefatigable C. C. L. Hirschfeld, painter and professor of philosophy and fine art at Kiel University. He published firstly *Anmerkungen über die Landhaüser und die Gartenkunst* in 1773, but his main work was *Theorie der Gartenkunst* (5 vols., 1779–85), published simultaneously in German and in French as *Théorie de l'art des jardins*. From the point of view of tracing English influence on the Continent Hirschfeld's importance is that he supports Walpole's version of the rise of the landscape garden. Thus, he not only saw it as an English phenomenon, but also as one largely due to William Kent, and was opposed to the fussy artificiality of the *jardin anglo-chinois*. His extensive theoretical, historical and aesthetic survey of eighteenth-century gardens throughout Europe and Russia has not been equalled in modern times; as a product of German industry it is akin to Hermann Muthesius's *Das englische Haus* (3 vols., 1904–5). Hirschfeld was followed by C. L. Stieglitz who published *Gemählde von Gärten* in 1796, translated in 1802 as *Descriptions pittoresques de jardins du goût le plus moderne*, in which his marked anglophilia led him to stress the work of Brown and Repton, whom he attempted to defend from the attacks of Price and Knight.

The park at Wörlitz and the writings of Hirschfeld turned the attention of Goethe to garden design and inspired him to lay out the park at Weimar from 1778. In 1793 the Landgrave Wilhelm of Hesse caused the ruins of a mock castle, which he called Felsenburg, to be erected in the baroque gardens at Wilhelmshöhe. His architect Simon-Louis du Ry had already prepared a scheme in 1786 for adding a substantial classical range *in ruins* to the schloss at Wilhelmshöhe. A sentimental interest in chivalry was reflected in the Rosicrucian League at the court of the Prussian king, Friedrich Wilhelm II, and also in the mock ruined castle built for him in 1794–6 by the royal carpenter Johann Gottlieb Brendel on the Peacock Island in the river Havel near Berlin. The delectable Peacock Island, developed by the king as a small but picturesque retreat, is part of a vast area of royal gardens and parkland between Berlin and Potsdam, including Sans Souci as well as the later parks at Schinkel's Schloss Glienicke and Schloss Babelsberg.

The name of Karl Friedrich Schinkel (1781–1841) brings us to a new phase of anglomania in the history of the Picturesque in Germany. One of the leading architects of his day in Europe, he frequently worked in close association with his friend and patron the Prussian Crown Prince (1795–1861), an architect *manqué* who succeeded to the throne as Friedrich Wilhelm IV in 1840. In the grounds of Sans Souci, Schinkel and the prince designed a small villa called Schloss Charlottenhof for the prince and his young wife in 1826. It was beautifully related to its garden which was designed with the help of the court gardener Peter Joseph Lenné (1789–1866), who had visited England in 1822–3 to study landscape

(*Above*) Roman Baths, Schloss Charlottenhof, Potsdam, 1829-33, by Karl Friedrich Schinkel for Crown Prince Friedrich Wilhelm of Prussia in a setting landscaped by P. J. Lenné. The gardener's house with its Italianate tower lies at the heart of a picturesque group of much complexity and delicacy.

(*Right*) Roman Baths interior. Schinkel's genius is revealed in his control of space and light in this imaginatively conceived neo-antique interior.

gardens. In 1829–36 Schinkel, his assistant Ludwig Persius and the prince designed and built an asymmetrical group of buildings in the grounds of Schloss Charlottenhof intended to suggest a Roman villa. The gardener's house, a tea house and Roman bath form an enchanting composition interlocking with canals and pergolas. In a similar vein was Schloss Glienicke, also with a Lenné park, built by Schinkel from 1824 for the Crown Prince's brother Karl. The composition pivots on an asymmetrically placed Italianate tower like Thomas Hope's The Deepdene and the later garden buildings at Schloss Charlottenhof. For the king's second son, Prince Wilhelm, Schinkel built Schloss Babelsberg in 1833, a Tudor Gothic fantasy recalling in plan and elevation a country house by Nash such as East Cowes Castle on the Isle of Wight. Schinkel, who had visited England to study architecture in 1826, was obliged to take account of sketch designs for Schloss Babelsberg by Wilhelm's anglophile wife Princess Augusta and by the Crown Prince. She had evidently studied English pattern books such as those by Lugar and Papworth while the Crown Prince proposed a variety of solutions in different styles, Italianate vernacular, Romanesque and Tudor Gothic – each characterised by an asymmetrically placed tower.

Urged by the Crown Prince, Schinkel prepared elaborate and fantastic designs in the 1830s for two dream palaces, one of 1834 for the King of Greece on the Acropolis in Athens, and another four years later for the Empress of Russia at Orianda on the Crimean coast. There were strong German connections in each case, the first King of Greece being the former Prince Otto of Bavaria, while the Empress was the Crown Prince's sister. The Acropolis palace represented in some ways the quintessence of the Picturesque movement in that the Parthenon itself was at last reduced to the status of a garden ornament! Schloss Orianda was even more spectacular. Its central picturesque garden-court was dominated by a great Ionic temple rising on a massive substructure which contained a sculpture museum and was as high as the main ranges of the palace itself. The temple, surrounded by trees and vegetation, thus appeared in distant views to float miraculously above the roofs of the palace. Architecture had become landscape and the whole was recorded in a series of dazzling lithographs by Schinkel, who must have realised that such a palace would never be built. As is often the case with the Picturesque, representation was as important as reality.

Though Schinkel dominated the architecture of mid-nineteenth-century Germany, his picturesque imagination found few imitators, except perhaps in the design of suburban villas. The Friedrichshain and the Tiergarten in Berlin were laid out as Reptonian public parks from the 1840s in a style which had been brought to Germany by Prince Hermann von Pückler-Muskau, the dashing and eccentric rake whose leading passion, amongst many, was what he called '*parkomanie*'. He spent the years 1814–16 and 1826–8 in England where, while looking for an heiress, he was especially influenced by Repton's work, for example at Cassiobury, Ashridge and Cobham. He published *Andeutungen über Landschaftsgärtnerei* (Hints on Landscape Gardening) in 1834 and laid out his own parks at Muskau on the river Neisse in Silesia from 1815–45 and later at Schloss Branitz near Cottbus. In typical Reptonian fashion he put little emphasis on garden buildings or the arousing of sentimental associations, but created green wooded landscapes and, near the house, flower gardens and even carpet beds. However, at Branitz he formed two earth pyramids of which the larger, surrounded by a lake, became his tomb, apparently inspired by a sentence from the Koran, 'Graves are the mountain-tops of a distant lovely land'.

Sweden was especially receptive to English picturesque gardens. The founding of the Swedish East India Company in 1731 had forged links between Sweden

Liselund, Island of Møn, Denmark. Thatched Palace, 1793, for Antoine de la Calmette, decorated by J. C. Lillie. Intended for occasional retreat from the Calmettes' principal seat, where they already had a *jardin anglais*, Liselund incorporates English, French and German influences into an example of the *cottage orné* at its most idyllic.

and the Far East which led to an appreciation of Chinese gardens. In 1753 the celebrated Chinese House, a rococo fantasy subsequently rebuilt in stone, was constructed of wood at Drottningholm for Queen Louisa Ulrica, and four years later Carl Ekeberg published *An Account of Chinese Husbandry*. More importantly, a young architect called Fredrik Magnus Piper (1746–1824) left Stockholm in 1772 to study garden design in England, almost certainly with a letter of introduction to William Chambers. Piper travelled round England for four years with a copy of Whately's *Observations on Modern Gardening* (1770), making attractive illustrated notes, many of which survive, on Stourhead, Painshill, Stowe and Kew. He then spent a further two years studying gardens in Italy and finally two more years in England from 1778–80. In 1771 the future King Gustaf III of Sweden had bought the estate of Haga just north of Stockholm to serve as a modest rural retreat. Ten years later, following his return from England, Piper began transforming the grounds on the west bank of Brunnsvik lake into a lake-landscape surrounded by meadowland and wooded slopes. In 1786 he built the hexagonal Turkish pavilion, but Haga was never fully completed to a unified scheme and Piper's elaborate boathouse for gondolas in the form of a grotto crowned by a Temple of Neptune was, alas, never executed. In 1777 the king had asked the English gardener William Phelan to prepare a plan for landscaping the grounds of the royal residence of Drottningholm to the west of Stockholm. Three years later Piper made a fresh start on this project and helped to create an attractive but scarcely spectacular park centred on a serpentine canal.

On the Island of Møn in south-east Denmark, Antoine de la Calmette and his wife Lisa created in the 1790s a charming rococo landscape which breathes to perfection the frivolous spirit of pre-revolutionary France. Known as Liselund, its pools and beechwoods are the setting for an enchanting *hameau* containing a miniature thatched palace, or *cottage orné*, a Chinese Tent, Norwegian Hut and Swiss Cottage. These buildings, which have recently been carefully restored, are in a rustic style reminiscent of Nash and Repton with sophisticated painted interiors and furniture inspired by France as well as by Henry Holland, Hepplewhite and Nash.

In Hungary the English garden arrived rather later than in Germany and lasted longer. The nobility, attracted by the social life of Vienna, tended to spend their time in palaces there rather than on their remote estates. However, fashions had changed by the end of the eighteenth century when the Esterházy family set an important trend by creating English gardens on their estates at Csákvár, Tata and Kismarton. At Tata in 1801 an artificial ruin was picturesquely assembled by Charles de Moreau from fragments of Roman and mediaeval buildings in the neighbourhood. In the early 1820s Michael Pollack created picturesque parks at Alcsut near Budapest for the Hungarian Palatine Duke, Joseph Hapsburg, and at Dég for the Festetich family. Virtually every garden in the country was transformed into an English park in the first quarter of the nineteenth century and by *c*.1850 there were about two hundred of them. One of the largest was Martonvásár laid out for the Brunswicks, the friends and patrons of Beethoven. The Hungarians, however, did not design accompanying picturesque asymmetrical houses, but often favoured a solemn Greek Revival style. As for the public parks, the first in Hungary seems to have been the Orczy garden in Pest designed by Bernhard Petri (1768–1853), who had spent four years studying garden design in England. Henry Nebbien, who was French or Belgian by origin and a profound admirer of Repton, laid out the city park of Varosliget in Budapest from 1817. He may also have designed the garden for the Palatine Duke Joseph on Saint Margaret Island in the Danube at Budapest.

Picturesque parks in Poland were largely the creation of two interrelated families, the Czartoryskis and the Poniatowskis. Such families spoke French rather than Polish and their gardens seem to have been inspired by *jardins anglais* in France rather than directly by English models. The leading designer was Szymon Bogumił Zug (1733–1807) who contributed an important chapter on Polish gardens to the fifth volume of Hirschfeld's *Theorie der Gartenkunst* (1785). After his return from Italy in 1772, Zug laid out an estate at Solec south of Warsaw for Kasinierz Poniatowski, the King's elder brother. In the later 1770s he was working at Ksiazece, at the nearby estate of Góra and at Powąski on the edge of Warsaw. His most important commission was Arkadia near Łowicz for Helen Radziwiłłowa where he worked from 1778–98. The best preserved eighteenth-century garden in Poland, Arkadia is still in a half-rococo taste with inscriptions and a Rousseau island inspired by Ermenonville. In the same years Izabella Czartoryski created at Puławy on the Vistula a romantic garden with the help of her English head gardener James Savage, and an Irish gardener called Denis McClear (1762–1840). Amongst the most notable surviving buildings there is an impressive Temple of the Sybil built in 1798–1801 on the edge of a cliff.

English ideas made even less headway in the eighteenth century in Bohemia and Moravia. The most impressive garden was that at Lednice (Eisgrub) in Moravia laid out from 1794 onwards until well into the nineteenth century for Alois Josef von Liechtenstein and his brother Johann I as a lake landscape. Work began with the great minaret and the Temple of the Sun in the 1790s and ended with the formal flower gardens of the 1860s.

The story of the Picturesque in Russia begins with Catherine the Great and the surprising career of James Cameron (*c.*1743–1812) whom she employed as court architect from 1778. A pupil of Isaac Ware, Cameron had studied antique architecture in Rome where he came under the influence of Clérisseau and formed a style akin to Adam's, though with greater polychromatic strength. From 1779–94 he extended the palace of Tsarskoe Selo near St. Petersburg for the Empress Catherine with a striking complex of buildings on a sloping site which may have reminded him of Titus's Baths in Rome. Above the Cold Baths he placed the Agate Pavilion and, at right angles to it, the Cameron Gallery, a long open colonnade terminating in a splendidly inviting external staircase. The masterly handling of levels, the varied forms, the blending of interior and exterior space, create a pictorial drama which reveals Cameron as a master of the Picturesque. In the park at Tsarskoe Selo, which Catherine had laid out from *c.*1770 as a *jardin anglais*, Cameron built for her a number of pagoda-like pavilions which were intended to form part of a Chinese village. Among other bizarre follies in the park was a half-buried ruined column supporting a Gothic pavilion which was executed from designs by Y. M. Velten in 1774 and painted by Hubert Robert in 1783.

In 1782–5 Cameron designed and built the palace of Pavlosk for the Empress's son, the Grand Duke Paul. Of the sixty odd garden buildings which Cameron and others provided in the park at Pavlosk the finest is the Temple of Friendship of

Tsarskoe Selo, near St. Petersburg. The Cameron Gallery, 1779-85, by James Cameron for the Empress Catherine. The sweeping curved staircase leads up to the Gallery with its open colonnades which may have been inspired by Palladio's Palazzo Chiericati in Vicenza. Set back between the Ionic columns are bronze busts of Catherine's thirty favourite philosophers; though mainly antique they included Charles James Fox. The complex of hanging gardens, terraces and steps incorporates the sumptuous Agate Pavilion.

Temple of Friendship, Pavlosk, 1779-80, by James Cameron for the Grand Duke Paul. Other surviving classical garden buildings by Cameron in the huge landscaped park at Pavlosk include the Apollo Colonnade and cascade, Pavilion of the Graces, Cold Bath and Centaur Bridge, Aviary and Obelisk.

Tsaritsyno, near Moscow, *c.* 1787, begun by Kazakov and continued by Bazhenov for the Empress Catherine. This uncompleted mediaevalising palace was set in a picturesque park dotted with garden buildings. Its curious style failed to please its patron and the building rapidly became ruinous.

1779–80 with its impressive ring of sixteen Doric columns – the first monument of the Greek Revival in Russia. There was also a now destroyed rustic village probably inspired by the *hameau* at Chantilly which Paul and his wife may have seen in 1782.

Catherine's interest in picturesque associations led her to adopt a mediaeval Russian style which anticipated the nineteenth-century revival of national styles for political and patriotic purposes. Kazakov built the Petrovski Palace for her on the outskirts of Moscow in 1775–82 in a curious neo-Russian style. Shortly after, he and Bazhenov began but never completed a similarly exotic palace for her at Tsaritsyno surrounded by a picturesque park crowded with garden buildings. Her grandson Nicholas I continued the eclectic development of the park at Tsarskoe Selo in the 1820s, employing the Scottish architect Adam Menelaws to grace it with a ruined chapel containing an Egyptian sarcophagus from Alexandria, a Turkish elephant house and the massive Egyptian Gate clad in cast-iron bas reliefs.

Lastly in Russia it is worth mentioning one of the best of the villas in picturesque English parks built around 1800. The neo-Palladian Bratsevo near Moscow was designed by Andrei Voronikhin for a member of the Stroganov family who, interestingly, confined his wife to it as a punishment for having led too social a life in St. Petersburg. The central circular hall is notable for its frescoes of the house viewed from the artificial lake in the park.

The Picturesque came comparatively late to Italy where the formidable inheritance of Renaissance and baroque gardens may have served as a natural barrier. However, the gardens of the Villa Borghese in Rome were developed picturesquely in the 1780s and 1790s by Antonio Asprucci and his son Mario, and in the 1820s by Luigi Canina. The Aspruccis had the help of a Scottish landscape painter Jacob More, and Antonio's Temple of Aesculapius of 1787 recalls the ruined temple in the grounds of Cardinal Albani's Villa Albani in Rome. Another early *jardin anglais* was the little watery wilderness created in the 1780s at the suggestion of Sir William Hamilton on the edge of the formal gardens of the palace of Caserta near Naples. In the 1790s Leopoldo Pollack, with help from Selva and Amati, produced the first picturesque park in Milan at the Villa Belgioioso, later called the Villa Reale.

The most important picturesque theorist in Italy was Count Ercole Silva of Milan who had visited English parks and gardens such as Blenheim and Stowe in 1786. Following his return he laid out in the English style his own grounds at the Villa Silva-Ghirlanda at Cinisello Balsamo near Milan, and in 1801 published an illustrated study, *Dell'arte de' giardini inglesi* which was reprinted in an expanded form in 1813. He wanted gardens to evoke sensations of pleasing melancholy and believed that ruins, hermitages and grottoes were more effective for that purpose than temples or pagodas. His own garden thus contained an artificial Roman ruin which he had induced a shepherd and his family to occupy. A knowledgeable botanist, he devoted many pages of his book to a list of flowering plants appropriate to landscaped gardens, but found to his regret that they had to be imported to Italy from England or Holland. His influence spread to several parks in the country round Milan and in the neighbouring province of Venetia, for example the Villa Cusani at Desio, which he illustrated in his book, and the Villa Reale at Monza.

Villa Borghese, Rome. Temple of Antoninus and Faustina, 1792, by A. and M. Asprucci and C. Unterberger for Prince Marcantonio Borghese. This sham temple front, which may incorporate some genuine fragments, was inspired by the Corinthian Temple of Antoninus and Faustina in the Roman Forum. To erect a mock ruin in a city where so many real ones abound suggests unusual faith in the virtues of the Picturesque.

Giuseppe Valadier (1762–1839), probably the leading Italian architect of his day, built the enchanting Casino Valadier in 1809–14 on the top of the Pincian Hill in Rome. A building possessing characteristically picturesque intricacy and variety both in its exteriors and interiors, it is a fetching, lively composition with its colonnades, terraces, varied skyline and the different designs of its three main façades. It anticipates the more eclectic picturesque qualities of the Caffè Pedrocchi at Padua built between 1826 and 1842 by Giuseppe Jappelli (1783–1852) who had travelled extensively in England, Germany and France. This bizarre building grew gradually in a variety of styles in which Greek Doric is juxtaposed with richly ornamented Gothic. In 1817 Jappelli began work on the Villa dei Conti Vittadella Vigodarsere near Padua where he contrasted his austerely classical house with a romantic English park. Later he worked on the landscaped gardens of the Villa Torlonia in Rome which he laid out with exotic pavilions and ruins. In the 1820s and 1830s he was widely employed near Padua and in the Veneto to transform formal gardens and to create new picturesque parks.

There is something about the heroic scale and superb siting of some of the early nineteenth-century neo-classical buildings of Italy that justifies their classification as picturesque. The Villa Cagnola d'Adda at Inverigo built for himself from 1813–33 by Luigi Cagnola (1762–1833) with its domes and colonnades in a mountainous setting is a striking example, echoed in the stupendous Tempio del

179

Caffè Pedrocchi, Padua, 1826–42, by G. Jappelli. The Greek Doric wing on the right was built in 1826–31. Following his visit to England in 1836, Jappelli added the Pedrocchino on the left in 1837–42 in a strikingly constrasting Venetian Gothic style. The eclectic interiors in Egyptian, Moorish and French Empire styles may have been inspired by the study which Jappelli made of the work of Thomas Hope.

Canova at Possagno of 1819–33 by Giovanni Selva and others. The same megalomaniac scale, fulfilling the visions of Boullée and Ledoux, occurs in Niccolini's Teatro San Carlo (1810–44) and Bianchi's San Francesco di Paola (1817–46), both in Naples, and in Poccianti's Cisternone (1829–42) at Livorno, a waterworks with a picturesque but functionless coffered semi-dome rising menacingly above a Doric colonnade.

8

The Picturesque
in Village and Town

THE central figure in any discussion of the Picturesque in this chapter must be John Nash (1752–1835), for it was his daring and genius that brought it to London in Regent's Park and Regent Street and which also created the 'instant' picturesque village of Blaise Hamlet near Bristol. The image most likely to be evoked in the popular mind by the term Picturesque is the country cottage, preferably thatched and embosomed with flowers, especially hollyhocks. The dominance of this image is due to a many-faceted preoccupation from the end of the eighteenth century with the appeal of villages and vernacular architecture. It was some time before the visual principles implicit in Kent's revolution in garden design in the 1730s were applied to the layout of the villages which so often lay just outside the new gardens and parks. In his *An Essay on the Picturesque* in 1794 Sir Uvedale Price was to condemn the rigid symmetry of villages, such as Nuneham Courtenay which Lord Harcourt had built in the 1760s at the same time that he was laying out his park along picturesque and asymmetrical lines. 'An obvious and easy method of rebuilding a village', Price explained, '(and one which unfortunately has been put into practice) is to place the houses on two parallel lines, to make them of the same size and shape, and at equal distances from each other. Such a methodical arrangement saves all further thought and invention; but it is hardly necessary to say that nothing can be more formal and insipid'.[1]

Nuneham Courtenay may also have been the inspiration for Goldsmith's poem 'The Deserted Village' of 1770. Complaining of the enclosures that were altering the face of the countryside, Goldsmith described how

> . . . The man of wealth and pride
> Takes up a space that many poor supplied;
> Space for his lake, his park's extended bounds,
> Space for his horses, equipage, and hounds;
> The robe that wraps his limbs in silken sloth
> Has robbed the neighbouring fields of half their growth,
> His seat, where solitary sports are seen,
> Indignant spurns the cottage from the green.[2]

The destruction of the old village and church at Nuneham Courtenay to make way for the park was echoed even more strikingly at Milton Abbas in Dorset from 1773–86 by the 1st Lord Milton, later Earl of Dorchester. Profoundly irritated by the proximity of a substantial market town to his newly improved house, Lord Milton first of all threatened to flood its inhabitants out, then removed the bells from the church tower and finally destroyed the whole town. He replaced it with forty neat cottages, mainly semi-detached, in a steep fold of the downs about three quarters of a mile from the house. They were delectably sited, probably by Capability Brown, but though picturesquely located the village of Milton Abbas

Milton Abbas, Dorset. Model village, 1773-80, by Sir William Chambers and Capability Brown for the 1st Lord Milton. Views from the village towards Brown's artificial lake were as important as those of the village from the lake. The parish church was built in 1786, probably from designs by James Wyatt, to replace the abbey church which became Lord Milton's private chapel. As a final example of the conscious contrivance characteristic of Milton Abbas, the seventeenth-century almshouses from the destroyed town were re-erected here in 1779.

is not picturesquely planned. It was not until 1794 that detailed proposals were made by Sir Uvedale Price for the type of cottage and village building which have coloured the popular imagination, including that of speculative builders, up to the present day. 'In all that relates to cottages, hamlets, and villages, to the grouping of them, and their mixture with trees and climbing plants', Price claimed, 'the best instruction may be gained from the works of the Dutch and Flemish masters'.[3] According to him, 'There is, indeed, no scene where such a variety of forms and embellishments may be introduced at so small an expence, and without any thing fantastic, or unnatural, as that of a village'. Emphasising the visual charms of tall chimneys, trees, flowers, climbing plants, church towers, the village stream and bridge, Price argued that 'The characteristic beauties of a village, as distinct from a city, are intricacy, variety, and play of outline: and whatever is done, should be with a design to promote those objects'.[4]

In 1810 these recommendations were put into practice in the design of a new picturesque village, Blaise Hamlet, created for John Scandrett Harford, the Quaker banker. Nash's Blaise Hamlet set a pattern for the free grouping of modest

picturesque houses in gardens which in some respects is still being followed today. The absence of church, school, inn and shops at Blaise helps establish an unreal or escapist character which further underlines the parallel with 'exclusive' residential estates of modern times. Nash and Repton had been at work at Blaise since 1796 when Repton produced his Red Book for Blaise Castle and designed an elaborate Gothic lodge. Nash added a quadrant conservatory to the house and a picturesque thatched dairy nearby, and finally built the Hamlet for Harford's aged retainers. With their thatched or tiled roofs, quaint verandahs, prominent dormers and tall chimneys of elaborately carved brickwork, the nine cottages, freely grouped round a green, have all the picturesque variety, irregularity and roughness that Price could have desired. In his enthusiastic account of Blaise in his diary, the architect C. R. Cockerell makes it clear that early in the 1820s it had become a 'beauty spot'[5] attracting visitors from Clifton. In 1826 it was made the subject of a series of lithographs so that like many other picturesque buildings inspired by paintings it could not fully be appreciated until it had been translated back into graphic form. The care taken to create the required visual effect is clear in the letters to Harford from Nash's chief assistant George Repton (1786–1858). For example on 23 August 1810 he wrote from Nash's London office to explain that although the cellars and pantry were *inside* in some cottages, 'if we make them *all* so it will very much injure (if not entirely destroy) the picturesque effect of the different Cottages where so much depends on the leantoo's and Sheds etc to make a variety in their form'.[6]

Nash's sources at Blaise could have included the *hameau* of the French *jardin anglais* as well as the numerous English pattern books which had been appearing since Nathaniel Kent's *Hints to Gentlemen of Landed Property* (1775), possibly the

Blaise Hamlet, near Bristol, 1810-11, by John Nash for J. S. Harford. These picturesque cottages are almshouses grouped as though they were a village. The idea of giving the old people a cottage and garden each instead of housing them in a single pedimented range was suggested to Harford by Nash. An expensive idea, if attractive both visually and practically, its realisation cost Harford nearly twice the £2,000 he had intended to spend on the almshouses.

(*Above*) Swiss Cottage, Cahir, County Tipperary, *c.* 1817, perhaps by John Nash for the Earl of Glengall. A *cottage orné* striking an outlandish pose in its lush landscape. In 1828 Prince Pückler-Muskau admired how 'the cottage is more than two-thirds hidden by the wood which clothes the whole hill'. The sitting-room contains contemporary panoramic wallpapers, 'Rives du Bosphore' and 'Monuments de Paris', by Dufour.

(*Right*) The Thornery, Woburn Abbey, Bedfordshire. Humphry Repton worked extensively in the grounds of Woburn for the 6th Duke of Bedford from *c.* 1806 and this little-known building, a 'picturesque morceau' (as it was described thirty years later), may be his work. Its rustic exterior is belied by the complexity and sophistication of its interior where there is an octagonal umbrella vault, painted decoration in the form of flowered trellises, and, in the basement, a white-tiled barrel-vaulted kitchen.

first to contain plans for labourers' cottages. John Plaw provided plans for villages in his *Ferme Ornée; or Rural Improvements. A Series of Domestic and Ornamental Designs* (1795), while other significant publications in the fifteen years before Blaise Hamlet include C. T. Middleton, *Picturesque and Architectural Views for Cottages, Farm-Houses, and Country Villas* (1793), J. T. Smith, *Remarks on Rural Scenery, with Twenty Etchings of Cottages from Nature* (1797), James Malton, *An Essay on British Cottage Architecture: Being an Attempt to Perpetuate on Principle, that Peculiar Mode of Building, which was originally the Effect of Chance* (1798), Edmund Bartell Jr, *Hints for Picturesque Improvements in Ornamental Cottages, and their Scenery: Including Some Observations on the Labourer and his Cottage* (1804), William Atkinson, *Views of Picturesque Cottages with Plans* (1805), Edward Gyfford, *Designs for Small Picturesque Cottages and Hunting Boxes* (1806) and W. F. Pocock, *Architectural Designs for Rustic Cottages, Picturesque Dwellings, Villas, &c.* (1807). This series of books came to a climax in 1833 with J. C. Loudon's immense *Encyclopaedia of Cottage, Farm and Villa Architecture and Furniture*, reprinted in a yet more expanded form in 1842.

The Rousseauesque preoccupation with the rustic had long buried roots in French architectural theory. Laugier, for example, had illustrated a primitive hut fashioned from tree trunks and branches in the second edition (1755) of his influential *Essai sur l'architecture* (Paris 1753). He had hailed this as the origin of all architecture and had argued that the modern rational architect should never lose sight of it. It emerged in designs like those by Soane for a dairy at Hamels, Hertfordshire, of 1781–3 with Doric columns in the form of tree trunks, but by the time of Blaise Hamlet all traces of French primitivism had gone. The *cottage orné* was one of the principal fruits of the rustic mania. Even the King had one at Windsor: Royal Lodge or King's Cottage designed by Nash in 1812 with careful planting to conceal its size. The game of rural make-believe in which the rich pretended for a moment they were poor was especially popular in Ireland where one of the finest of all *cottages ornés* survives, the Swiss Cottage at Cahir built for the Earl of Glengall in *c*.1817, probably by Nash. Girt with two-storeyed verandahs, trellises and thatch it is extravagantly picturesque. Close English parallels are Houghton Lodge, Hampshire, of *c*.1800 with its circular domed drawing-room, and Repton's enchanting thornery at Woburn, 'a most picturesque morceau of huge and fantastic oaks, grotesque old thorns, hazels and dogwoods; on ground abruptly varied'.[7] Yet more eccentric is Samuel Russell Collett's Gothick house of *c*. 1820, the Jungle at Eagle in Lincolnshire, which, once embedded in thorn trees, is built of overburnt vitrified bricks run together in rough masses and has door and window frames made from oak branches fashioned into Gothic arches. It was surrounded by a zoo which in 1826 included kangaroos, buffalo, American deer, pheasants and goldfish.

The new and almost obsessive interest in the cottage was naturally accompanied by an appreciation of the potential visual appeal of the cottagers themselves, so that in 1832 William Sawrey Gilpin envisaged the possibility of a path in a landscaped park with 'the occasional groups of villagers supplying an additional embellishment to the landscape'.[8] Thus tenants and cottagers now fulfilled exactly the role of sheep and cattle in the classic landscapes of Capability Brown. Lord Ongley laid out a picturesque village at Old Warden in Bedfordshire from the 1830s with cottages sporting thatched roofs, prominent dormers and red

(*Above*) The Jungle, Eagle, Lincolnshire, *c.* 1820 for S. R. Collett. Close in mood and form to Alfred's Hall at Cirencester Park (p. 46) of a century earlier, this building demonstrates the continuity of picturesque sensibility.

(*Right*) Old Warden, Bedfordshire, cottage group, *c.* 1830. These cottages were described in a guide as having been 'devised and arranged by Lord Ongley', as though the process involved was akin to staging a play. The inhabitants played their role in the pictorial effect, sitting before the doors of their 'quaint houses with curved barge-boards and red painted doors and windows and some covered with ivy and honeysuckle and all Picturesque'.

painted doors and windows, in which 'the inhabitants, by aid of red cloaks and tall hats were made to harmonise with their dwellings'. At Somerleyton in Suffolk Sir Morton Peto, railway contractor and Liberal M.P., laid out a village of twenty-eight cottages in *c*.1848 for estate workers round a green. The architect was probably John Thomas who had evidently studied Blaise closely as well as the numerous pattern books which were by then available. For the industrialist Jesse Watts Russell, Sir Gilbert Scott built a picturesque village in the 1850s at Ilam in a part of Staffordshire long admired by romantically minded travellers. The upper floors of Scott's cottages are an early example of the revival of tile-hanging, a technique which was scarcely indigenous to the neighbourhood. In 1865 the millionaire philanthropist Baroness Burdett Coutts chose to house her elderly servants in a group of nine cottages, two of them forming an elaborate gateway, known as Holly Village, Highgate. Designed by H. A. Darbishire, the asymmetrical cottages with their barge-boards, creepers and curious carvings, are grouped round a spacious green liberally planted with conifers. As at Blaise there is no church, inn or shop.

Appreciation of the charm produced by fortuitous circumstances in the development of the streets of London was expressed as early as 1786 by Sir Joshua Reynolds in his celebrated Thirteenth Discourse at the Royal Academy in which he recommended architects to imitate the picturesque movement in Vanbrugh's buildings and skylines. He argued that

The forms and turnings of the streets of London, and other old towns, are produced by accident, without any original plan or design; but they are not always the less pleasant to the walker or spectator, on that account. On the contrary, if the city had been built on the regular plan of Sir Christopher Wren, the effect might have been, as we know it is in some new parts of the town, rather unpleasing; the uniformity might have produced weariness, and a slight degree of disgust.[9]

In his proposals for a new road linking the newly developed Regent's Park with Charing Cross Nash described his Quadrant as 'a bending street, resembling, in that respect, the High-Street at Oxford'.[10] He also introduced further picturesque interest by varying the design of the many differently sized blocks of buildings of which Regent Street was composed. The few buildings in the new street that were not designed by Nash fitted equally well into the contrived pictorial irregularity of the whole. Thus we know that even the classically minded C. R. Cockerell conceived of his own twin-towered Hanover Chapel, just below Oxford Circus, as essentially 'picturesque'[11] in character. In the same vein, when Wilkins designed the National Gallery in Trafalgar Square in 1832 he was forced to set back his original building line by fifty feet in order to preserve the view from Pall Mall of Gibbs's St. Martin-in-the-Fields: a characteristically picturesque constraint with which the rigid Wilkins could not sympathise.

Regent's Park with its terraces and trees, villas and water, is the stylish climax of Nash's whole scheme. It began with his proposals for the 554 acres of Marylebone Park presented in March 1811 to the Chief Commissioner of the Office of Woods, Forests and Land Revenues. Nash intended to develop the area with a tight network of streets, squares, circuses and crescents inspired by the Woods' work at Bath. However, these were to interpenetrate with areas of picturesque parkland which were themselves to be dotted with numerous villas.

Village inn, from P. F. Robinson's
*Village Architecture . . . illustrating
Observations contained in the Essay on the
Picturesque, by Sir Uvedale Price* (1830),
an imaginatively eclectic and popular
book which had reached its 4th edition
by 1837.

Park Village East, Regent's Park, London, 1824–8, by J. Nash, from J. Elmes, *Metropolitan Improvements* (1829). Nash's first plan for the street layout of December 1823 shows a scheme closer to Blaise Hamlet with *cottages ornés* on continuous open lawns. As built, the houses were more substantial as can be seen from this engraving which shows the west fronts (facing on to the now filled-in canal) of some of the surviving houses on the west side of the road. The styles range from Tudor at the north end (not shown in this view) to broad-eaved Italianate and humbler Swiss.

In connection with this plan Nash presented two long panoramas which may have been the work of his two assistants, the Frenchman A. C. Pugin and Humphry Repton's son George. These panoramic views in grey monochrome washes do not relate in all particulars to the plan. In particular, they minimise the dominance of the terraced houses and emphasise the arcadian character of the whole park-like setting. Moreover, the style of the buildings recalls the work of French architects such as Belanger rather than that of Nash himself. In August 1811 the Chancellor of the Exchequer, Spencer Perceval, recommended that Nash reduce the number of buildings: thus the park as eventually developed with terraces on three sides of a central landscaped area containing only a few villas, was in some ways closer to the mood of the imaginative panoramas than to the original plan. Architecture conceived as scenery has rarely been carried to greater extremes than in the varied designs of the stuccoed terraces surrounding the park. In the best tradition of picturesque make-believe the palatial façades bear no necessary relation to the formation of the individual houses behind them.

In 1823–7 there arose on the edge of the park a curious building known as the Colosseum, a Greek Doric version of the Roman Pantheon built from designs by the young Decimus Burton (1800–81), whose father had built much of Regent Street and the park terraces. From the 1780s to the 1860s Londoners could enjoy numerous panoramas and dioramas which exploited picturesque sensibility in the convincing representation of architecture, natural scenery, historical events, tempests and avalanches. The Regent's Park Colosseum housed an immense panorama of London viewed from the ball and cross of St. Paul's Cathedral. This was painted in 1822 by Thomas Horner, a failed landscape gardener. C. R. Cockerell was restoring St. Paul's at this time so it was possible for Wren's original ball and cross to be reassembled in the Colosseum to heighten the verisimilitude. Below the building there were romantic caves and conservatories leading by an underground passage to a Swiss Cottage, designed by P. F. Robinson, surrounded by rock scenery and waterfalls. The picturesque effect was heightened in 1845 with the addition of sham ruins of the temples of Theseus and Vesta.

The Prince Regent's decision not to build himself the proposed pleasure pavilion or *guingette* in the park, and his enlargement of Buckingham House into his principal London residence, meant that the court and nobility flocked to Belgravia instead of to Marylebone. In terms of influence, Nash's layout of Park Village East and West on the north-east edge of Regent's Park in 1824 was of more importance than his work on Buckingham Palace. As Blaise Hamlet of 1810 helped establish a cottage mode, so the Park Villages provided a model for the villadom which was to fringe so many Victorian and Edwardian towns throughout the British Isles. Nash's Italianate and Gothic villas of modest size nestle coyly among trees on gently winding roads separated from main traffic routes. Park Village West survives today, but unfortunately half of Park Village East was destroyed by the cutting for the railway. Nash's piquant clash of architectural style was reflected in the plates of books like P. F. Robinson's *Village Architecture, Being a Series of Designs for the Inn, the Schoolhouse, Almshouses, Markethouse, Shambles, Workhouse, Parsonage, Town Hall, and Church* (1830), and also in the estate village of Edensor in Derbyshire built for the 6th Duke of Devonshire from 1838 by Paxton and Robertson.

The Calverley Estate at Tunbridge Wells designed by Decimus Burton in 1828 was closer to Nash's Park Villages. Burton's Arcadian scheme, which used only half of the forty-six acre site, included twenty-four villas on the north and east sides standing well back from a roughly semi-circular drive so that they overlook each other as little as possible and also command good views into the attractively landscaped valley below. Designed in quietly asymmetrical Greek and Italianate styles, the villas have a spare refinement of detail which is emphasised by their construction in stone as opposed to the slipshod stucco of Nash's Park Villages. At

Pelham Crescent, Hastings, East Sussex, 1824-8, by Joseph Kay for the 1st Earl of Chichester. A stunning set-piece following the natural curve of the cliffs. The church of St. Mary in the Castle, burrowed into the rock, forms a surprising central feature.

the west end of Calverley Park, Burton added the Crescent in 1835, a gracious curve of seventeen houses with shops on the ground floor and a library and reading room in the centre. Its continuous one-storeyed colonnade of cast-iron columns echoes the original arrangement of the Quadrant in Nash's Regent Street. The indefatigable publisher and topographer John Britton quickly realised the picturesque charms of Calverley Park and published *Descriptive Sketches of Tunbridge Wells and the Calverley Estate* in 1832. Burton's father James developed an estate at St. Leonards near Hastings which he bought in 1828. Here he brought Regent's Park to the seaside by laying out a landscaped park known as St. Leonards Gardens on the site of a quarry behind his terraces. This was fringed with large villas mainly in the Tudor style to contrast with the flashy stuccoed classicism along the water front.

Spas and seaside resorts with their cheerful atmosphere of leisure and entertainment in the open air were outstandingly well suited to extensive experiments in Regency Picturesque. Between the 1790s and the 1840s Brighton, Hove, Hastings, Plymouth, Bath, Clifton, Cheltenham and Leamington were developed with sparkling terraces and comfortable villas enlivened with verandahs, colonnades and conservatories, all delightfully interlocking with parks and gardens. An interesting early stage in this process is represented by Henry Holland's Marine Pavilion of 1786 for the Prince of Wales at Brighton. Before its celebrated orientalisation by Nash in 1815–21 the garden front was a series of rippling balconied bows, the parent of many later terraces such as Pelham

Ker Street, Devonport, Devon, 1821-4, by John Foulston, from *The Public Buildings erected in the West of England . . . by John Foulston* (1838). Amazingly, all the buildings in the engraving were executed though the Corinthian terrace and the chapel no longer survive. Foulston explained that 'it occurred to him that if a series of edifices, exhibiting the various features of the architectural world, were erected in conjunction, and skilfully grouped, a happy result might be obtained'. He therefore 'was induced to try an experiment (not before attempted) for producing a picturesque effect'.

Crescent at Hastings, built in 1824–8 by Joseph Kay (1775–1847), a pupil of S. P. Cockerell. Rising as it curves, Pelham Crescent is dramatically broken in the middle by the Ionic portico of Kay's church of St. Mary-in-the Castle. Further curvaceous movement is provided by the shallow balconied bows of different sizes on the two main floors of each house, and also by the semi-circular Diocletian windows in the top storey. Finally, the whole composition has a superb backdrop of towering cliffs surmounted by the remains of Hastings Castle.

One of the several architects involved in the layout of Cheltenham was John Buonarotti Papworth (1775–1847), perhaps the most prolific and versatile exponent of the lighter side of Regency Picturesque taste. He exploited the potentialities of the aquatint process in the coloured plates which he published as *Select Views in London* in Ackermann's *Repository of Arts* (1809–28). He reprinted these separately in 1816 and at the same time published *Architectural Hints* which he reprinted in 1818 and 1832 as *Rural Residences, consisting of a Series of Designs for Cottages, small villas, and other ornamental Buildings*. He followed this in 1823 with his no less delectable *Hints on Ornamental Gardening*. His fetching designs for *cottages ornés*, villas, park entrances, dairies, fishing lodges, icehouses, garden seats and verandahs have always been recognised as the quintessence of the Picturesque. And his improbable role as architect to the King of Württemberg seems in the end no less fitting than that he should have designed a sherbet service for the Pasha of Egypt, a glass throne for the Shah of Persia, a paddle steamer for the Thames and a monument to Colonel Gordon on the field of Waterloo in the form of a broken column. Following his design of 1815 for a 'Tropheum' to commemorate the Battle of Waterloo his friends persuaded him to add 'Buonarotti' to his name in recognition of a talent which seemed to them of Michelangelesque proportion.

John Foulston (1772–1842) was responsible for the similarly unexpected development of Devonport in the 1820s with a school in the Egyptian style, a Greek Doric Town Hall, a 'Hindoo' non-conformist chapel and a street of houses fronted with Corinthian columns. Even more remarkably all these buildings were contrived to form a single picturesque group and as such were subsequently recorded by their architect in the lithographic plates of his book, *The Public Buildings, erected in the West of England, as designed by John Foulston, F.R.I.B.A.* (1838). Unfortunately the chapel and Corinthian houses have now been demolished. In the grounds of 'Athenian Cottage', the house Foulston built for himself near Plymouth, he diverted a stream so as to echo in miniature the effect of the Niagara Falls. Travelling around Plymouth in a vehicle he had designed in imitation of an antique war chariot, he resembled 'Ictinus, of the Parthenon, "out for a lark"', according to his young partner George Wightwick.[12]

Charles Barry (1795–1860), destined to be a greater architect than Papworth or Foulston, made elaborate plans for a development at Brighton in 1829 to be known as Queen's Park. This was inspired by Nash's Park Villages and Burton's Calverley Park but only one of its many villas was ever built: an elegant Italianate residence for Thomas Attree, a prominent local solicitor, which was, alas, demolished in 1971. Sir Joseph Paxton, who had designed the picturesque estate village of Edensor, laid out Birkenhead Park in 1843–7 with numerous villas and terraces à la Nash. The result, at least in its present state, is not visually coherent and the landscaped park, contrived out of marshland, is punctuated by small but arresting hillocks which are too obviously artificial to command respectful attention.

A new phase was initiated thirty years later by Richard Norman Shaw in the work he carried out at Bedford Park, Turnham Green, on the edge of London, for Jonathan T. Carr (1845–1915), a cloth merchant, property speculator and dilettante. Bedford Park was a self-congratulatory artistic community where the middle classes could indulge their advanced artistic and social tastes. One resident recorded that the American artist Edwin Abbey 'took great interest in our village of antique houses, all newly built, in going about which he said pleasantly that he felt as though he were walking through a water-colour'.[13] If Nash had provided the original idea, Shaw now clothed it in the form in which it was to be repeated for the next sixty years. His solid and sensible brick-built houses with spacious bay windows, no basements and modest back gardens are set in quiet tree-lined roads near a railway station, shopping parade and church. Something of the atmosphere of Bedford Park was applied to very different purposes at Port Sunlight in Cheshire where from 1888 the soap manufacturer William Hesketh Lever (created Viscount Leverhulme in 1922) developed a mildly picturesque, model village for his employees. The result is perhaps of more sociological than strictly architectural interest but, as Edward Hubbard has pointed out,[14] represents an influential confluence of two separate traditions which met here for the first time: the sylvan suburb inspired by Nash, and the Victorian philanthropic movement for the improvement of working-class dwellings. The temperance hotel, men's and women's dining-halls, girls' hostel and technical institute, variously rough-cast, tile-hung and half-timbered, all survive today, serving new functions. Sadly, the copy of Anne Hathaway's cottage was demolished between the wars.

At the luxury end of the scale was the astonishing development at Hever Castle, Kent, which had been bought in 1903 by the American William Waldorf Astor. In order to increase the accommodation without impairing the integrity of the

Hever Castle, Kent, 1903-8, by F. L. Pearson for W. W. Astor. A twentieth-century version of Blaise Hamlet for an American millionaire, in which the apparently detached cottages, containing accomodation for guests and servants, are connected to each other and, by means of a covered bridge over the moat, to the restored mediaeval castle itself.

moated mediaeval castle, Astor's architect Frank L. Pearson (1864–1947) built an extensive complex nearby in 1903–8 comprising service and guest ranges cleverly grouped to suggest a feudal village nestling beneath the walls of its lord's residence. Solidly constructed of stone and half-timbering, Pearson's buildings recall Devey's cottages of half a century earlier only a few miles away at Penshurst. The impact of Nash's Blaise Hamlet did not end with Hever. It was felt right into the twentieth century in the design of new model villages such as that of 1900 at Ashton, Northamptonshire, for the Hon. Charles Rothschild; of 1914 at Briantspuddle, Dorset, for Sir Ernest Debenham by Halsey Ricardo and MacDonald Gill; and of 1917 at Ardeley, Hertfordshire, by F. C. Eden.

In the meantime, an uneducated London clerk called Ebenezer Howard (1850–1928) who had spent some time in Chicago published *Tomorrow; a Peaceful Path to Real Reform* (1898) which he reissued in 1902 under the more suggestive and influential title *Garden Cities of Tomorrow*. Howard adopted a sentimental Ruskinian rhetoric to proclaim a new world of Utopian socialism built around communal kitchens and gardens. More important was his theme of the Town-Country Magnet which he used to argue for new Garden Cities of fixed population and area, served by planned industries and surrounded by a Green Belt. In 1903 the Garden City Association was founded and work was begun soon after on its first practical expression, Letchworth Garden City. The architects Barry Parker and Raymond Unwin produced a low-key picturesque layout in which their own architectural contributions and those of many other well-known architects have never risen above the second-rate.

Far more successful than Letchworth was Hampstead Garden Suburb, planned by the same architects and founded in 1905 largely through the endeavours of Dame Henrietta Barnett, whose husband had founded Toynbee Hall in the East End of London. Hampstead, which had rather different origins

'View of the Garden Suburb as it will appear from the Heath in another year or two', from a booklet of 1909 by Raymond Unwin and Baillie Scott advertising Hampstead Garden Suburb. The Arts and Crafts spire of Lutyens's St. Jude's presides unexpectedly over this cosily domestic version of a fortified German town.

from Letchworth, similarly represented the convergence of two traditions: the preservation of the countryside in the face of increasing industrial and urban sprawl, and the theories of romantic socialism which led Mrs Barnett to suppose that if the different classes lived close enough together the divisions between them would be broken down. The new social order envisaged at Hampstead never fully materialised and its wooded hilly lanes soon became the preserve of the prosperous middle and upper-middle classes. In 1909 Unwin and Baillie Scott summed up the escapist pastoral atmosphere they had been at such pains to create:

The houses themselves, among their trees and boscage, their gardens and greens, are a stirring picture of what our cities may be one day when other things are thought of than the highest possible sum to be wrung in ground rents out of a certain area. The visitor is struck by the home-like appearance of the houses . . . It seems a restful place to live in; there is a serene atmosphere about it. As one strolls along the roadways – there are no real streets – one recalls the satisfying old brick houses of elderly, airy, unspoilt towns like Evesham and the quiet dignified by-ways of such places as Haarlem. The greens, laid out country fashion, the treasured old oaks in unexpected places, the new hedges of privet, sweetbriar, yew, holly and quick, the treillage clothed with honeysuckle and jasmine, that forms a welcome substitute for garden walls – the sunk lawns, the roadside trees – often fruit trees, and not singly but several rows deep – help in the making of what is indeed a grateful retreat from 'London's central roar'.[15]

The planning of Hampstead Garden Suburb, which made careful visual use of accidents of terrain and planting, as well as creating new 'accidents', revived whether consciously or not, the principles of Price and Knight. The tall Germanic shops by Unwin in Temple Fortune Lane and the 'fortified' wall with watch-towers separating the houses from Hampstead Heath Extension, suggest the mediaeval walled towns of Germany such as Rothenburg which features prominently in Unwin's comprehensive and attractive study, *Town Planning in Practice, an Introduction to the Art of Designing Cities and Suburbs* (1909). Indeed Hampstead seems to echo the work of the Viennese architect and planner Camillo Sitte (1843–1903) who had published in German an influential volume of essays

Street junction, from Raymond Unwin's *Town Planning in Practice* (1909), showing how a professional town-planner combined an English feeling for the picturesque village with the systematic study of historic town layout on the Continent, which Camillo Sitte had published in 1889.

called *City Planning According to Artistic Principles* (1889), translated inaccurately into French in 1902. Sitte studied the apparently jumbled or picturesque planning of the centres of the mediaeval and baroque towns of Europe in order to extract a set of principles which could be applied both to the design of new streets, squares and monuments, and to the remodelling and preservation of existing historic towns. He was thus at the centre of the unsuccessful battles to prevent the destruction of the core of old Vienna in the 1890s. The concern for urban preservation is again a parallel to the rural preservation which was at the heart of the Hampstead Garden Suburb experiment: the Trustees at Hampstead included not only W. H. Lever of Port Sunlight and George Cadbury of the model industrial village of Bournville, but also Sir Robert Hunter who was one of the three founders and the first Chairman of the National Trust. The impulse to preserve the image of nature unsullied by nineteenth-century progress had provided the characteristic passion and beauty of much of Ruskin's compellingly influential work. It was Ruskin, Morris, J. S. Mill, T. H. Huxley and their associates who formed the Society to Protect Commons, Open Spaces, and Footpaths in 1865. The Commons Society ran successful campaigns to preserve from enclosure Hampstead Heath, Berkhamstead, Plumstead, Tooting, Wandsworth and Wimbledon Commons, and Epping and Ashdown Forests. Sir Robert Hunter, a solicitor, who was a leading member of the society from 1868, subsequently joined Octavia Hill and Canon Rawnsley in founding its logical successor, The National Trust for Places of Historic Interest or Natural Beauty. Miss Hill's work as a philanthropist had led her to appreciate the need of the working classes for access to open space, while Canon Rawnsley, who lived in and loved the Lake District of Gilpin, Wordsworth and Ruskin, had vigorously opposed the railway with which it was proposed to connect Buttermere and Braithwaite.

The continuing preoccupation with the rural scene is one of the strongest features of English literary life up to the Second World War. The seemingly endless flow of novels by Sheila Kaye-Smith (1887–1956) and Mary Webb

Portmeirion, Gwynedd, 1926-39 and 1954-70 by Sir Clough Williams-Ellis. One of the most substantial of all picturesque follies, this evocation of an Italian coastal village has been compared by its architect with the recent creation of a Mediterranean harbour town at Port Grimaud on the gulf of St. Tropez. Like a Rex Whistler *trompe l'oeil* or a Panini *capriccio*, Portmeirion effortlessly digests a combination of real and invented buildings of different periods, including fragments brought from Dawpool, Hooton Hall, Arnos Court, Nercwys Hall and Emral Hall.

(1881–1927) exalted the supposed richness and sincerity of a life close to the soil, as did the many books of H. J. Massingham (1888–1952), agriculturalist and journalist. The Catholic-orientated Distributist and 'Back to the Land' movements were a part of this way of thinking, and it is no coincidence that Sheila Kaye-Smith and Massingham were Catholic converts. The alarming engulfment of the countryside between the wars with the ribbon development, seaside bungalows and petrol stations of modern suburbia also provoked brilliant reaction from the architect Clough Williams-Ellis (1883–1978) in the form of his polemical study *England and the Octopus* (1928) and a book of essays which he edited under the title *Britain and the Beast* (1938). From 1926 he gave practical expression to his ideals in his truly astonishing village of Portmeirion where he showed how a section of coastline could be developed in the twentieth century without ruining its natural charms. Part stage set, part Italian hill town and part fishing village,

Laundry and workers' housing, Drury Lane, Knutsford, Cheshire, 1898, by R. H. Watt. The chimney stack masquerading as a minaret was copied from one Watt had seen in Palestine. Watt's habit of standing up in his carriage to admire his picturesque creations cost him his life in 1913 when his horse shied and threw him to the ground in front of one of his exotic villas.

Portmeirion was continually growing and changing between 1926 and 1939 and again between 1954 and 1970. The result is undoubtedly the most complete expression of picturesque principle in this century. The nearest modern parallel is probably the freakish buildings with which Richard Harding Watt (1842–1913), glove-maker and amateur architect, enlivened the little Cheshire town of Knutsford between 1895 and 1908. There, the Ruskin Rooms, Gaskell Memorial Tower, King's Coffee House, numerous villas and cottages, and the laundry with its soaring minaret, are experiments in such diverse styles as the Italianate, castellated, Byzantine and Art Nouveau.

Portmerion is picturesque in its make-believe quality, its principle of growth, use of accident, whimsical contrast of styles, re-use of earlier buildings transplanted from other parts of the country and, above all, in its emphatically *visual* basis. Clough Williams-Ellis recorded how when he showed Portmerion with some trepidation to Frank Lloyd Wright, 'to my profound astonishment, he took it all without a blink, seeming instantly to see the point of all my wilful pleasantries, the calculated naïveties, eye-traps, forced and faked perspectives, heretical constructions, unorthodox colour mixtures and general architectural levity'.[16]

Portmeirion is not just a fantasy. Its hotel and holiday houses bring in an essential income, and it also plays a deliberately didactic role for, as Williams-Ellis has written, 'I was aiming at winning as yet uninterested and uniformed popular support for architecture, planning, landscaping, the use of colour and indeed for design generally, by a gay, light-opera sort of approach, whereby the casual visitor who had perhaps only turned up to bathe, or to eat, or out of vague curiosity, might be ensnared into taking a really intelligent interest in the things that give some of us fortunate ones such intense and abiding pleasure'.[17]

Christopher Hussey's impressive book, *The Picturesque, Studies in a Point of View* (1927) was published at the moment of conception of Portmeirion. Indeed, he put Williams-Ellis's views in a nutshell in his definition of picturesque architecture as 'not, except in rare instances, a style, but a method of using and combining styles'.[18] We have already seen how Hussey's tastes and perceptions

Hallfield Housing Scheme, Bishop's Bridge Road, Paddington, London, 1948-50, by Tecton, Lasdun and Drake. Townscape drawing by Gorden Cullen, published in the *Architectural Review*, February 1954, in which the picturesque stock-in-trade of asymmetry, variety, surprise, contrasting textures, blending of indoors and outdoors, and use of sculpture, was deployed in an attempt to make tower blocks seem cheerful and acceptable for residential use.

were formed by his admiration for Lutyens and for the English landscape tradition as developed, for example, in his own family place, Scotney Castle in Kent. In 1923 he wrote characteristically of Lutyens's Ednaston Manor in Derbyshire that 'when a house is built a little bit of England is permanently changed'.[19] This profoundly felt perception of the link between architecture and setting, which he had learned from the Picturesque, lay at the heart of all he tried to do in his fifty-year-long career at *Country Life*.

Further important work on the history of the Picturesque was undertaken by the emigré German scholar, Nikolaus Pevsner. As part of an art-historical outlook dependent on Hegelian notions of the *Zeitgeist*, Pevsner was anxious to see art as an expression of national character. The Picturesque appealed to him as a uniquely English contribution to European aesthetics and he therefore published essays in the 1940s, mainly in the *Architectural Review*, on 'Sir William Temple and Sharawaggi', 'The Genesis of the Picturesque', Payne Knight, Uvedale Price and Humphry Repton, and followed these with a book in 1956 called *The Englishness of English Art*. Deeply concerned with the problem of post-war reconstruction, Pevsner used his position as an editor of the *Architectural Review* to argue for the application of picturesque principles to modern urban design. Claiming that the work of Gropius and Le Corbusier was picturesque, Pevsner argued in 1954 that 'the Modern revolution of the early twentieth century and the Picturesque revolution of a hundred years before had all their fundamentals in common. The qualities of the modern movement were not developed to please the eye, but ... no other existing aesthetic theory fits the demands of modern architecture and planning so well as that of Price and Knight'.[20] The result of this preoccupation came to be known as 'Townscape' and was extensively illustrated in the *Architectural Review* in crudely impressionistic sketches by Gorden Cullen which always included windswept patios and outdoor cafés enlivened with metal

South Woodham Ferrars, Essex, 1977-9, by the Holder and Mathias Partnership. One of the most thoroughgoing of the many recent attempts to produce a kind of picturesque folk-architecture in reaction to the lack of historical resonance in modern architecture. Opened by H. M. The Queen in May 1981, South Woodham Ferrars is an example of the continuing English preoccupation with the charms of the village which dates back at least to the late eighteenth century.

furniture and shallow concrete flower-tubs. These supposedly picturesque ideals bore meagre fruit in the pedestrian precincts of the New Towns such as Harlow, begun in 1947, which were further prevented from achieving any real picturesque quality by their overall architectural bankruptcy.

If the need for post-war reconstruction stimulated a revival of picturesque planning theory, then the bombing raids on English cities created ruins which were immediately seen as picturesque. Ravishing photographs of ruined buildings appeared in the *Architectural Review* in the 1940s and were published in book form by John Summerson and James Richards as *The Bombed Buildings of Britain* (1942; enlarged ed. 1947). In September 1947 John Piper published in the same journal an article called 'Pleasing Decay' in which he claimed that 'Bomb damage has revealed new beauties in unexpected appositions – a rich source of information for the planner who would retain picturesque elements from the past that can be opposed in size, colour and shape to new buildings and groups of buildings, whether by way of contrast or agreement. As to texture, modern painters have left few possibilities unexplored: surely their works are source-books that can inspire architecture in the future, as painters have inspired architects in the past?'[21] Piper later incorporated this article in a charming topographical book called *Buildings and Prospects* (1948) which, like his own style in painting, was a picturesque celebration of the texture of English landscape and buildings.

Pevsner's colleague at the *Architectural Review*, Sir James Richards, published in 1946 *The Castles on the Ground, the Anatomy of Suburbia*. This attractive eulogy of the leafy picturesque retreats of the middle classes, written by a Communist dedicated to the furtherance of Modern Movement architecture, surprised and annoyed many. However, as Richards later observed with some justice, he had 'attempted to establish architectural criticism as criticism of the *results* of building, not of buildings as such; a direction in which today's emphasis on the environment also leads'.[22] Though the sociological approach implicit in this claim is not without dangers for the art historian, it has its usefulness in describing picturesque suburbia. Indeed Richards's book of 1946 was not the last published tribute to the potency of the Picturesque, for in 1973 Nicholas Taylor, the first Environmental Correspondent of the *Sunday Times*, published a vigorous and historically well-informed study of urban housing called *The Village in the City, Towards a New Society*. More recently Gillian Darley has published *Villages of Vision* (1975), an attractive essay on the history of the Arcadian ideal, and Nigel Temple *John Nash and the Village Picturesque* (1979). In the meantime, with the death of the Modern Movement, stylistic pluralism has been established as the architectural fashion of the 1980s. Presumably Price and Knight would have approved.

Notes

Preface   pp. vii–xi

1 H. Walpole, *Anecdotes of Painting in England*, ed. J. Dallway, 5 vols., 1828, IV, p. 278.

2 W. Gilpin, *Observations ... on ... Cumberland, and Westmoreland*, 1786, II, p. 253.

3 J. Harris, 'English Country House Guides, 1740–1840', *Concerning Architecture*, ed. J. Summerson, 1968, pp. 58–74.

4 E. Burke, *A Philosophical Enquiry into the Origin of our Ideas of the Sublime and Beautiful*, 5th ed., 1767, p. 137.

5 T. Blaikie, *Diary of a Scotch Gardener at the French Court at the End of the Eighteenth Century*, ed. F. Birrell, 1931, pp. 166–7.

6 *The Complete Works of Sir John Vanbrugh*, IV, *The Letters*, G. Webb ed., 1928, p. 30.

7 Sir U. Price, *Three Essays on the Picturesque*, 1810, II, p. 116.

8 Ibid., I, pp. 37–40.

9 *The Works of John Ruskin*, E. T. Cook & A. Wedderburn eds, 39 vols., 1903–12, VIII, pp. 235–7.

10 C. Meeks, *The Rail-Road Station, an Architectural History*, New Haven & London, 1957, pp. 3–8.

11 *R.I.B.A. Journal*, vol. 55, Dec. 1947. p. 58.

12 J. Gage, *Colour in Turner*, 1969, p. 57.

13 C. Hussey, *The Picturesque, Studies in a Point of View*, 1927, p. 4.

Chapter 1   pp. 1–30

1 S. H. Monk ed., *Five Miscellaneous Essays by Sir William Temple*, Ann Arbor, 1963, p. 30.

2 *Spectator*, 4th ed. 1718, VI, No. 414, 25 June 1712, pp. 70–1.

3 *Guardian*, 1714, II, No. 173, 29 Sept 1713, pp. 493–4.

4 Cooper, A. A., 3rd Earl of Shaftesbury, *The Moralists, a Philosophical Rhapsody* (1709), *Characteristicks of Men, Manners, Opinions, Times*, II, 1723, pp. 393–4.

5 R. Wittkower, *Palladio and English Palladianism*, 1974, pp. 177–90.

6 S. Switzer, *Ichnographia Rustica*, 1718, III, p. 5.

7 Ibid, II, p. 201.

8 Ibid., III, p. 6.

9 Ibid., III, p. 1.

10 H. Walpole, *Anecdotes of Painting in England*, J. Dallaway ed., 5 vols., 1828, IV, pp. 263–4 and p. 278.

11 K. Downes, *Vanbrugh*, 1977, p. 109.

12 A. Young, *A Six Months Tour through the North of England*, 1770, II, p. 83.

13 *The Complete Works of Sir John Vanbrugh*, IV, *The Letters*, G. Webb ed., 1928, pp. 29–30.

14 H. Walpole, op. cit., IV, p. 263.

15 Historical Manuscripts Commission Report, 42, Carlisle MSS, pp. 143–4. Robinson to Carlisle, 23 December 1734.

16 H. Walpole, op. cit., IV, p. 264.

17 P. Willis, *Charles Bridgeman and the English Landscape Garden*, 1977, pp. 110–11 (Perceval to Dering, 14 August 1724. BL, Add MS 47030, fos 156–59).

18 J. Spence, *Observations, Anecdotes, and Characters of Books and Men collected from Conversation*, 2 vols., Oxford, 1966, I, p. 423.

19 G. B. Clarke, 'Grecian Taste and Gothic Virtue. Lord Cobham's Gardening Programme and its Iconography', *Apollo*, June 1973, pp. 566–71.

20 *The Correspondence of Alexander Pope*, G. Sherburn ed., Oxford, 1956, II, p. 513.

21 K. Woodbridge, *Landscape and Antiquity*, Oxford, 1971, p. 35 (Hoare to Lord Bruce, 23 Dec. 1765. Tottenham House Archive, Savernake).

22 C. Hussey, *English Gardens and Landscapes 1700–50*, 1967, p. 164.

23 K. Woodbridge, op. cit., p. 53 (Hoare to Lady Bruce, 23 Oct. 1762. Ailesbury Archives, Savernake).

Chapter 2   pp. 31–44

1 J. Harris, *Gardens of Delight, the Rococo English Landscape of Thomas Robins the Elder*, 1978, p. 44.

2 E. J. Climenson, *Elizabeth Montagu, the Queen of the Blue-Stockings, her Correspondence from 1720 to 1761*, 1906, II, p. 150.

3 W. Chambers, *Design of Chinese Buildings*, 1757, p. (ii).

4 E. J. Climenson ed., *Passages from the Diaries of Mrs. Philip Lybbe Powys ... 1756–1808*, 1899, p. 114.

Chapter 3   pp. 45–66

1 *The Correspondence of Alexander Pope*, ed. cit., III, pp. 299–300.

2 *The Autobiography and Correspondence of Mary Granville, Mrs Delany*, Lady Llanover ed., 6 vols 1861–2, I, p. 421.

3 A. Young, op. cit., II, p. 90.

4 D. Stroud, *Capability Brown*, 1975, p. 139.

5 W. Gilpin, *Observations . . . on several parts of Great Britain; particularly the High-Lands of Scotland*, 1789, I, pp. 21–3.

6 H. W. Hawkes, 'Sanderson Miller of Radway, 1716–1780, Architect', Diploma Thesis, Cambridge 1964, p. 43 (Dacre to Miller, Jan. 1749. Newdigate Papers, Warwickshire Record Office).

7 W. Shenstone, *Letters*, M. Williams ed., Oxford 1939, p. 147.

8 J. Heely, *Letters on the Beauties of Hagley, Envil and the Leasowes*, 1777, I, p. 73.

9 H. Walpole, *Correspondence*, ed. W. S. Lewis, XXXV, 1973, pp. 148–9.

10 Hawkes, op. cit., p. 1 (Lyttleton to Miller, 1 June 1749. Newdigate Papers, Warwickshire Record Office).

11 Wimpole Red Book, 1801, quoted in G. Jackson-Stops, *Wimpole Hall, Cambridgeshire*, 1979, p. 42.

12 W. Gilpin, *Observations on the Coasts of Hampshire, Sussex, and Kent, relative chiefly to Picturesque Beauty made in the summer of the year 1774*, 1804, pp. 97–8.

13 H. Walpole, *Anecdotes of Painting*, ed. cit., IV, p. 398.

14 J. Fleming, *Robert Adam and his Circle in Edinburgh and Rome*, 1962, p. 135.

15 W. Chambers, *Plans, Elevations . . . of the Gardens and Buildings at Kew*, 1763, p. 7.

16 T. J. McCormick, 'Charles-Louis Clérisseau and the Roman Revival', Ph.D. Thesis, Princeton, 1970, p. 35 (Diary of Robert Adam, Jan. 1755. Edinburgh Register House).

17 McCormick, op. cit., p. 36 (Robert Adam to James Adam, 19 Feb. 1755. Edinburgh Register House).

18 R. P. Knight, *The Landscape*, 1794, p. 54.

19 W. Gilpin, *Observations . . . on . . . Cumberland, and Westmoreland*, 1786, II, pp. 184 and 188.

20 H. von Pückler-Muskau, *Tour of Germany, Holland and England . . .*, 1832, IV, p. 202.

21 Port Eliot Red Book, 1792, quoted in D. Stroud, *Humphry Repton*, 1962, p. 69.

22 R. P. Knight, op. cit., pp. 52–3.

7 W. Chambers, *A Dissertation on Oriental Gardening*, 1772, p. 161 and pp. 106–7.

8 Ibid., pp. 40–1.

9 H. von Pückler-Muskau, op. cit., III, pp. 241–2.

10 W. Gilpin, *An Essay upon Prints; containing remarks upon the principles of picturesque beauty*, 1768, p. 2.

11 J. Reynolds, *Discourses on Art*, R. R. Wark ed., San Marino, 1959, p. 243.

12 U. Price, op. cit., I, pp. 37–40.

13 Ibid., I, pp. 50–1.

14 *The Poems of Alexander Pope*, F. W. Bateson ed., III, ii, 1951, p. 138.

15 M. Allentuck, 'Price and the Picturesque Garden', *The Picturesque Garden and its Influence outside the British Isles*, N. Pevsner ed., Dumbarton Oaks, 1974, p. 76 (Price to Lady Beaumont, 9 June 1804. Coleorton Papers, Pierpont Morgan Library).

16 J. W. Goethe, transl., 'Tagebuch einer Reise nach Sicilien von Henry Knight' [i.e. R. P. Knight], in *Philipp Hackert: Biographische Skizze*, Tübingen, 1811.

17 R. P. Knight, op. cit., p. 31.

18 Ibid., pp. 15–16.

19 H. Repton, *The Landscape Gardening and Landscape Architecture of the Late Humphry Repton, Esq. Being his entire works on these subjects*, J. C. Loudon ed., 1840, p. 99.

20 Ibid., p. 603.

21 Ibid., p. 460.

22 N. Pevsner, *Studies in Art, Architecture and Design*, 1968, I, p. 152.

23 H. Repton, op. cit., p. 330.

24 Ibid., p. 528.

25 Ibid., p. 536.

26 E. Croft-Murray, *Decorative Painting in England 1537–1837*, II, 1970, p. 61.

27 B. Jones, *Follies and Grottoes*, 2nd ed., 1974, p. 250.

28 *Country Life*, XLVI, 9 Aug. 1919, p. 176.

29 Ibid., XVIII, 5 Aug. 1905, p. 162.

30 R. Gathorne Hardy ed., *Ottoline, The Early Memoirs of Lady Ottoline Morrell*, 1963, p. 128.

Chapter 4 pp. 67–88

1 E. Burke, op. cit., p. 213 and p. 300.

2 R. H. Benson, *The Conventionalists*, 1908, p. 307.

3 L. Dickins & M. Stanton, *An Eighteenth Century Correspondence*, 1910, p. 416.

4 *The Autobiography . . . of . . . Mrs Delany*, op. cit., III, p. 611.

5 T. Whately, *Observations on Modern Gardening*, Dublin, 1770, pp. 195–6.

6 H. Walpole, *Correspondence*, ed. W. S. Lewis, XXIX, 1955, p. 85.

Chapter 5 pp. 89–130

1 J. Reynolds, op. cit., pp. 241–2.

2 *The Complete Works of Sir John Vanbrugh*, loc. cit., p. 14.

3 H. Walpole, *Correspondence*, W. S. Lewis et al. eds., XXXVII, pp. 269–70.

4 Ibid., XIX, p. 497.

5 Ibid., XX, p. 111.

6 Ibid. XX, p. 127.

7 Ibid., XX, p. 372.

8 Ibid., XXI, p. 306.

9 L. Melville, ed., *The Life and Letters of William Beckford*, 1910, p. 299.

10 R. P. Knight, *An Analytical Inquiry into the Principles of Taste*, 4th ed. 1808, p. 225.

11 Ibid., p. 223.

12 *The Works in Architecture of Robert and James Adam*, I, 1773, p. v.

13 M. Girouard, *Life in the English Country House*, New Haven & London, 1978, p. 199.

14 H. Walpole, *Correspondence*, ed. cit. XIX p. 497 & XX, p. 16.

15 *Country Life*, CXLV, 17 April 1969, p. 955.

16 B. H. Malkin, *The Scenery, Antiquities and Biography of South Wales*, 2nd ed. 1807, II, pp. 71–2.

17 Ibid., II, pp. 87–9.

18 G. Borrow, *Wild Wales, its People, Language and Scenery* (1862), 1977 ed., p. 433.

19 R. P. Knight, *The Landscape*, p. 53.

20 *Architectural Review*, LXXXVII, June 1940, pp. 207–10.

21 *The Cornhill Magazine*, No. 970, Spring 1947, pp. 275–83.

22 *Life at Fonthill 1807–1822 . . . from the Correspondence of William Beckford*, B. Alexander transl. and ed., 1957, p. 128.

23 H. Walpole, *Correspondence*, ed. cit., XII, p. 111.

24 Ibid., XII, p. 136.

25 J. Rutter, *Delineations of Fonthill and its Abbey*, Shaftesbury and London, 1823, p. 110.

26 *Life at Fonthill*, op. cit., pp. 80–1.

27 See C. Wainwright, 'Some Objects from William Beckford's Collection now in the Victoria and Albert Museum', *Burlington Magazine*, CXII, May 1971, pp. 254–64.

28 J. C. Loudon ed., *The Gardener's Magazine*, XI, 1835, pp. 442–3.

29 *Life at Fonthill*, op. cit., pp. 97–8.

30 G. Lipscomb, *Journey into South Wales: in the year 1799*, 1802, p. 163.

31 C. R. Cockerell, Diary, 21 Jan. 1823, quoted in D. J. Watkin, *The Life and Work of C. R. Cockerell, R.A.*, 1974, pp. 69–71.

32 H. Repton, op. cit., pp. 593–4.

33 R. P. Knight, *An Analytical Inquiry into the Principles of Taste*, 4th ed. 1808, pp. 221–2.

34 B. Hofland, *A Descriptive Account of the Mansion and Gardens of White Knights* (1819), introd. by T. Hope (1808), pp. 11–13.

35 C. R. Cockerell, 'Ichnographica Domestica', 1825 (Crichton Collection), quoted by J. Harris in *Architectural History*, 14, 1971, p. 13.

36 U. Price, op. cit., II, p. 180.

37 J. Harris, loc. cit., p. 13.

38 J. Soane, *Description of . . . the Residence of Sir John Soane, Architect*, 1835, p. 58.

39 *The Works of John Ruskin*, ed. cit., XIII, p. 308.

40 J. Soane, *Lectures on Architecture*, ed. A. T. Bolton, 1929, p. 126.

41 A. Michaelis, *Ancient Marbles in Great Britain*, Cambridge, 1882, p. 473.

Chapter 6   pp. 131–160

1 A. J. C. Hare, *The Story of Two Noble Lives*, 1893, I, p. 178.

2 A. W. N. Pugin, *The True Principles of Pointed or Christian Architecture*, 1841, pp. 62–3.

3 *The Builder*, VIII, 27 July 1850, p. 355.

4 M. J. Dobson, *A Memoir of John Dobson*, 1885.

5 Ibid.

6 *The Builder*, XXXIV, 27 May 1876, p. 507.

7 M. Girouard, *The Victorian Country House*, Oxford, 1971, p. 57.

8 Ibid., p. 74.

9 Ibid., p. 118.

10 *The Works of John Ruskin*, ed. cit., I, p. 9.

11 Ibid., I, p. 187.

12 Ibid., XII, p. 33.

13 Ibid., XII, p. 50.

14 Ibid., VIII, pp. 235–7.

15 Ibid., VIII, pp. 240–1.

16 Ibid., XI, pp. 225–6.

17 E.-E. Viollet-le-Duc, *Habitations modernes*, Paris, 1875, I, p. 15.

18 *British Architect*, 1894, XLI, p. 308.

19 A. Saint, *Richard Norman Shaw*, New Haven and London, 1976, p. 219.

20 *The Builder*, LIX, 18 Oct. 1890, p. 309.

21 C. Hussey, *The Life of Sir Edwin Lutyens*, 1950, p. 23.

22 G. Jekyll, *Home and Garden*, 1900, pp. 4–5.

23 Ibid., pp. 14–15.

24 Lutyens Correspondence, R.I.B.A. Library, Lutyens to Lady Emily Lutyens, 8 Aug. 1933.

25 C. Hussey, op. cit., p. 86.

26 E. S. Prior, *The Cathedral Builders in England*, 1905, p. 25.

27 A. S. G. Butler, *The Architecture of Sir Edwin Lutyens*, 1950, I, p. 46.

28 W. G. Newton, *The Work of Ernest Newton, R.A.*, 1925, p. 4.

29 L. Weaver, *Small Country Houses of Today*, I, 3rd ed. 1922, pp. 28–9.

30 C. V. Balsan, *The Glitter and the Gold*, 1953, pp. 163–4.

31 I. Nairn & N. Pevsner, *The Buildings of England, Surrey*, 2nd ed. Harmondsworth, 1971, p. 396.

32 Idem., *The Buildings of England, Sussex*, Harmondsworth, 1965, p. 98.

Chapter 7   pp. 161–180

1 H. Walpole, *Correspondence*, ed. cit., XXXV, pp. 125–6.
2 T. Blaikie, op. cit., p. 210.
3 Ibid., p. 132.
4 Ibid., p. 179.

Chapter 8   pp. 181–200

1 U. Price, op. cit., II, p. 346.
2 *The Works of Oliver Goldsmith*, P. Cunningham ed., 4 vols., 1854, I, p. 49.
3 U. Price, op. cit., II, pp. 341–2.
4 Ibid., II, p. 346.
5 D. J. Watkin, op. cit., p. 81.
6 N. Temple, *John Nash and the Village Picturesque*, Gloucester, 1979, p. 136 (G. S. Repton to J. S. Harford, 23 Aug. 1810. Harford Papers, Bristol Record Office).
7 J. C. Loudon ed., *The Gardener's Magazine*, XII, 1836, pp. 292–3.
8 W. S. Gilpin, *Practical Hints upon Landscape Gardening*, 1832, p. 187.
9 J. Reynolds, op. cit., p. 243.
10 J. Summerson, *The Life and Work of John Nash, Architect*, 1980, p. 204 (n. 18).
11 D. J. Watkin, op. cit., p. 138.
12 G. Wightwick, 'The Life of an Architect', *Bentley's Miscellany*, XLII, 1857, p. 297.
13 M. D. Conway, *Autobiography, Memories and Experiences*, 1904, II, p. 341.
14 N. Pevsner & E. Hubbard, *The Buildings of England, Cheshire*, Harmondsworth, 1971, pp. 3–4.
15 *Town Planning and Modern Architecture at the Hampstead Garden Suburb with contributions by Raymond Unwin and M. H. Baillie Scott*, 1909, pp. 83–7.
16 C. Williams-Ellis, *Architect Errant*, 1971, p. 210.
17 Ibid., p. 209.
18 C. Hussey, *The Picturesque, Studies in a Point of View*, 1927, p. 217.
19 *Country Life*, LIII, 24 March 1923, p. 404.
20 *Architectural Review*, CXV, April 1954, p. 229.
21 Ibid., CII, Sept. 1947, p. 93.
22 J. Richards, *The Castles on the Ground*, 2nd ed. 1973, p. 2.

Bibliography

Place of publication is London unless otherwise stated.
Abbreviations:
AH *Architectural History, Journal of the Society of Architectural Historians of Great Britain*
AR *Architectural Review*
CL *Country Life*

Primary Sources

Ackermann, R. *The Microcosm of London*, 3 vols. (1805).
Ackermann, R. ed. *The Repository of Arts, Literature, Commerce, Manufactures, Fashions and Politics*, 35 vols. (1809–29).
Adam, R. *Ruins of the Palace of the Emperor Diocletian at Spalatro, in Dalmatia* (1764).
Adam, R. & J. *Works in Architecture*, 3 vols. (1773–1822).
Addison, J. 'The Pleasures of the Imagination', *Spectator*, 21 June–4 July and 6 Sept. 1712.
Aikin, E. *Designs for Villas* (1808).
Alison, Rev. A. *Essays on the Nature and Principles of Taste* (Edinburgh, 1790).
Allason, T. *Picturesque Views of the Antiquities of Pola, in Istria* (1819).
Alphand, A. *Les Promenades de Paris* (Paris, 1868).
Annals of the Fine Arts (5 vols. 1817–20).
Atkinson, W. *Views of Picturesque Cottages with Plans* (1805).
Angus, W. *Seats of the Nobility and Gentry* (1787).
Attiret, J.-D. *Lettres édifiantes et curieuses, écrits des Missions étrangères de la Compagnie de Jésus*, XXVII, (Paris, 1749).
A Walk Round Mount Edgcumbe (Plymouth, c.1808 etc.).
Barber, W. *Farm Buildings; or Rural Economy. Containing Designs for Cottages, Farm-Houses, Lodges, Farm-yards* (1802).
Barry, A. *The Life and Works of Sir Charles Barry* (1867).
Bartell, E, Jr. *Hints for Picturesque Improvements in Ornamented Cottages, and their Scenery* (1804).
Baumgartner, F. G. ed. *Neue Gartenbaukunst* (Leipzig, 1818–20).
Beckford, W. *Italy; with Sketches of Spain and Portugal*, 2 vols. (1834).
—, *Recollections of an Excursion to the Monasteries of Alcobaça and Batalha in 1794* (1835).
—, *The Journal of William Beckford in Portugal and Spain* (written 1787–8, published 1954).
—, *Vathek* (written in French 1782; published in English 1786).
Bickham, G. *The Beauties of Stowe* (1750).

Blaikie, T. *Diary of a Scotch Gardener at the French Court at the End of the Eighteenth Century*. F. Birrell ed. (1931).

Boullée, E.-L. *Architecture. Essai sur l'art* (c.1790; ed. Pérouse de Montclos, Paris, 1968).

Bridgeman, S. *A General Plan of the Woods, Park and Gardens of Stowe* (1739).

Britton, J. *Bath and Bristol* (1829).

—, *Descriptive Sketches of Tunbridge Wells and the Calverley Estate* (1832).

—, *Devonshire and Cornwall Illustrated* (1832).

—, *Graphical and Literary Illustrations of Fonthill Abbey* (1823).

—, *Graphical Illustrations of Toddington* (1840).

—, *History, &c. of Deepdene* (MS. 1821–6).

—, *Illustrations of the Deepdene* (MS. 1826).

—, *Modern Athens or Edinburgh in the Nineteenth Century* (1829).

—, *Picturesque Antiquities of the English Cities* (1830).

—, *Picturesque Views of the English Cities* (1828).

—, & Brayley, E. W. *The Beauties of England and Wales*. 18 vols. (1801–16).

—, —, *The History and Description . . . of Cassiobury Park* (1837).

— & Pugin, A. C. *The Public Buildings of London*. 2 vols. (1825–8).

—, —, *The Union of Architecture, Sculpture and Painting* (1827).

Brooks, S. H. *Designs for Cottage and Villa Architecture* (1839).

Brown, R. *Domestic Architecture* (n.d. 1842).

Buckler, J. & J. C. *Views of Eaton Hall*, 1826.

Burke, E. *A Philosophical Enquiry into the Origin of our Ideas of the Sublime and the Beautiful* (1757).

Busby, C. A. *A Series of Designs for Villas and Country Houses* (1808).

—, *A Collection of Designs for Modern Embellishments* (1810).

Burton, J. *Views at St Leonards, near Hastings* (n.d. 1828).

Cameron, C. *The Baths of the Romans explained and illustrated* (1772).

Campbell, C. *Vitruvius Britannicus*, 3 vols. (1717–25); continued by T. Badeslade & J. Rocque, 1 vol. (1739), and by J. Wolfe & J. Gandon, 2 vols. (1767–71).

Carlisle, N. *Hints on Rural Residences* (1825).

Carrogis, L. (Carmontelle) *Jardin de Monceau, près de Paris* (Paris, 1779).

Castell, R. *The Villas of the Ancients Illustrated* (1728).

Caylus, Comte de *Recueil d'antiquités égyptiennes, étrusques, grecques et romaines* (title of vols. 3–7 expanded to include *et gauloises*) 7 vols. (Paris, 1752–67).

Chambers, W. *Designs of Chinese Buildings* (1757).

—, *A Dissertation on Oriental Gardening* (1772).

—, *Plans, Elevations, Sections and Perspective Views of the Gardens and Buildings at Kew in Surrey* (1763).

Choiseul-Gouffier, M.-G.-H.-F. *Voyage pittoresque de la grèce*, 2 vols. (Paris, 1782, 1809).

Collard, W. & Ross, M. *Architectural and Picturesque Views in Newcastle-upon-Tyne* (Newcastle-upon-Tyne, 1841).

Colt-Hoare, R. *A Description of the House and Gardens at Stourhead* (Bath, 1818).

Combe, W. *The Tour of Dr Syntax in Search of the Picturesque, a Poem* (1812).

Cozens, A. *A New Method of Assisting the Invention in drawing Original Compositions of Landscapes* (n.d., c.1785).

Cumberland, G. *An Attempt to describe Hafod* (1796).

Davies, H. *A View of Cheltenham in its Past and Present State* (Cheltenham, 1843).

Dearn, T. D. W. *Sketches in Architecture*, 2 vols. (1806–7).

—, *Designs for Lodges and Entrances to Parks, Paddocks and Pleasure-Grounds* (1811).

—, *An Historical, Topographical and Descriptive Account of the Weald of Kent* (Cranbrook, 1814).

Decker, P. *Chinese Architecture* (1759).

—, *Gothic Architecture Decorated* (1759).

Desgodetz, A. *Les édifices antiques de Rome* (Paris, 1682).

Dézallier d'Argenville, A.-J. *La Théorie et la pratique du jardinage* (Paris, 1709; English transl. by J. James, *The Theory and Practice of Gardening*, 1712).

Dodsley, R. *Description of the Leasowes* (1764).

Downing, A. J. *The Architecture of Country Houses* (New York, 1850).

—, *Rural Essays* (New York, 1853).

—, *A Treatise on the Theory and Practice of Landscape Gardening adapted to North America* (New York and London, 1841).

Dugdale, W. *Monasticon Anglicanum*, 3 vols. (1655–73).

Eastlake, C. L. *A History of the Gothic Revival* (1872).

Elmes, J. *Metropolitan Improvements* (1829).

English, E. F. *Views of Lansdown Tower by Willes Maddox* (1844).

Elsam, R. *An Essay on Rural Architecture* (1803).

Farington, J. *Diary 1793–1821*. In process of publication under the editorship of K. Garlick & A. Macintyre (New Haven and London, 1978–)

Fischer von Erlach, J. B. *Entwurff einer historischen Architectur* (Vienna, 1721).

Foulston, J. *The Public Buildings, erected in the West of England . . .* (1838).

Gandy, J. M. *Designs for Cottages* (1805).

—, *The Rural Architect* (1805).

—, 'The Philosophy of Architecture', *The Magazine of the Fine Arts*, I, 1829, 289, 370.

The Gentleman's Magazine, 103 vols. (1731–1833).

Gilpin, W. *A Dialogue Upon the gardens . . . of Stow* (Buckingham, 1748).

—, *Observations on the River Wye and several parts of South Wales, etc., relative chiefly to Picturesque Beauty* (1782).

Gilpin, W. *Observations . . . on . . . Cumberland, and Westmoreland*, 2 vols. (1786).

—, *Observations . . . on Several Parts of Great Britain* (1789).

—, *An Essay upon Prints* (1768).

—, *Remarks on Forest Scenery* (1791).

—, *Three Essays: on Picturesque Beauty; on Picturesque Travel; and on Sketching Landscape. To which is added a Poem on Landscape Painting* (1792).

—, *Observations on the Western Parts of England* (1798).

—, *Observations on the Coasts of Hampshire, Sussex, and Kent* (1804).

—, *Observations on . . . Cambridge, Norfolk, Suffolk, and Essex . . . Also on several parts of North Wales* (1809).

Gilpin, W. S. *Practical Hints upon Landscape Gardening: with some remarks on Domestic Architecture as connected with Scenery* (1832).

Gimson, Ernest: His Life and Work (Stratford on Avon, 1924).

Girardin, R.-L. de *De la composition des paysages* (Geneva, 1777; English transl. by D. Malthus, *An Essay on Landscape*, 1783).

Goldsmith, O. *The Deserted Village*, 1770.

Goodwin, F. *Domestic Architecture*, 2 vols. (1833–4).

—, *Rural Architecture* (1835).

—, *Cottage Architecture* (1835).

Green, W. *The Tourist's New Guide, Containing a Description of . . . Cumberland, Westmoreland and Lancashire*, 2 vols. (Kendal, 1819).

Gyfford, E. *Designs for Elegant Cottages and Small Villas* (1806).

—, *Designs for Small Picturesque Cottages and Hunting Boxes* (1806–7).

Halfpenny, W. *New Designs for Chinese Temples &c.* (1750).

—, *Rural Architecture in the Gothic Taste* (1752).

—, *Chinese and Gothic Architecture properly ornamented* (1752).

—, *Rural Architecture in the Chinese Taste* (1752, 1755).

Hassell, J. *A Picturesque Guide to Bath . . . and the adjacent country* (1793).

—, *Picturesque Rides and Walks . . . 30 miles round the Metropolis*, 2 vols. (1817–18).

—, *Views of Noblemen and Gentlemen's Seats* (1804–5).

Havell, R. *A Series of Picturesque Views of Noblemen's and Gentlemen's Seats* (1823).

Heath's Picturesque Annual, 14 vols. (1832–45).

Heely, J. *Letters on the Beauties of Hagley, Envil, and the Leasowes*, 2 vols. (1777).

Hirschfeld, C. C. L. *Theorie der Gartenkunst*, 5 vols. (Leipzig, 1779–85; simultaneously published in France as *Théorie de l'art des jardins*).

Hofland, B. *A Descriptive Account of the Mansion and Gardens of White Knights* (1819).

Hogarth, W. *The Analysis of Beauty* (1753).

Hope, T. *Household Furniture and Interior Decoration executed from Designs by Thomas Hope* (1807).

—, 'On the Art of Gardening', *Review of Publications of Art*, 1808, No. II, pp. 133–44 (reprinted in B. Hofland, *A Descriptive Account . . . of White Knights*, 1819, pp. 3–13).

—, *Anastasius or the Memoirs of a Modern Greek*, 3 vols. (1819).

Howard, E. *Garden Cities of Tomorrow* (1902).

Hunt, T. F. *Architettura Campestre* (1827).

—, *Designs for Parsonage-houses, Alms houses, etc.* (1827).

—, *Exemplars of Tudor architecture adapted to modern habitations* (1830, 1841).

—, *Half-a-dozen Hints on Picturesque Domestic Architecture* (1825, 1826, 1833, 1841).

Hutchinson, W. *An Excursion to the Lakes in Westmoreland and Cumberland in the years 1773 and 1744* (1776).

Jekyll, G. *Home and Garden* (1900).

—, *Wood and Garden* (1899).

Jones's Views of the Seats, Mansions, Castles, etc. of Noblemen and Gentlemen in England, Wales, Scotland and Ireland, 3 vols. (1829).

Kent, N. *Hints to Gentlemen of Landed Property* (1775).

Kip, J. & Knyff, L. *Britannia Illustrata* (1707 etc.).

Kircher, A. *China Monumentis qua sacris qua profana illustrata* (Amsterdam, 1667; French translation, 1670).

—, *Turris Babel* (Amsterdam, 1679).

Knight, R. P. *An Analytical Inquiry into the Principles of Taste* (1805).

—, *An Account of the Remains of the Worship of Priapus* (1786).

—, *The Landscape, a Didactic Poem* (1794).

—, *An Inquiry into the symbolical language of ancient art and mythology* (1818).

Knight, W. *Memorials of Coleorton being letters to Sir George and Lady Beaumont 1803 to 1834*, 2 vols. (Edinburgh, 1887).

La Belle Assemblée, 15 vols. (1806–32).

Krafft, J.-C. *Plans de plus beaux jardins pittoresques de France, d'Angleterre et d'Allemagne*, 2 vols. (Paris, 1809–10).

—, *Recueil de plus jolies maisons de Paris et de ses environs* (Paris, 1809).

Laborde, A.-L.-J. de *Description des nouveaux jardins de la France* (Paris, 1808–15).

Laborde, J.-B. de *Description générale et particulière de la France*, 12 vols. (Paris, 1781–96; title changed to *Voyage pittoresque de la France* with vol. 5).

Laing, D. *Hints for Dwellings* (1804).

—, *Plans, Elevations, and Sections, of Buildings, Executed in Various Parts of England* (1818).

Lamb, E. B. *Studies of Ancient Domestic Architecture* (1846).

Landi, G. *Architectural Decorations* (1810).

Langley, B. *Ancient Architecture Restored and Improved* (1741–2).

—, *New Principles of Gardening . . .* (1728).

—, *A Sure Method of Improving Estates by Plantations . . .* (1728;

republished as *The Landed Gentleman's Useful Companion*, 1741).

Laugier, M.-A. *Essai sur l'architecture* (Paris, 1753).

—, *Observations sur l'architecture* (The Hague, 1764).

Le Camus de Mézières, N. *Le génie de l'architecture, ou l'analogie de cet art avec nos sensations* (Paris, 1780).

Ledoux, C.-N. *L'Architecture considérée sous le rapport de l'art, des moeurs et da la législation*, 2 vols. (Paris, 1804, 1846).

Leeds, W. H. *Studies and Examples of the Modern English School of Architecture: The Travellers' Club House by Charles Barry, Architect* (1839).

Le Rouge, G.-L. *Détails des nouveaux jardins à la mode*, 10 cahiers (Paris, 1776–88).

Le Roy, J.-D. *Les Ruines des plus beaux monuments de la Grèce*, 2 vols. (Paris, 1770).

Lewis, J. *Original Designs in Architecture*, 2 vols. (1779–97).

Lewis, S. *A Topographical Dictionary of England*, 4 vols. (1831); *Ireland*, 2 vols. (1837); *Scotland*, 2 vols. (1846); *Wales*, 2 vols. (1833).

Library of the Fine Arts, or Monthly Repertory, 25 vols. (1831–3).

Lipscomb, G. *Journey into South Wales in the year 1799* (1802).

Loudon, J. C. *A Treatise on Forming, Improving and Managing Country Residences*, 2 vols. (1806).

—, *An Encyclopaedia of Gardening* (1822).

—, *An Encyclopaedia of Agriculture* (1825).

—, *Hints on the Formation of Gardens and Pleasure Grounds* (1812).

—, *The Suburban Gardener and Villa Companion* (1838).

Loudon, J. C., ed. *The Architectural Magazine*, 5 vols. (1834–8).

—, *The Gardener's Magazine*, 19 vols. (1826–43).

—, *Encyclopaedia of Cottage, Farm and Villa Architecture and Furniture* (1833).

—, *The Landscape Gardening and Landscape Architecture of the Late Humphry Repton, Esq. Being his entire works on these subjects* (1840).

Lugar, R. *Architectural Sketches for Cottages, Rural Dwellings, and Villas* (1805).

—, *The Country Gentleman's Architect* (1807).

—, *Plans and Views of Buildings executed in England and Scotland* (1811).

—, *Villa Architecture* (1828).

Malkin, B. H. *The Scenery, Antiquities and Biography of South Wales* (1804).

Malton, J. *An Essay on British Cottage Architecture . . .* (1798).

—, *Collection of Designs for Rural Retreats* (1802).

Malton, T. *A Picturesque Tour through the Cities of London and Westminster* (1792–1801).

Mansa, J. L. *Plans de jardins dans le goût anglais* (Copenhagen, 1798).

Mason, W. *The English Garden* (1772–9).

—, *An Heroic Epistle to Sir William Chambers* (1772).

Mason, W. H. *Goodwood, its House, Park and Grounds* (1839).

Mawson, T. H. *The Life and Work of an English Landscape Architect. An Autobiography* (1927).

Meason, G. L. *The Landscape Architecture of the Great Painters of Italy* (1827).

Michaelis, A. *Ancient Marbles in Great Britian* (Cambridge, 1882).

Middleton, C. *Designs for Gates and Rails suitable to Parks, Pleasure Grounds, Balconys, etc.* (n.d.).

—, *Picturesque and Architectural Views for Cottages, Farm Houses, and Country Villas* (1793).

—, *The Architect and Builder's Miscellany, or Pocket Library* (1799).

Miller, J. *The Country Gentleman's Architect* (1787, 1791, 1805).

Milner, H. E. *The Art and Practice of Landscape Gardening* (1890).

Mitchell, R. *Plans and Views . . . of Buildings Erected in England and Scotland* (1801).

Morel, J.-M. *Théorie des jardins* (Paris, 1776).

Morris, F. O. *A Series of Picturesque Views of the Seats of the Noblemen and Gentlemen of Great Britain and Ireland*, 5 vols. (1866–80).

Morris, R. *Rural Architecture* (1750, reissued as *Select Architecture*, 1755).

—, *The Architectural Remembrancer . . . Designs, of Ornamental Buildings and Decorations for Parks, Gardens, Woods &c.* (1751).

Morison, R. *Designs in Perspective for Villas in the Ancient Castle and Grecian Styles* (1794).

Murphy, J. C. *Plans . . . and Views of the Church of Batalha* (1795).

Murray, J. F. *A Picturesque Tour of the River Thames* (1853).

Nash, John *The Royal Pavilion at Brighton* (1826).

Nash, Joseph *The Mansions of England in the Olden Time*, 3 vols. (1839–49).

Neale, J. P. *Views of Seats*, 11 vols. (1818–29).

Newton, W. G. *The Work of Ernest Newton, R.A.* (1923).

Nichols, J. B. *Historical Notices of Fonthill Abbey* (1836).

Nieuhof, J. *An Embassy from the East India Company of the United Provinces to the Grand Tartar Cham Emperor of China*, trans. by J. Ogilby, 1669 (reprinted Scolar Press, Menston, Yorkshire, n.d.).

Nuneham-Courtenay (1783).

Over, C. *Ornamental Architecture in the Gothic, Chinese and Modern Taste* (1758).

Overton, T. C. *Original Designs of Temples* (1766). Some copies entitled *The Temple Builder's Most Useful Companion*.

Papworth, J. B. *Architectural Hints* (1813–14 and 1816–17, the second series being republished as *Rural Residences*, 1818).

—, *Hints on Ornamental Gardening* (1823).

—, *Select Views of London* (1816).

Papworth, W. *John B. Papworth. A Brief Record of his Life and Works* (1879).

Parker, C. *Villa Rustica* (1832–41).

Paterson's Roads, 2 vols. (1785; 18th ed. 1826).

Peacock, J. *OIKIΔIA, or, Nutshells: Being Ichnographic Distributions for Small Villas* (1785, published under pseudonym of 'Jose Mac Packe').

Petit, V. *Habitations champêtres . . . constructions pittoresques pour la décoration des parcs . . .* (Paris, c.1870).

Piranesi, G. B. *Prima Parte di Architetture e Prospettive* (Rome, 1743).

—, *Invenzioni capric di Carceri* (Rome, c.1745).

—, *Opere Varie* (Rome, c.1750).

—, *Le Antichità Romane* (Rome, 1756).

—, *Della Magnificenza ed Architettura de' Romani* (Rome, 1761).

—, *Diverse Maniere d'adornare i cammini* (Rome, 1769).

Plaw, J. *Ferme Ornée; or Rural Improvements* (1795).

—, *Rural Architecture; or Designs from the Simple Cottage to the Decorative Villa* (1785).

—, *Sketches for Country Houses, Villas and Rural Dwellings* (1800).

Pocock, W. F. *Architectural Designs for Rustic Cottages, Picturesque Dwellings, Villas, with appropriate scenery* (1807).

—, *Modern Finishings for Rooms . . . to which are added some designs for villas and porticos* (1811).

Pococke, R. *Travels through England During 1750, 1751 and later years*, 2 vols. (1888–9).

Pope, A. *Guardian*, 29 Sept. 1713.

—, *An Epistle to the Right Honourable Richard, Earl of Burlington* (1731).

—, *The Correspondence of Alexander Pope*, 5 vols., G. W. Sherburn, ed. (Oxford, 1956).

Powys, Mrs Lybbe *Diaries 1756–1808* (1899).

Price, Sir Uvedale *Essay on the Picturesque* (1794, expanded in the final edition of 1810 into 3 vols. under the title *Three Essays on the Picturesque*).

Pückler-Muskau, H. von *Tour of Germany, Holland and England, in the years 1826, 1827 and 1828*, 4 vols. (1832).

—, *Andeutungen über Landschaftsgärtnerei* (Stuttgart, 1834; trans. as *Hints on Landscape Gardening*, Boston and New York, 1917).

Pugin, A. W. N. *The True Principles of Pointed or Christian Architecture* (1841).

Pyne, W. H. *The History of the Royal Residences*, 3 vols. (1819).

Randall, J. *Designs for Mansions, Casinos, Villas, Lodges and Cottages in the Grecian, Gothic and Castle Styles* (1806).

Repton, H. *An Enquiry into the Changes of Taste in Landscape Gardening* (1806).

—, *Designs for the Pavilion at Brighton* (1808).

—, *Observations on the Theory and Practice of Landscape Gardening* (1803).

—, *Sketches and Hints on Landscape Gardening* (1794).

—, *Fragments on the Theory and Practice of Landscape Gardening* (1816).

Reynolds, J. *Discourses on Art* (R. R. Wark, ed. Huntington Library, San Marino, 1959).

Ricauti, T. J. *Rustic Architecture* (1840).

—, *Sketches for Rustic Work* (1842).

Ricci, M. *Histoire de l'expedition Chrétienne au royaume de la Chine* (Lyon, 1616).

Richardson, C. J. *Picturesque Designs in Architecture* (1870).

Richardson, G. *New Designs in Architecture* (1792).

Robertson, W. *Designs in Architecture for Garden Chairs, Small Gates for Villas, Park Entrances, Aviarys, Temples, Boat Houses, Mausoleums, and Bridges* (1800).

Robinson, P. F. *A New Series of Designs for Ornamental Cottages and Villas* (1838).

—, *Designs for Farm Buildings* (1830).

—, *Designs for Lodges and Park Entrances* (1833).

—, *Designs for Ornamental Villas* (1825–7).

—, *Village Architecture, being a Series of Designs . . . illustrative of the Observations contained in the Essay on the Picturesque, by Sir Uvedale Price* (1830).

—, *Domestic Architecture in the Tudor Style* (1837).

—, *Rural Architecture* (1823, 5th ed. 1850).

Robinson, W. *The Parks, Promenades and Gardens of Paris* (1869).

Rodenhurst, T. *A Description of Hawkstone* (1783).

Rousseau, J.-J. *La Nouvelle Héloïse* (Paris, 1759).

Ruskin, J. *Lectures on Architecture and Painting* (delivered at Edinburgh, November 1853).

—, *Modern Painters*, 5 vols. (1843–60).

—, *The Poetry of Architecture* (articles in the *Architectural Magazine*, 1837–8, reprinted 1892).

—, *The Seven Lamps of Architecture* (1849).

—, *The Stones of Venice*, 2 vols. (1851–3).

Rutter, J. *Delineations of Fonthill and its Abbey* (Shaftesbury and London, 1823).

Scott, M. H. Baillie *Houses and Gardens* (1906).

Scott, J. & Nash, F. *Picturesque Views of the City of Paris and its Environs*, 2 vols. (1820–3).

Scott, Sir Walter *The Provincial Antiquities and Picturesque Scenery of Scotland*, 2 vols. (1826).

Seacombe, J. *The Eaton Tourist* (Chester, 1825).

Seeley, J. (pub.) *Stowe. A Description of the House and Gardens* (London and Buckingham, 1797).

Serle, J. *A Plan of Mr. Pope's Garden as it was Left at his Death, with a Plan and Perspective View of the Grotto* (1745).

Shaftesbury, 3rd Earl of *Letter Concerning the Art or Science of Design* (1712).

—, *The Moralists* (1709).

Shaw, E. *Rural Architecture* (Boston, 1843).

Shaw, R. N. *Architectural Sketches from the Continent* (1858).

Shenstone, W. 'Unconnected Thoughts on Gardening', *Works*, 1764, II, 125–47.

Silva, E. *Dell'arte de'giardini inglesi* (Milan, 1801; 2nd ed., 2 vols., 1813, reprinted Milan, 1976).

Simond, L. *Journal of a Tour and Residence in Great Britain*, 2 vols. (Edinburgh, 1815).

Sitte, C. *Der Städte-Bau nach seinen künstlerischen Grundsätzen* (Vienna, 1889; trans. by G. R. & C. C. Collins as *City Planning according to Artistic Principles* (London and New York, 1965).

Smith, J. E. *A Tour to Hafod* (1810).

Smith, J. T. *Remarks on Rural Scenery, with Twenty Etchings of Cottages from Nature* (1797).

Soane, Sir J. *Description of . . . the Residence of John Soane* (1830 etc.).

—, *Designs for Public and Private Buildings* (1828).

—, *Designs in Architecture* (1778).

—, *Plans . . . of Buildings erected in . . . Norfolk, Suffolk, &c.* (1788).

—, *Sketches in Architecture* (1793).

Stevens, F. *Views of Cottages and Farm Houses in England and Wales* (1815).

Stieglitz, C. L. *Gemählde von Gärten* (Leipzig, 1796; trans. as *Descriptions pittoresques de jardins du goût le plus moderne*, Leipzig, 1802).

Storer, J. *A Description of Fonthill Abbey* (1812).

Stukeley, W. *Itinerarium Curiosum . . . an Account of the Antiquities and Remarkable Curiosities in Nature or Art observed in Travels through Great Britain* (1724).

Switzer, S. *Ichnographia, or The Nobleman, Gentleman, and Gardener's Recreation* (1715; revised and enlarged as *Ichnographia Rustica*, 3 vols., 1718).

Temple, Sir W. 'Upon the Gardens of Epicurus: or, of Gardening, in the Year 1685', and 'Of Heroic Virtue', repr. in *Five Miscellaneous Essays by Sir William Temple*, ed. S. Monk (Ann Arbor, 1963).

Thiéry, L.-V. *Guide des amateurs et des étrangers voyageurs aux environs de Paris* (Paris, 1788).

Thomson, J. *The Seasons* (1730).

Thomson, J. *Retreats: a Series of Designs . . . for Cottages, Villas, and Ornamental Buildings* (1827).

Thomas, W. *Original Designs in Architecture* (1783).

Trendall, E. W. *Original Designs for Cottages and Villas, in the Grecian, Gothic and Italian Styles of Architecture* (1831).

Unwin, R. *Town Planning in Practice* (1909).

Vassas, L.-F. *Grandes vues pittoresques en Grèce* (Paris, 1813).

Vertue, G. MS. notes on English Art, compiled 1713–56, published by the Walpole Society, vols. 18, 20, 22, 24, 26, 29 and 30 (1930–55).

Viollet-le-Duc, E.-E. *Habitations modernes*, 2 vols. (Paris, 1875–7).

Vanbrugh, Sir John *The Complete Works*, 4 vols., Dobrée, B., & Webb, G. F., eds. (1927–8).

Walpole, H. *The Yale Edition of Horace Walpole's Correspondence*, Lewis, W. S., et al., eds. (London and New Haven, 1937 etc.).

—, *A Description of the Villa . . . at Strawberry Hill* (Strawberry Hill, 1774).

—, *Anecdotes of Painting in England*, ed. J. Dallaway, 5 vols. (1828).

—, *The History of the Modern Taste in Gardening* (1780).

—, 'Journals of Visits to Country Seats, Etc.', *Walpole Society*, XVI, 1927–8, pp. 9–80.

Watelet, C.-H. *Essai sur les jardins* (Paris, 1774).

Watts, W. *Seats of the Nobility and Gentry* (1779).

Weaver, L. & Randal Phillips, R. *Small Country Houses of Today*, 3 vols. (1910–25).

West, G. *Stowe: the Garden* (1732).

Wetten, R. G. *Designs for Villas in the Italian Style of Architecture* (1830).

Whately, T. *Observations on Modern Gardening* (Dublin, 1770).

Williams-Ellis, C. *Portmeirion; the place and its meaning* (1963).

Whittaker, G. & W. B. *The New Guide to Fonthill Abbey* (1822).

Williams, C. F. *Guide to Illustrations of Knowle Cottage* (Sidmouth, 1834).

Wood, J., the elder *Description of Bath* (1742).

Wood, J., the younger *A Series of Plans, for Cottages . . .* (1781).

Wood, R. *The Ruins of Balbec* (1757).

—, *The Ruins of Palmyra* (1753).

Wright, T. *Six Original Designs of Arbours* (1755).

—, *Six Original Designs of Grottos* (1758).

Wrighte, W. *Grotesque Architecture or Rural Amusements* (1767).

Wyatt, L. W. *A Collection of Architectural Designs, rural and ornamental, executed . . . in Caernarvonshire and Cheshire* (1800–1).

Young, A. *A Six Weeks' Tour through the Southern Counties of England and Wales* (1768).

—, *A Six Months Tour through the North of England*, 4 vols. (1770).

Unpublished Theses

Allibone, J. 'Salvin' (Ph.D., London University, 1975).

Hawkes, H. W. 'Sanderson Miller of Radway, 1716–1780, Architect' (Diploma thesis, Cambridge, 1964).

Leach, P. 'The Life and Work of James Paine' (D.Phil., Oxford, 1975).

Lewis, C. D. 'Greece and the Greek Revival: 1759–1809' (B.A., Cambridge, 1962).

McCormick, T. J. 'Charles-Louis Clérisseau and the Roman Revival' (Ph.D., Princeton, 1970).

Raggett, S. G. 'The Work of George Devey' (B.A., Cambridge, 1967).

Rowan, A. J. 'The Castle Style in British Domestic Architecture in the 18th and early 19th centuries' (Ph.D., Cambridge, 1965).

Samuels, A. 'Rudolph Ackermann' (Ph.D., Cambridge, 1972).

Secondary Sources

BOOKS

Abbey, J. R. *Life in England in Aquatint and Lithography, 1770–1860* (1953).

—, *Scenery of Great Britain and Ireland in Acquatint and Lithography, 1770–1860. From the Library of J. R. Abbey. A Bibliographical Catalogue* (1952).

[Académie de France à Rome], *Piranèse et les Français 1740–1790* (Rome, 1976).

Adams, W. H. *The French Garden 1500–1800* (1979).

Addison, W. *English Spas* (1951).

Alexander, B. *England's Wealthiest Son, a Study of William Beckford* (1962).

—, *Life at Fonthill, 1807–22* (1957).

Allen, B. Sprague *Tides in English Taste, 1619–1800*, 2 vols. (Cambridge, Mass., 1937).

Altick, R. *The Shows of London* (Harvard, 1978).

Arisi, F. *Gian Paolo Panini* (Piacenza, 1961).

[Arts Council], *The Romantic Movement: Council of Europe Exhibition Catalogue* (1972).

—, *Charles Cameron* (1968).

—, *The Age of Neo-Classicism* (1972).

—, *Lutyens* (1981–2).

Barbier, C. P. *William Gilpin: his drawings, teaching and theory of the Picturesque* (Oxford, 1963).

Bate, W. J. *From Classic to Romantic, Premises of Taste in Eighteenth-century England* (Cambridge, Mass., 1946).

Beard, G. *The Work of Robert Adam* (Edinburgh and London, 1978).

Beckford Exhibition Catalogue (Salisbury and Bath, 1976).

Betjeman, Sir John *First and Last Loves* (1952).

Boase, T. S. R. *English Art, 1800–1870* (Oxford, 1959).

Börsch-Supan, E. *Garten, – Landschafts, – und Paradiesmotive in Innenraum* (Berlin, 1967).

Bolton, A. T. *The Architecture of Robert and James Adam*, 2 vols. 1922).

—, *The Portrait of Sir John Soane* (1927).

—, *The Works of Sir John Soane, R.A.* (1924).

Braham, A. *The Architecture of the French Enlightenment* (1980).

Brockman, H. A. N. *The Caliph of Fonthill* (1956).

Brownell, M. *Alexander Pope and the Arts of Georgian England* (Oxford, 1978).

Burda, H. *Die Ruine in den Bildern Hubert Roberts* (Munich, 1967).

Burke, J. *English Art 1714–1800* (Oxford, 1976).

Butler, A. S. G. *The Architecture of Sir Edwin Lutyens*, 3 vols. (1950).

Butler, E. M. *The Tyranny of Greece over Germany* (Cambridge, 1935).

—, *A Regency Visitor, the English Tour of Prince Pückler-Muskau* (1957).

[Caisse Nationale des Monuments Historiques et des Sites], *Jardins en France 1760–1820, Pays d'illusion, Terre d'expériences* (Paris, 1977).

Carritt, E. F. *A Calendar of British Taste from 1669 to 1800* (1949).

Chadwick, G. F. *The Park and the Town: Public Landscape in the 19th and 20th centuries* (1966).

Chapman, G. *Beckford* (1937).

Charlton, J. *A History and Description of Chiswick House and Gardens* (1958).

Chase, I. W. U. *Horace Walpole: Gardenist. An Edition of Walpole's 'The History of the Modern Taste in Gardening', with an Estimate of Walpole's Contribution to Landscape Architecture* (Princeton, N.J., 1943).

Childe-Pemberton, W. A. *The Earl Bishop: Frederick Harvey, Bishop of Derry, Earl of Bristol*, 2 vols. (1925).

Clark, H. F. *The English Landscape Garden* (1948; reprinted 1980).

Clark, K. *The Gothic Revival* (1928).

Clarke, M. et al. *The Arrogant Connoisseur: Richard Payne Knight 1751–1824* (Manchester, 1982).

Clifford, D. *A History of Garden Design* (1962).

Coffin, D. R., ed. *The Italian Garden* (Washington, D.C., 1972).

Collins, P. *Changing Ideals in Modern Architecture, 1750–1950* (1965).

Collins, G. R. & C. C. *Camillo Sitte and the Birth of Modern City Planning* (1965).

Colvin, H. M. *A Biographical Dictionary of British Architects 1600–1840* (1978).

Colvin, H. M., ed. *The King's Works*, 6 vols. (1963–80).

Colvin, H. M. & Harris, J., ed. *The Country Seat* (1970).

Conner, P. *Oriental Architecture and the West* (1979).

Cornforth, J. *English Interiors, 1790–1848, the Quest for Comfort* (1978).

Coult, D. *A Prospect of Ashridge* (1980).

Croft-Murray, E. *Decorative Painting in England, 1537–1837*, 2 vols. (1962–70).

Crook, J. M. *The Greek Revival, Neo-Classical Attitudes in British Architecture 1760–1870* (1972).

Cust, L. & Colvin, S. *History of the Society of Dilettanti* (1898).

Dale, A. *James Wyatt, Architect, 1746–1813* (1936; rev. ed. 1956).

—, *Fashionable Brighton 1820–1860* (1947).

Darley, G. *Villages of Vision* (1975).

Davis, T. *John Nash* (1966).

—, *The Architecture of John Nash* (1960).

—, *The Gothick Taste* (1974).

Dickins, L. & Stanton, M. *An Eighteenth Century Correspondence* (1910).

Dobai, J. *Die Kunstliteratur des Klassizismus und der Romantik in England, 1700–1840*, 3 vols. (Bern, 1974–7).

Downes, K. *Vanbrugh* (1977).

Eitner, L. E. A. *Neoclassicism and Romanticism, 1750–1850*, 2 vols. (Englewood, 1970).

Erdberg, E. von *Chinese Influence on European Garden Structures* (Cambridge, Mass., 1936).

Evans, J. *A History of the Society of Antiquaries* (Oxford, 1956).

Fiddes, V. & Rowan, A. *Mr David Bryce 1803–1876. Exhibition Catalogue* (Edinburgh, 1976).

[Fitzwilliam Museum], *Beauty, Horror and Immensity, Picturesque Landscape in Britain, 1750–1850. Exhibition Catalogue* (Cambridge, 1981).

Fleming, J. *Robert Adam and his Circle in Edinburgh and Rome* (1962).

Fothergill, B. *Beckford of Fonthill* (1979).

—, *Sir William Hamilton, Envoy Extraordinary* (1969).

—, *The Mitred Earl, an Eighteenth-Century Eccentric* (1974).

Frankl, P. *The Gothic, Literary Sources and Interpretations through Eight Centuries* (Princeton, 1960).

Franklin, J. *The Gentleman's Country House and its Plan 1835–1914* (1981).

Frey, D. *Englisches Wesen in der bildenden Kunst* (Stuttgart, 1942).

Gallet, M. *Claude-Nicolas Ledoux* (Paris, 1980).

Garden History, the Journal of the Garden History Society (1972–).

Garrigan, K. O. *Ruskin on Architecture, his Thought and Influence* (Wisconsin, 1973).

Germann, G. *Gothic Revival in Europe and Britain: Sources, Influences and Ideas* (1972).

Gill, R. *Happy Rural Seat, the English Country House and the Literary Imagination* (New Haven and London, 1972).

Girouard, M. *Life in the English Country House* (New Haven and London, 1978).

—, *Sweetness and Lght, the 'Queen Anne' Movement, 1860–1900* (Oxford, 1977).

—, *The Victorian Country House* (2nd ed., New Haven and London, 1979).

—, *The Return of Camelot* (New Haven and London, 1981).

Gloag, J. *Mr Loudon's England* (1970).

Goodhart-Rendel, H. S. *English Architecture since the Regency* (1952).

Gothein, M. L. *Geschichte der Gartenkunst*, 2 vols. (Jena, 1914; trans. as *A History of Garden Art*, 2 vols., 1928).

Gradidge, R. *Dream Houses, the Edwardian Ideal* (1980).

Graves, A. *The Royal Academy of Arts*, 8 vols. (1905–6).

Greaves, M. *Regency Patron: Sir George Beaumont* (1966).

Green, D. *Blenheim Palace* (1951).

—, *Gardener to Queen Anne. Henry Wise (1653–1738) and the Formal Garden* (1956).

Grigson, G. *The Harp of Aeolus* (1946).

Hadfield, M. *A History of British Gardening* (1969).

Hardie, M. *Water-Colour Painting in Britain*, 3 vols. (1966–7).

Harris, E. *Thomas Wright Arbours and Grottos, a facsimile . . . with a catalogue of Wright's work in architecture and garden design* (1979).

Harris, J. *A Catalogue of British Drawings for Architecture, Decoration, Sculpture and Landscape Gardening 1550–1900 in American Collections* (New Jersey, 1971).

—, *A Country House Index* (Isle of Wight, 1971).

—, *Gardens of Delight, the Rococo English Landscape of Thomas Robins the Elder* (1978).

—, *Sir William Chambers* (1970).

—, *The Artist and the Country House* (1979).

—, ed. *The Garden* (Victoria and Albert Museum Exhibition Catalogue, 1979).

—, Bellaigue, G. de, and Millar, O. *Buckingham Palace* (1968).

Headlam, Sir Cuthbert *George Abraham Crawley* (1929).

Herrmann, F. *The English as Collectors* (1972).

Herrmann, L. *British Landscape Painting of the 18th century* (1973).

Herrmann, W. *Laugier and Eighteenth-Century French Theory* (1962).

Hersey, G. L. *High Victorian Gothic, a study in Associationism* (Baltimore and London, 1972).

Hipple, W. J. *The Beautiful, the Sublime, and the Picturesque in 18th century British Aesthetic Theory* (Carbondale, 1957).

Hitchcock, H.-R. *Architecture: 19th and 20th centuries* (Harmondsworth, 1958, 1963).

—, *Early Victorian Architecture in Britain*, 2 vols. (New Haven, 1954).

Hobhouse, H. *A History of Regent Street* (1975).

Honour, H. *Chinoiserie, The Vision of Cathay* (1961).

—, *Neo-Classicism* (Harmondsworth, 1968).

—, *Romanticism* (1979).

Hunt, J. D. *The Figure in the Landscape: Poetry, Painting, and Gardening during the Eighteenth Century* (Baltimore and London, 1977).

Hunt, J. D. & Willis, P., eds. *The Genius of the Place. The English Landscape Garden, 1620–1820* (1975).

Hussey, C. *English Country Houses: Early, Mid and Late Georgian*, 3 vols. (1954–8).

—, *English Gardens and Landscapes 1700–50* (1967).

—, *The Life of Sir Edwin Lutyens* (1950).

—, *The Picturesque, Studies in a Point of View* (1927).

—, *Sir Robert Lorimer* (1931).

Hyams, E. *Capability Brown and Humphry Repton* (1971).

Ilyin, M. *Moscow Monuments of Architecture, 18th – the First Third of the 19th century*, 2 vols. (Moscow, 1975).

Impey, O. *Chinoiserie* (Oxford, 1977).

Inglis-Jones, E. *Peacocks in Paradise* (1950).

Inskip, P. *Edwin Lutyens* (1979).

Irwin, D. *English Neoclassical Art* (1966).

Ison, W. *The Georgian Buildings of Bath* (1948).

—, *The Georgian Buildings of Bristol* (1952).

Jones, B. *Follies and Grottoes* (1953; rev. ed. 1974).

Jourdain, *The Work of William Kent* (1948).

Journal of Garden History (1981–).

Kaufmann, E. *Architecture in the Age of Reason* (Cambridge, Mass., 1955).

Kornwolf, J. D. *M. H. Baillie Scott and the Arts and Crafts Movement* (Baltimore and London, 1972).

Lees-Milne, J. *Earls of Creation* (1962).

—, *The Age of Adam* (1947).

—, ed. *The National Trust* (1945).

—, *William Beckford* (Tisbury, 1976).

Lewis, L. *Connoisseurs and Secret Agents in 18th century Rome* (1961).

Lewis, W. S. *Horace Walpole* (1961).

Lindsay, I. & Cosh, M. *Inveraray and the Dukes of Argyll* (Edinburgh, 1973).

Linstrum, D. *Sir Jeffry Wyatville* (Oxford, 1972).

Liscombe, R. W. *William Wilkins 1778–1839* (Cambridge, 1980).

Lovejoy, A. O. *Essays in the History of Ideas* (1948).

Macaulay, J. *The Gothic Revival 1745–1845* (Glasgow and London, 1975).

Macaulay, R. *Pleasure of Ruins* (1953).

Mack, M. *The Garden and the City. Retirement and Politics in the later poetry of Pope, 1731–43* (Toronto, Buffalo and London, 1969).

Malins, E. *English Landscaping and Literature, 1660–1840* (1966).

—, ed. *The Red Books of Humphry Repton* (1976).

— & the Knight of Glin, *Lost Demesnes, Irish Landscape Gardening 1660–1845* (1976).

— & Bowe, P. *Irish Gardens and Demesnes from 1830* (1980).

Manwaring, E. *Italian Landscape in Eighteenth-Century England* (New York, 1925).

Masson, G. *Italian Gardens* (1961).

Mayoux, J.-J. *Richard Payne Knight et le pittoresque* (Paris, 1932).

Meeks, C. *Italian Architecture 1750–1914* (New Haven, Conn., 1966).

—, *The Rail-Road Station, an Architectural History* (New Haven and London, 1957).

Melville, L. *Life and Letters of William Beckford* (1910).

Messmann, F. J. *Richard Payne Knight, the Twilight of Virtuosity* (The Hague, 1973).

Moir, E. *The Discovery of Britain: the English Tourists* (1964).

Monk, S. H. *The Sublime, a Study of Critical Theories in 18th century England* (New York, 1935).

Murray, P. *Piranesi and the Grandeur of Ancient Rome* (1971).

Musgrave, C. *Royal Pavilion* (1959).

Muthesius, H. *Das englische Haus*, 3 vols. (Berlin, 1904–5; abridged English trans. 1979).

Nicolson, M. H. *Mountain Gloom and Mountain Glory: the Development of the Aesthetics of the Infinite* (New York, 1959).

Ogden, H. V. S. & M. S. *English Taste in Landscape in the 17th century* (Ann Arbor, 1955).

Olmsted, F. L. & Kimball, T. *Frederick Law Olmsted, Landscape Architect, 1822–1903*, 2 vols. (1922, 1928; reprinted 1 vol., New York, 1970).

O'Neill, D. *Sir Edwin Lutyens, Country Houses* (1980).

Oppé, A. P. *Alexander and John Robert Cozens* (1952).

—, *The Drawings of Paul and Thomas Sandby in the Collection of His Majesty the King at Windsor Castle* (1947).

—, *Thomas Rowlandson, his Drawings and Water-colours* (1923).

Parreaux, A. & Plaisant, M., eds. *Jardins et paysages: le style Anglais*, 2 vols. (Lille, 1977).

Paulson, R. *Emblem and Expression, Meaning in English Art of the 18th century* (1975).

Pérouse de Montclos, J.-M. *Etienne-Louis Boullée* (Paris, 1969).

Pevsner, Sir Nikolaus *The Buildings of England*, 46 vols. (Harmondsworth, 1951–74).

—, ed. *The Buildings of Scotland* (Harmondsworth, 1978–).

—, ed. *The Buildings of Ireland* (Harmondsworth, 1979–).

—, ed. *The Buildings of Wales* (Harmondsworth, 1979–).

—, ed. *The Picturesque Garden and its Influence outside the British Isles* (Washington, D.C., 1974).

—, *Studies in Art, Architecture and Design*, 2 vols. (1968).

—, *The Englishness of English Art* (1956).

Pilcher, D. *The Regency Style* (1947).

Piper, J. *Buildings and Prospects* (1948).

Praz, M. *Gusto Neoclassico* (Florence, 1940; English trans. 1969).

—, *The Romantic Agony* (Oxford, 1931; New York, 1956).

Prince, H. C. *Parks in England* (Isle of Wight, 1967).

Raval, M. & Moreux, J.-Ch. *Claude-Nicolas Ledoux 1756–1806* (Paris, 1956).

Rave, P. O., ed. *Karl Friedrich Schinkel Lebenswerk* (Berlin, 1941–).

Reilly, P. *An Introduction to Regency Architecture* (1948).

Riesenfeld, E. P. *Erdmannsdorff* (Berlin, 1913).

Reudenbach, B. *G. B. Piranesi: Architektur als Bild* (Munich, 1979).

Richards, Sir James *The Castles on the Ground, the Anatomy of Suburbia* (1946, 1973).

Richardson, Sir Albert *Monumental Classic Architecture in Great Britain and Ireland during the 18th and 19th centuries* (1914).

— et al. *Southill, a Regency House* (1951).

— & Gill, C. L. *Architecture in the West of England* (1924).

Roberts, H. D. *History of the Royal Pavilion, Brighton* (1939).

Roberts, J. F. A. *William Gilpin and Picturesque Beauty* (Cambridge, 1944).

Robinson, J. M. *The Wyatts, an Architectural Dynasty* (Oxford, 1979).

Robson-Scott, W. D. *German Travellers in England, 1400–1800* (Oxford, 1953).

—, *The Literary Background of the Gothic Revival in Germany* (Oxford, 1965).

Rosenblum, R. *Transformations in Late 18th century Art* (Princeton, N.J., 1967).

Rowan, A. *Garden Buildings* (1968).

Royal Commission on Ancient and Historical Monuments, *Inventories* (1910–).

Royal Institute of British Architects Drawings Collection Catalogues (1969–).

Saint, A. *Richard Norman Shaw* (New Haven and London, 1976).

Saunders, A. *Regent's Park* (Newton Abbot, 1969; 2nd ed. 1981).

Saxl. F. & Wittkower, R. *British Art and the Mediterranean* (Oxford, 1948).

Scott, G. *The Architecture of Humanism* (1914).

[Scottish Arts Council], *Robert Adam and Scotland: the Picturesque Drawings* (1972).

Service, A. *Edwardian Architecture* (1977).

—, ed. *Edwardian Architecture and its Origins* (1975).

Siren, O. *China and Gardens of Europe of the 18th century* (New York, 1950).

Sitwell, E. *English Eccentrics* (1933; enlarged ed. 1958).

Stanton, P. *Pugin* (1971).

Smith, B. *European Vision and the South Pacific* (Oxford, 1960).

Spencer, T. *Fair Greece, Sad Relic* (1954).

Steegman, H. E. *Consort of Taste, 1830–70* (1950).

—, *The Rule of Taste from George I to George IV* (1936).

Steele, H. R. & Yerbury, F. R. *The Old Bank of England* (1930).

Stroud, D. *Capability Brown* (1950; new ed. 1975).

—, *Henry Holland* (1966).

—, *George Dance, Architect, 1741–1825* (1971).

—, *Humphry Repton* (1962).

—, *The Architecture of Sir John Soane* (1961).

Summers, M. *The Gothic Quest, a History of the Gothic Novel* (1938).

Summerson, Sir John *Architecture in Britain, 1530–1830* (Harmondsworth, 1953, 1970).

—, *Heavenly Mansions* (1949).

—, *Sir John Soane* (1952).

—, *The Life and Work of John Nash, Architect* (1980).

Survey of London (1896–).

Tait, A. A. *The Landscape Garden in Scotland, 1735–1835* (Edinburgh, 1980).

Templeman, W. D. *The Life and Work of William Gilpin* (Urbana, 1939).

Taylor, G. *Some Nineteenth Century Gardeners* (1951).

—, *The Victorian Flower Garden* (1952).

Taylor, N. *The Village in the City, Towards a New Society* (1973).

Temple, N. *John Nash and the Village Picturesque* (Gloucester, 1979).

Tunnard, C. *Gardens in the Modern Landscape* (1938; rev. ed. London and New York, 1948).

Turner, A. R. *The Vision of Landscape in Renaissance Italy* (Princeton, N.J., 1966).

Turnor, R. *James Wyatt* (1950).

Unrau, J. *Looking at Architecture with Ruskin* (1978).

Unwin, R. *Town Planning in Practice* (1909).

Victoria History of the Counties of England (1904–).

Waterhouse, E. *Painting in England 1530–1790* (Harmondsworth, 1953; 1969).

Watkin, D. J. *Athenian Stuart, Pioneer of the Greek Revival* (1982).

—, *The Buildings of Britain, Regency, a Guide and Gazetteer* (1982).

—, *The Life and Work of C. R. Cockerell, R.A.* (1974).

—, *The Triumph of the Classical, Cambridge Architecture 1804–34* (Cambridge, 1977).

—, *Thomas Hope (1769–1831) and the Neo-Classical Idea* (1968).

— & Middleton, R. D. *Neo-Classical and 19th-century Architecture* (New York, 1980).

Whiffen, M. *Stuart and Georgian Churches . . . outside London* (1947–8).

Whistler, L. *The Imagination of Vanbrugh and his Fellow Artists* (1954).

— et al. *Stowe. A Guide to the Gardens* (1956; rev. ed. 1974).

White, C. *English Landscape 1630–1850, Drawings, Prints and Books from the Paul Mellon Collection* (New Haven, 1977).

Whitney, L. *Primitivism and the Idea of Progress in English Popular Literature of the 18th century* (Baltimore, 1934).

Wiebenson, D. *Sources of Greek Revival Architecture* (1969).

—, *The Picturesque Garden in France* (Princeton, N.J., 1978).

Williams-Ellis, C. *Architect Errant* (1971).

—, *Around the World in Ninety Years* (Portmeirion, 1978).

—, ed. *Britain and the Beast* (1938).

—, *England and the Octopus* (1928).

—, *Lawrence Weaver* (1933).

Willis, P. *Charles Bridgeman and the English Landscape Garden* (1977).

—, ed. *Furor Hortensis. Essays on the History of the English Landscape Garden in Memory of H. F. Clarke* (Edinburgh, 1974).

Wilton, A. *Turner and the Sublime* (1980).

Wilton-Ely, J. *The Mind and Art of Giovanni Battista Piranesi* (1978).

Wittkower, R. *Palladio and English Palladianism* (1974).

Wood, A. C. & Hawkes, W. *Sanderson Miller* (Banbury Historical Society, 1969).

Woodbridge, K. *Landscape and Antiquity, Aspects of English Culture at Stourhead, 1718–1838* (Oxford, 1971).

Youngson, A. J. *The Making of Classical Edinburgh* (Edinburgh, 1966).

ARTICLES

Allentuck, M. 'Sir Uvedale Price and the Picturesque Garden: the Evidence of the Coleorton Papers', N. Pevsner, ed., *The Picturesque Garden*, pp. 57–76.

Aslet, C. 'Rhapsodies on a Tudor Theme', CL, 19 June 1980.

Bald, R. C. 'Sir William Chambers and the Chinese Garden', *Journal of the History of Ideas*, II, No. 3, June 1959, pp. 287–320.

Banham, R. 'Revenge of the Picturesque: English Architectural Polemics, 1945–1965', J. Summerson, ed., *Concerning Architecture*, pp. 265–73.

Batey, M. 'Oliver Goldsmith: an indictment of landscape gardening', P. Willis, ed., *Furor Hortensis*, pp. 57–71.

Binney, M. 'The Travels of Sir Charles Barry', CL, 28 Aug., 4–11 Sept. 1969.

—, 'The Villas of Sir Robert Taylor', CL, 6–13 July 1967, 17–24 April 1969.

—, 'The Peacock Island, Berlin', CL, 1–8 Nov. 1979.

Blutman, S. 'Books of Designs for Country Houses, 1780–1815', AH, vol. 11, 1968, pp. 25–33.

Bolton, A. T. 'The Classical and Romantic Compositions of Robert Adam', AR, vol. LVII, Jan.–May 1925.

Carré, J. 'Lord Burlington's Garden at Chiswick', *Garden History*, I, No. 3, Summer 1973, pp. 23–30.

Clark, H. F. 'Eighteenth-Century Elysiums. The Role of "Association" in the Landscape Movement', *Journal of the Warburg and Courtauld Institutes*, VI, 1943, pp. 165–89.

Clark, H. F. 'Lord Burlington's Bijou, or Sharawaggi at Chiswick', AR, May 1944, pp. 125–9.

Clarke, G. B. 'The Gardens of Stowe', *Apollo*, June 1973, pp. 558–65.

—, 'Grecian Taste and Gothic Virtue. Lord Cobham's Gardening Programme and its Iconography', *Apollo*, June 1973, pp. 566–71.

—, 'William Kent. Heresy in Stowe's Elysium', *Furor Hortensis*, R. Willis ed., pp. 48–56.

Colton, J. 'Kent's Hermitage for Queen Caroline at Richmond', *Architectura*, IV, No. 2, Munich, 1974, pp. 181–91.

Cornforth, J. 'Portmeirion Revisted', CL, 16–23 Sept. 1976.

—, 'The Husseys and the Picturesque', CL, 10–17 May 1979.

—, 'Liselund, Denmark', CL, 17 March 1977.

Country Life (1897–) contains articles on most of the houses and gardens described in the present book; an index is published twice a year.

Crook, J. M. 'The Villas in Regent's Park', CL, CXLIV, 1968, pp. 22–5, 84–7.

—, 'John Britton and the Genesis of the Gothic Revival', J. Summerson, ed., *Concerning Architecture*, 1968, pp. 98–119.

—, 'Grange Park Transformed', H. M. Colvin & J. Harris, eds., *The Country Seat*, 1970, pp. 220–8.

—, 'The Architecture of Thomas Harrison', CL, 15 and 22 April, 6 May 1971.

—, 'Xanadu by the Black Sea, the Woronzow Palace at Aloupka', CL, 2 March 1972.

—, 'Strawberry Hill Revisited', CL, 7–21 June 1973.

de Wolfe, I. 'Townscape: a Plea for an English Visual Philosophy founded on the True Rock of Sir Uvedale Price', AR, 106, Dec. 1949, pp. 354–74.

Fleming, J. 'A "Retrospective View" by John Clerk of Eldin, with some Comments on Adam's Castle Style', J. Summerson, ed., *Concerning Architecture*, pp. 75–84.

Gemmett, R. J. 'Beckford's Fonthill: the Landscape as Art', *Gazette des Beaux-Arts*, LXXX, 1972, pp. 335–56.

Gibbon, M. J. 'Stowe House, 1680–1779', *Apollo*, June 1973, pp. 552–7.

—, 'Stowe, Buckinghamshire: the house and garden buildings and their designers', AH, 20, 1977, pp. 31–44.

Girouard, M. 'George Devey in Kent', CL, 1–8 April 1971.

Gray, B. 'Lord Burlington and Father Ripa's Chinese Engravings', *British Museum Quarterly*, XXII, Feb. 1960, pp. 40–3.

Grigson, G. 'Kubla Khan in Wales', *The Cornhill Magazine*, No. 970, Spring 1947, pp. 275–83.

Harris, E. 'Burke and Chambers on the Sublime and the Beautiful', *Essays in the History of Architecture Presented to Rudolf Wittkower*, 1967, pp. 207–13.

Harris, J. 'Exoticism at Kew', *Apollo*, August 1963, pp. 103–8.

—, 'C. R. Cockerell's "Ichnographica Domestica"', AH, 14, 1971, pp. 5–29.

—, 'English Country House Guides, 1740–1840', J. Summerson, ed., *Concerning Architecture*, 1968, pp. 58–74.

Honour, H. 'An Epic of Ruin Building', CL, 10 Dec. 1953.

—, 'Adaptations from Athens', CL, CXXIII, 1958, pp. 1120–1.

—, 'English Gardens in Italy', CL, 23 Nov. 1961.

—, 'Capricci Cinesi. The Vogue for Chinoiserie in Italy', *Connoisseur Year Book*, 1962, pp. 42–9.

—, 'The Regent's Park Colosseum', CL, 2 Jan. 1953.

Hunt, J. D. 'Emblem and Expressionism in the Eighteenth-Century Landscape Garden', *Eighteenth-Century Studies*, IV, 1971, pp. 294–317.

—, 'Gardening, and Poetry, and Pope', *The Art Quarterly*, XXXVI, no. 1, 1974, pp. 1–30.

—, 'Sense and Sensibility in the Landscape Designs of

Humphry Repton', *Studies in Burke and his Time*, vol. 19, No. 1, 1978, pp. 3–28.

Hussey, C. 'Calverley Park, Tunbridge Wells', CL, CXLV, 1969, pp. 1080–3, 1166–9.

—, 'The Picturesque', *Encylopedia of World Art*, XI, New York, Toronto and London, 1966, pp. 335–40.

Jenkins, F. I. 'John Foulston and his Public Buildings in Plymouth, Stonehouse and Devonport', *Journal of the Society of Architectural Historians* (U.S.A.), XXVII, 1968, pp. 124–35.

Kimball, F. 'Romantic Classicism in Architecture', *Gazette des Beaux-Arts*, 1944, pp. 95–112.

Kindler, R. A. 'Periodical criticism 1815–40: originality in architecture', AH, 17, 1974, pp. 22–37.

Knox, B. 'The arrival of the English Garden in Poland and Bohemia', N. Pevsner, ed., *The Picturesque Garden*, pp. 99–116.

Lang, S. 'The Genesis of the English Landscape Garden', N. Pevsner, ed., *The Picturesque Garden*, pp. 1–29.

—, 'St James's Park. The Rise and Threatened Decline of a Model Landscape', AR, Nov. 1951, pp. 292–8.

—, 'Payne Knight and the Idea of Modernity', J. Summerson, ed., *Concerning Architecture*, pp. 85–97.

Leach, P. 'The architecture of Daniel Garrett', CL, 12, 19, 26 Sept. 1974.

Lewis, L. 'Stuart and Revett: their Literary and Architectural Careers', *Journal of the Warburg and Courtauld Institutes*, II, 1938–9, pp. 128–46.

McCarthy, M. 'Eighteenth-Century Amateur Architects and their Gardens', N. Pevsner, ed., *The Picturesque Garden*, pp. 31–55.

McCormick, T. J. & Fleming, J. 'A Ruin Room by Clérisseau', *Connoisseur*, CXLIX, 1962, pp. 239–43.

McMordie, M. 'Picturesque Pattern Books and Pre-Victorian Designers', AH, 18, 1975, pp. 44–60.

Meeks, C. V. L. 'Creative Eclecticism', *Journal of the Society of Architectural Historians* (U.S.A.), XII, 1953, pp. 15–18.

—, 'Picturesque Eclecticism', *Art Bulletin*, XXXII, 1950, pp. 226–35.

Neumayer, E. M. 'The Landscape Garden as a Symbol in Rousseau, Goethe and Flaubert', *Journal of the History of Ideas*, VIII, April 1947, pp. 187–217.

O'Donnell, R. M. 'W. J. Donthorn (1799–1859)', AH, 21, 1978, pp. 83–92.

Oppé, P. 'Robert Adam's Picturesque Compositions', *Burlington Magazine*, LXXX, March 1942, pp. 56–9.

Panofsky, E. '*Et in Arcadia Ego*', R. Klibansky & H. J. Paton, eds., *Philosophy and History*, Oxford, 1936, pp. 223–54; reprinted in *Meaning in the Visual Arts*, New York, 1955.

Patten, J. 'The Chase and the English Landscape', CL, 16–23 Sept. 1971.

Paulson, R. 'The Pictorial Circuit and Related Structures in Eighteenth-Century England', P. Hughes & D. Williams, eds., *The Varied Pattern. Studies in the Eighteenth Century*, Toronto, 1971, pp. 165–87.

Pérouse de Montclos, J.-M. 'De la villa rustique d'Italie au pavillon de banlieu', *Revue de l'art*, 1976, No. 3, pp. 23–36.

Pevsner, N. 'Price on Picturesque Planning', AR, 95, Feb. 1944, pp. 47–50; repr. in *Studies in Art, Architecture and Design*, II.

—, 'The Genesis of the Picturesque', AR, 96, Nov. 1944, pp. 139–46; repr. in *Studies in Art, Architecture and Design*, II.

—, 'Humphry Repton: a Florilegium', AR, 103, Feb. 1948, pp. 53–9; repr. in *Studies in Art, Architecture and Design*, II.

—, 'Sir William Temple and Sharawaggi' (with S. Lang), AR, 106, Dec. 1949, pp. 391–3; repr. in *Studies in Art, Architecture and Design*, II.

—, 'Richard Payne Knight', *The Art Bulletin*, 31, No. 4, Dec. 1949, pp. 293–320; repr. in *Studies in Art, Architecture and Design*, II.

—, 'Twentieth century Picturesque: an answer to Basil Taylor's broadcast', AR, 115, April 1954, pp. 227–9.

—, 'The Picturesque in Architecture', *R.I.B.A. Journal*, 55, Dec. 1947, pp. 55–61.

—, 'Heritage of Compromise', AR, 91, Feb. 1942, pp. 37–8.

—, 'The Egyptian Revival' (with S. Lang), AR, 119, May 1956, pp. 242–54; repr. in *Studies in Art, Architecture and Design*, II.

—, 'Apollo or Baboon' (with S. Lang), AR, 104, Dec. 1948, pp. 271–9; repr. in *Studies in Art, Architecture and Design*, II.

—, 'Fischer von Erlach, 1656–1723', AR, 120, Oct. 1956, pp. 215–17.

—, 'An Italian Miscellany: Pedrocchino and some allied problems', AR, 122, Aug. 1957, pp. 112–15.

—, 'Roehampton: LCC housing and the Picturesque tradition', AR, 126, July 1959, pp. 21–35.

Price, M. 'The Picturesque Moment', F. W. Hilles & H. Bloom, eds., *From Sensibility to Romanticism*, New York, 1965, pp. 259–92.

Ross Williamson, R. P. 'John Buonarotti Papworth', AR, 79, June 1936, pp. 279–81.

—, 'Staffordshire's Wonderland' [Alton Towers], AR, 87, May 1940, pp. 157–64.

Rowan, A. 'After the Adelphi: forgotten years in the Adam brothers' practice', *Journal of the Royal Society of Arts*, CXXII, 1974, pp. 659–710.

Rowan, A. 'Batty Langley's Gothic', G. A. Robertson & G. Henderson, eds., *Studies in Memory of David Talbot Rice*, Edinburgh, 1975, pp. 197–215.

—, 'Japelli and Cicognara', AR, 143, March 1968, pp. 225–8.

—, 'Japellianum Miscellany', AR, 145, April 1969, pp. 297–8.

—, 'Downton Castle, Herefordshire', H. M. Colvin & J. Harris, eds., *The Country Seat*, pp. 170–3.

Sambrook, A.J. 'Pope's Neighbours. An Early Landscape

Garden at Richmond', *Journal of the Warburg and Courtauld Institutes*, XXX, 1967, pp. 444–6.

—, 'The Size and Shape of Pope's Garden', *Eighteenth-Century Studies*, V, 1972, pp. 450–5.

Steegman, J. 'Bayham Abbey, Designs for a House and View by Humphry Repton', AR, 80, Nov. 1936, pp. 195–200.

—, 'Humphry Repton at Blaize Castle', AR, 83, May 1938, pp. 249–51.

Stillman, D. 'Robert Adam and Piranesi', *Essays in the History of Architecture presented to Rudolf Wittkower*, 1967, pp. 197–206.

Stroud, D. 'The Gardens at Claremont', *The National Trust Year Book*, 1975–6, pp. 32–7.

—, 'A forgotten landscape at Wembley Park', *Furor Hortensis, Essays on the History of the English Landscape Garden in Memory of H. F. Clark*, pp. 72–5.

Summerson, Sir John 'The Vision of J. M. Gandy', *Heavenly Mansions*, 1949, pp. 111–34.

—, 'Soane: the Case-History of a Personal Style', *R.I.B.A. Journal*, 58, 1951, pp. 831–91.

—, 'The Beginning of Regents Park', AH, 20, 1977, pp. 56–62.

—, 'Sir John Soane and the Furniture of Death', AR, 163, March 1978, pp. 147–55.

—, 'Gandy and the Tomb of Merlin', AR, 89, April 1941, pp. 89–90.

—, 'J. M. Gandy: Architectural Draughtsman', *Image*, No. 1, Summer 1949, pp. 40–50.

Sunderland, J. 'Uvedale Price and the Picturesque', *Apollo*, March 1971, pp. 197–203.

Sykes, M. & Neve, C. 'A Laundry from Damascus, R. H. Watt in Knutsford', CL, 4 March 1976.

Tait, A. A. 'The Picturesque Drawings of Robert Adam', *Master Drawings*, IX, 1971, pp. 161–71.

Tatton Brown, A. & W. 'An Unprofessional Genius' [R. H. Watt], AR, 88, 1940, pp. 109–12.

Taylor, N. 'The Awful Sublimity of the Victorian City', H. J. Dyos & M. Wolff, eds., *The Victorian City: Images and Realities*, vol. 2, 1972, pp. 431–47.

Thomas, J. 'The Architectural Development of Hafod: 1786–1882', *Ceredigion, Journal of the Ceredigion Antiquarian Society*, VI, 1973, pp. 152–69, VII, 1974–5, pp. 215–29.

Tudor-Craig, P. 'The Evolution of Ickworth', CL, 17 May 1973.

Walker, D. 'William Burn: the country house in transition', J. Fawcett, ed., *Seven Victorian Architects*, 1976, pp. 8–31.

Watkin, D. J. 'Karl Friedrich Schinkel: Royal Patronage and the Picturesque', *Architectural Design*, 49, Nos. 8–9, 1979, pp. 56–71.

Whiffen, M. 'Academical Elysium. The Landscaping of the Cambridge Backs', AR, 101, Jan. 1947, pp. 13–18.

Wiebenson, D. 'Greek, Gothic and Nature: 1750–1820', *Essays in Honor of Walter Friedlander*, New York 1965, pp. 187–94.

Wilton-Ely, J. 'A Model for Fonthill Abbey, Wiltshire', H. M. Colvin & J. Harris, eds., *The Country Seat*, 1970, pp. 199–204.

Wittkower, R. 'English Neo-Palladianism, the Landscape Garden, China, and the Enlightenment', *Palladio and English Palladianism*, 1974, pp. 175–90.

Woodbridge, K. 'William Kent as Landscape Gardener: A Reappraisal', *Apollo*, Aug. 1974, pp. 126–37.

—, 'William Kent's Gardening: the Rousham Letters', *Apollo*, Oct. 1974, pp. 282–91.

Zádor, A. 'The English Garden in Hungary', N. Pevsner, ed. *The Picturesque Garden*, pp. 77–98.

List of Illustrations

The author and publishers would like to thank the museums, galleries, private collectors, photographers, publishers, photographic agencies and institutions who provided photographic material and kindly permitted its reproduction. Special thanks are due to Nigel Luckhurst for photographing plans and engravings, Mrs Olive Cook, Dr Peter Willis and Miss Elisabeth Hunt. All other photographic sources are credited in brackets.

Index

The index refers jointly to captions and text. Page references in italics, however, refer specifically to illustrations.